ITALIAN
Phrase book

Carol Stanley and Philippa Goodrich

BBC Books

Language consultants: Augusto Zucconi and Clara Romano

Published by BBC Books,
a division of BBC Enterprises Limited,
Woodlands, 80 Wood Lane, London W12 0TT

ISBN 0 563 21517 8

First published 1991
© Carol Stanley and Philippa Goodrich 1991
Published in consultation with the
BBC Continuing Education Advisory Council

Set in Times Roman by Ace Filmsetting Ltd, Frome
Printed and bound in Great Britain
by Richard Clay Ltd, Bungay
Cover printed by Richard Clay Ltd, Norwich

Contents

How to use this book	5
Pronunciation	7
The Italian alphabet	10
General conversation	12
Arriving in the country	23
Directions	26
Road travel	32
Taxis	46
Air travel	49
Travelling by train	54
Buses and coaches	63
Underground travel	68
Boats and ferries	70
At the tourist office	74
Accommodation	77
Telephones	87
Changing money	91
Eating and drinking	94
Menu reader	105
Shopping	118
Business trips	129
Sightseeing	134
Entertainments	138
Sports and activities	144
Health	149
Problems and complaints	159
Basic grammar	167
Days, months, dates	177
Time	181
Countries and nationalities	184
General signs and notices	187
Conversion tables	189
National holidays	192

Useful addresses   193
Numbers   195
Dictionary   197
    Italian/English   198
    English/Italian   222
Emergencies   267
Emergency telephone numbers 268
All-purpose phrases   inside back cover

HOW TO USE THIS BOOK

Communicating in a foreign language doesn't have to be difficult – you can convey a lot with just a few words (plus a few gestures and a bit of mime). Just remember: keep it simple. Don't try to come out with long, grammatically perfect sentences when one or two words will get your meaning across.

Inside the back cover of this book is a list of All-purpose phrases. Some will help you to make contact – greetings, 'please' and 'thank you', 'yes' and 'no'. Some are to help you understand what people are saying to you. And some are questions like 'do you have ...?' and 'where is ...?', to which you can add words from the Dictionary at the back of the book.

The book is divided into sections for different situations, such as Road travel, Shopping, Health and so on. In each section you'll find

● A selection of words and phrases that you'll see on signs or in print
● Useful tips and information
● Phrases you are likely to want to say
● Things that people may say to you.

Many of the phrases can be adapted simply by using another word from the Dictionary. For instance, take the question **È lontano l'aeroporto?** (Is the airport far away?) If you want to know if the *station* is far away, just substitute **la stazione** (the station) for **l'aeroporto** to give **È lontano la stazione?**

All the phrases have a simple pronunciation guide underneath based on English sounds – this is explained in Pronunciation (page 7).

If you want some guidance on how the Italian language works, see Basic Grammar (page 167).

There's a handy reference section (starts page 177) which contains lists of days and months, countries and nationalities, general signs and notices that you'll see, conversion tables, national holidays and useful addresses.

The 5000-word Dictionary (page 197) comes in two sections – Italian–English and English–Italian.

Numbers are printed inside the front cover for easy reference (see also page 195), and towards the end of the book is an Emergencies section (which we hope you *won't* have to use).

Wherever possible, work out in advance what you want to say – if you're going shopping, for instance, write out a shopping list in Italian. If you're buying travel tickets, work out how to say where you want to go, how many tickets you want, single or return, etc.

Practise saying things out loud – the cassette that goes with this book will help you get used to the sounds of Italian.

Above all – don't be shy! It'll be appreciated if you try to say a few words, even if it's only 'good morning' and 'goodbye' – and in fact those are the very sorts of phrases that are worth learning, as you'll hear them and need to use them all the time.

If you would like to learn more about Italian, BBC Books also publish *Buongiorno Italia* and *Get by in Italian*.

BBC phrase books are also available for the following languages: French, German and Spanish. Future titles include Arabic, Greek, Portuguese and Turkish.

The authors would welcome any suggestions or comments about this book, but in the meantime – **buon viaggio!**

PRONUNCIATION

You don't need perfect pronunciation to be able to communicate – it's enough to get the sounds approximately right and to stress words in the correct place. If you want to hear real Italian voices and practise trying to sound like them, then listen to the cassette.

Italian pronunciation is very regular – you can tell how a word is pronounced from the way it's written, once you know what sound each letter (or group of letters) represents. A pronunciation guide is given with the phrases in this book. The system is based on English sounds, as described below.

Many Italian consonants are pronounced in a similar way to English. If there is a double consonant each letter is pronounced making a prolonged sound.

Italian vowels are pronounced the same wherever they occur, except for **e** and **o** where there are two slightly different ways of pronouncing each letter. For simplicity's sake only one sound is represented in the phrases. The final **e** on a word is always pronounced.

For the Italian alphabet, see page 10.

Stress

1 In most cases, the stress is on the last but one syllable: *amico, amore, pagare, andare.*

2 If there is a written accent, the stress is where the accent is: *città, possibilità.*

3 In some long words, the stress is on the last syllable but two, e.g. third person plural forms of verbs: *vengono* (they come); *prendono* (they take).

In this book, a stressed syllable is shown in the pronunciation guide by bold type: *statsyone, peetsa.*

Vowels

	Approx. English equivalent	Shown in book as	Example	
a	a in 'car'	a	nave	*nave*
ai	i in 'pile'	iy	gennaio	*jenniyo*
ao, au	ow in 'cow'	ow	autobus	*owtoboos*
e	e in 'met'	e	bello	*bello*
ei	ay in 'lay'	e-ee	lei	*le-ee*
i	ee in 'meet'	ee	amico	*ameeko*
or sometimes	y in 'yet'	y	possiamo	*possyamo*
o	o in 'lot'	o	notte	*notte*
oi	oy in 'boy'	oy	poi	*poy*
u	oo in 'moon'	oo	una	*oona*
or sometimes	w in 'wobble'	w	può	*pwo*

Consonants

	Approx. English equivalent	Shown in book as	Example	
b	b in 'but'	b	**bagno**	*banyo*
c followed by e or i	ch in 'church'	ch	**cena**	*chena*
ch	c in 'can'	k	**che**	*ke*
c otherwise	c in 'can'	k	**camera**	*kamera*
d	d in 'dog'	d	**dove**	*dove*
f	f in 'feet'	f	**famiglia**	*fameelya*
g followed by e or i	j in 'jet'	j	**gettone**	*jettone*
gh	g in 'got'	g	**ghiaccio**	*gyacho*
gl	lli in 'million'	ly	**gli**	*lyee*
gn	ni in 'onion'	ny	**gnocchi**	*nyokkee*
g otherwise	g in 'got'	g	**gamba**	*gamba*
h	always silent	–	**hotel**	*otel*
j	y in 'you'	y	**Juventus**	*yooventoos*
l	l in 'look'	l	**libro**	*leebro*
m	m in 'mat'	m	**mano**	*mano*
n	n in 'not'	n	**nome**	*nome*
p	p in 'pack'	p	**persona**	*persona*
qu	qu in 'quick'	kw	**quanto**	*kwanto*
r	rolled as in Scottish accent	r	**Roma**	*roma*
rr	strongly rolled	rr	**birra**	*beerra*
s	s in 'set'	s	**solo**	*solo*
or	z in 'zoo'	z	**bisogna**	*beezonya*
sc followed by i or e	sh in 'shin'	sh	**lasciare**	*lashare*
sc otherwise	sk in 'skin'	sk	**scusi**	*skoozee*
t	t in 'tin'	t	**tenda**	*tenda*
v	v in 'vain'	v	**vino**	*veeno*
z	ts in 'hits'	ts	**stazione**	*statsyone*
or	ds in 'roads'	dz	**zio**	*dzee-o*

THE ITALIAN ALPHABET

In the Italian alphabet, the letters **j**, **k**, **w**, **x** and **y** are only found in words borrowed from other languages.

Spelling

How is it spelt?
Come si scrive?
kome see skreeve

Letter	Pronounced
A	*a*
B	*bee*
C	*chee*
D	*dee*
E	*e*
F	*effe*
G	*gee*
H	*akka*
I	*ee*
J (i lungo)	*ee loongo*
K	*kappa*
L	*elle*
M	*emme*
N	*enne*
O	*o*
P	*pee*
Q	*koo*
R	*erre*
S	*esse*
T	*tee*
U	*oo*
V	*voo*

W (voo doppio)	*voo doppyo*
X (ics)	*eeks*
Y (ipsilon)	*eepseelon*
Z (zeta)	*tseta*

GENERAL CONVERSATION

● Italians tend to shake hands on meeting people more than the British do. Friends and young people may greet each other with a kiss on both cheeks.

● **Buon giorno** is the general expression for 'hello', 'good day', and is used in the morning and early afternoon. **Buona sera** means 'good evening' and is used from the middle of the afternoon onwards. **Buona notte** is simply 'good night'. **Ciao** means 'hello' and 'goodbye' and is used between friends.

● There is more than one word for 'you' in Italian. **Lei** is the more formal word and is used between people who don't know each other or between younger and older people. **Tu** is used between friends and young people. The ending of the verb changes depending on whether you are addressing someone as **lei** or **tu**. Both forms are given in the phrases; the **lei** form is given first.

● Adjectives (descriptive words) change their ending in Italian depending on whether they are describing a masculine or feminine word or object. The masculine ending is usually 'o', e.g. **è brutto tempo**, and the feminine ending 'a', e.g. **la giornata è bellissima**. Both endings are given where necessary in the phrases.

Greetings

Hello!
Ciao!
chow

Good day/morning/
   afternoon
Buon giorno
bwonjorno

Good night
Buona notte
bwonanotte

Good evening
Buona sera
bwonasera

Goodbye
Arrivederci
arreevederchee

Bye!
Ciao!
chow

See you later
A più tardi
a pyoo tardee

Hello, how are things?
Ciao, come va?
chow kome va

How are you?
Come sta?/stai?
kome sta/stiy

Fine, thanks
Bene, grazie
bene gratsye

And you?
E lei?/tu?
e le-ee/too

Introductions

My name is . . .
Mi chiamo . . .
mee kyamo

This is . . .
Questo è . . .
kwesto e

This is Mr Brown
Questo è il signor Brown
kwesto e eel seenyor Brown

This is Mrs Clark
Questa è la signora Clark
kwesta e la seenyora Clark

This is my husband/son
Questo è mio marito/figlio
kwesto e mee-o mareeto/feelyo

This is my wife/daughter
Questa è mia moglie/figlia
kwesta e mee-a molye/feelya

Pleased to meet you
Piacere
pyachere

Pardon?
Come?
kome

Talking about yourself and your family

(see Countries and nationalities, *page 184)*

I am English
Sono inglese
sono eengleze

I am Scottish
Sono scozzese
sono skotseze

I am Irish
Sono irlandese
sono eerlandeze

I am Welsh
Sono gallese
sono galleze

We live in Newcastle
Abitiamo a Newcastle
abeetyamo a newcastle

I am a student
Sono studente *(male)*
sono stoodente
Sono studentessa *(female)*
sono stoodentessa

I am a nurse
Sono infirmiere *(male)*
sono eenfeermyere
Sono infirmiera *(female)*
sono eenfeermyera

I work in/for ...
Lavoro in/per ...
lavoro een/per

I work in a bank
Lavoro in una banca
lavoro een oona banka

I work for a computer firm
Lavoro per una società di informatica
lavoro per oona socheta dee eenformateeka

I work in an office/factory
Lavoro in un ufficio/in una fabbrica
lavoro een oon ooffeecho/ een oona fabbreeka

I am unemployed
Sono disoccupato *(male)*
sono deezokkoopato
Sono disoccupata *(female)*
sono deezokkoopata

I am married
Sono sposato/sposata
sono spozato/spozata

I am separated
Sono separato/separata
sono separato/separata

I am divorced
Sono divorziato/divorziata
sono deevortsyato/deevortsyata

I am a widower/widow
Sono vedovo/vedova
sono vedovo/vedova

I have a son/a daughter
Ho un figlio/una figlia
o oon feelyo/oona feelya

I have three children
Ho tre bambini
o tre bambeenee

I don't have any children
Non ho bambini
non o bambeenee

I have one brother
Ho un fratello
o oon fratello

I have three sisters
Ho tre sorelle
o tre sorelle

I'm on holiday here
Sono in vacanza qui
sono een vakantsa kwee

I'm here on business
Sono qui per affari
sono kwee per affaree

I'm here with my husband/
wife
**Sono qui con mio marito/mia
moglie**
*sono kwee kon mee-o
mareeto/mee-a molye*

I'm here with my family
Sono qui con mia famiglia
sono kwee kon mee-a fameelya

I speak a little Italian
Parlo un po' di italiano
parlo oon po dee eetalyano

My husband/wife is . . .
Mio marito/mia moglie è . . .
mee-o mareeto/mee-a molye e

My husband is a policeman
Mio marito è poliziotto
mee-o mareeto e poleetsyotto

My wife is an accountant
Mia moglie è ragioniera
mee-a molye e rajonyera

My husband/wife works
in . . .
**Mio marito/mia moglie
lavora in . . .**
*mee-o mareeto/mee-a molye
lavora een*

My son is five years old
Mio figlio ha cinque anni
*mee-o feelyo a cheenkwe
annee*

My daughter is eight years old
Mia figlia ha otto anni
mee-a feelya a otto annee

You may hear

Di dove è/sei?
dee dove e/say
Where are you from?

Come si chiama/ti chiami?
kome see kyama/tee kyamee
What's your name?

Che lavoro fa/fai?
ke lavoro fa/fiy
What do you do?

Che studia/studi?
ke stoodya/stoodee
What are you studying?

È sposato/a?
e spozato/spozata
Are you (*polite*) married?

Sei sposato/a?
say spozato/a
Are you (*familiar*) married?

Ha/hai bambini?
a/iy bambeenee
Do you have children?

Ha/hai fratelli o sorelle?
a/iy fratellee o sorelle
Do you have brothers and
  sisters?

Quanti anni hanno?
kwantee annee anno
How old are they?

Quanti anni ha/hai?
kwantee annee a/iy
How old are you?

È suo marito/ragazzo?
e soo-o mareeto/ragatso
Is this your (*polite*)
  husband/boyfriend?

È tuo marito/ragazzo?
e too-o mareeto/ragatso
Is this your (*familiar*)
  husband/boyfriend?

È sua moglie/ragazza?
e soo-a molye/ragatsa
Is this your (*polite*) wife/
  girlfriend?

È tua moglie/ragazza?
e too-a molye/ragatza
Is this your (*familiar*) wife/
  girlfriend?

Com'è carino/a!
kome kareeno/a
Isn't he/she sweet!

È molto simpatico/a
e molto seempateeko/a
He/she's very nice

Dove va/vai?
dove va/viy
Where are you going?

Dove abita/abiti?
dove abeeta/abeetee
Where are you staying?

Dove abita/abiti in Gran Bretagna?
dove abeeta/abeetee een gran bretanya
Where do you live in Great Britain?

Talking about Italy and your own country

I like Italy very much
Mi piace molto l'Italia
mee pyache molto leetalya

Italy is very beautiful
L'Italia è molto bella
leetalya e molto bella

It's the first time I have been to Italy
È la prima volta che vengo in Italia
e la preema volta ke vengo een eetalya

I come to Italy often
Vengo spesso in Italia
vengo spesso een eetalya

Do you live here?
Abita/abiti qui?
abeeta/abeetee kwee

Have you (*polite*) ever been to England/Scotland/Ireland/Wales?
È mai stato/a in Inghilterra/nella Scozia/in Irlanda/in Galles
e miy stato/a een eengeelterra/nella skotsya/een eerlanda/galles

Have you (*familiar*) ever been to . . . ?
Sei mai stato/a . . . ?
say miy stato/a

Did you (*polite*) like it?
Le è piaciuto/a?
le e pyachooto/a

Did you (*familiar*) like it?
Ti è piaciuto/a?
tee e pyachooto/a

You may hear

Le/ti piace l'Italia?
le/tee pyache leetalya
Do you like Italy?

È la sua/la tua prima volta in Italia?
e la soo-a/la too-a preema volta een eetalya
Is this your first time in Italy?

Quanto tempo si fermerà qui?
kwanto tempo see fermera kwee
How long are you (*polite*) here for?

Quanto tempo ti fermerai qui?
kwanto tempo tee fermeriy kwee
How long are you (*familiar*) here for?

Che ne pensa/pensi di . . . ?
ke ne pensa/pensee dee . . .
What do you think of . . . ?

Che ne pensa dell'Italia?
ke ne pensa delleetalya
What do you (*polite*) think of Italy?

Parla/parli molto bene l'italiano
parla/parlee molto bene leetalyano
Your Italian is very good

Likes and dislikes

I like …
Mi piace/piacciono …
mee pyache/pyachono

I like it
Mi piace
mee pyache

I like football
Mi piace il calcio
mee pyache eel kalcho

I like swimming
Mi piace nuotare
mee pyache nwotare

I like strawberries
Mi piacciono le fragole
mee pyachono le fragole

I don't like …
Non mi piace/piacciono …
non mee pyache/pyachono

I don't like it
Non mi piace
non mee pyache

I don't like beer
Non mi piace la birra
non mee pyache la beerra

I don't like playing tennis
Non mi piace giocare a tennis
non mee pyache jokare a tennees

Do you like it?
Le/ti piace?
le/tee pyache

Do you like ice-cream?
Le/ti piace il gelato?
le/tee pyache eel jelato

Invitations and replies

Would you like . . . ?
Vuole/vuoi . . . ?
vwole/vwoy

Yes, please
Sì, grazie
see gratsye

Would you like a drink?
Vuole/vuoi bere qualcosa?
vwole/vwoy bere kwalkoza

No, thank you
No, grazie
no gratsye

Would you like something
to eat?
**Vuole/vuoi mangiare
qualcosa?**
vwole/vwoy manjare kwalkoza

That's very kind
È molto gentile
e molto jenteele

Please go away
Se ne vada, per favore!
se ne vada per favore

Would you like to come
with us?
Vuole/vuoi venire con noi?
vwole/vwoy veneere kon noy

What are you doing tonight?
Che fa/fai stasera?
ke fa/fiy stasera

Would you like to go
dancing?
Vuole/vuoi andare a ballare?
vwole/vwoy andare a ballare

What time shall we meet?
A che ora ci incontriamo?
a ke ora chee inkontryamo

Would you like to go and
eat?
**Vuole/vuoi andare a
mangiare qualcosa?**
*vwole/vwoy andare a manjare
kwalkoza*

Where shall we meet?
Dove ci incontriamo?
dove chee inkontryamo

20

Good wishes and exclamations

Congratulations!
Complimenti!
kompleementee

Happy Birthday!
Buon compleanno!
bwon komple-anno

Happy Christmas!
Buon Natale!
bwon natale

Happy New Year!
Buon Anno!
bwon anno

Good luck!
Buona fortuna!
bwona fortoona

Have a good journey!
Buon viaggio!
bwon vyajo

Enjoy yourself/yourselves!
Divertiti!/divertitevi!
deeverteetee/deeverteetevee

Bless you!
Salute!
saloote

Enjoy your meal!
Buon appetito!
bwon appeteeto

Thank you, same to you
Grazie, altrettanto
gratsye altrettanto

Cheers!
Cin Cin!
cheen cheen

What a pity!
Che peccato!
ke pekkato

If only!
Magari!
magaree

Talking about the weather

The weather's very good
È bel tempo
e bel tempo

The weather's bad
È brutto tempo
e brootto tempo

It's very hot/cold
Fa molto caldo/freddo
fa molto kaldo/freddo

It's good/bad
È buono/brutto
e bwono/brootto

It's a wonderful day
È una bellissima giornata
e oona belleesseema jornata

I don't like the heat
Non mi piace il caldo
non mee pyache eel kaldo

It's hot!
Che caldo!
ke kaldo

It's very windy
C'è vento
che vento

Is it going to rain?
Pioverà?
pyovera

ARRIVING IN THE COUNTRY

● Whether you arrive by air, road or sea, the formalities (passport control and Customs) are quite straightforward; the only document you need is a valid passport.

● You will probably not need to say anything in Italian unless you are asked the purpose of your visit, or have something to declare at Customs. If you need to say what you have to declare (rather than just showing it), look up the words in the dictionary. EC duty-free allowances apply – you can get a leaflet with the details at your point of departure.

● According to Italian law, you must register with the police within three days of your arrival. If you check into a hotel, this is done automatically.

You may see

Altri passaporti	Other passports
Articoli da dichiarare	Goods to declare
Benvenuti	Welcome
CE	EC
Controllo passaporti	Passport control
Dogana	Customs
Niente da dichiarare	Nothing to declare

You may want to say

I am here on holiday
Sono in vacanza qui
sono een vakantsa kwee

I am here on business
Sono qui per affari
sono kwee per affaree

It's a joint passport
È un passaporto di famiglia
e oon passaporto dee fameelya

I have something to declare
Ho qualcosa da dichiarare
o kwalkoza da deekyarare

I have this
Ho questo
o kwesto

I have two bottles of whisky
Ho due bottiglie di whisky
o doo-e botteelye dee veeskee

I have two cartons of cigarettes
Ho due stecche di sigarette
o doo-e stekke dee seegarrette

I have a receipt (for this)
Ho una ricevuta (per questo)
o oona reechevoota per kwesto

Do I have to pay duty on
this?
Devo pagare un dazio per questo?
devo pagare oon datsyo per kwesto

You may hear

Il suo passaporto, per favore
eel soo-o passaporto per favore
Your passport, please

I suoi documenti, per favore
ee soo-o-ee dokoomentee per favore
Your documents, please

Qual è lo scopo della sua visita?
kwal e lo skopo della soo-a veezeeta
What is the purpose of your visit?

È qui in vacanza o per affari?
e kwee een vakantsa o per affaree
Are you here on holiday or business?

Quanto tempo rimane in Italia?
kwanto tempo reemane een eetalya
How long are you going to stay in Italy?

Per cortesia, apra questa borsa/valigia
per kortezee-a apra kwesta borsa/valeeja
Please open this bag/suitcase

Per cortesia, apra il portabagagli
per kortezee-a apra eel portabagalyee
Please open the boot

Dobbiamo perquisire la macchina
dobbyamo perkweezeere la makkeena
We have to search the car

Ha altro bagaglio?
a altro bagalyo
Do you have any other luggage?

Deve pagare un dazio per questo
deve pagare oon datsyo per kwesto
There is duty to pay on this

Venga con me/con noi
venga kon me/kon noy
Come with me/with us

DIRECTIONS

● Some general maps are available from the Italian State Tourist Office (*address, page 193*). A wide range of road maps and some more specialised maps, e.g. for walkers, are obtainable from bookshops and specialist mapsellers. Local tourist offices can provide town plans and regional maps.

● When you need to ask the way somewhere, the easiest thing is just to name the place you're looking for and add 'please', e.g. **Frascati, per favore?**. Or you can start with 'where is . . . ?': **Dov'è . . . ?**.

The question 'Where is the nearest (petrol station/bank)?' is rather complicated in Italian, so instead just ask 'Is there (a petrol station/bank) around here?': **C'è una stazione di servizio/ una banca qui vicino?**.

● If you're looking for a particular address, have it written down. It Italy, addresses are written with the street name first and the number afterwards, e.g. **Via Garibaldi 23**.

● When you're being given directions, listen out for the important bits (such as whether to turn left or right), and try to repeat each bit to make sure you've understood it correctly. If you can't understand anything, ask the person to say it again more slowly, prompting with **Come?** ('Pardon?') if necessary.

You may see

Al/Alla . . .	To the . . .
Calle	Street (in Venice)
Campo	Square
Castello	Castle
Cattedrale	Cathedral
Chiesa	Church

Corso	Avenue
Duomo	Cathedral
Fermata (dell'autobus)	Bus stop
Largo	Small square
Museo	Museum
Palazzo	Palace
Passaggio pedonale	Pedestrian crossing
Pedoni	Pedestrians
Piazza	Square
Piazzale	Large square
Sottopassaggio	Subway
Via	Street
Viale	Avenue
Vicolo	Alley
Zona pedonale	Pedestrian precinct

You may want to say

Excuse me, (please)
Mi scusi, per favore
mee skoozee per favore

Pardon?
Come?
kome

Can you repeat that, please?
Può ripetere, per favore?
pwo reepetere per favore

Slowly
Lentamente
lentamente

Again
Ancora una volta
ankora oona volta

I am lost
Mi sono perduto (*male*)/
perduta (*female*)
mee sono perdooto/perdoota

Where are we?
Dove siamo?
dove syamo

Where does this road/street
lead to?
Dove va questa strada?
dove va kwesta strada

Is this the right way to
Frascati?
Va bene per Frascati?
va bene per fraskatee

Is this the footpath for Subiaco?
È il sentiero per Subiaco?
e eel sentyero per soobyako

Can you show me on the map?
Può farmelo vedere sulla cartina?
pwo farmelo vedere soolla karteena

The station, please?
La stazione, per favore?
la statsyone per favore

The (town) centre, please?
Il centro (della città), per favore?
eel chentro (della cheeta) per favore

The road to Bologna, please?
La strada per Bologna, per favore?
la strada per bolonya per favore

How do I/we get to . . . ?
Per andare a . . . ?
per andare a

How do I/we get to Portofino?
Per andare a Portofino?
per andare a portofeeno

How do I/we get to the airport?
Per andare all'aeroporto?
per andare alliyroporto

How do I/we get to the beach?
Per andare alla spiaggia?
per andare alla spyaja

Where is . . . ?
Dov'è . . . ?
dove

Where is this? (*if you've got an address written down*)
Dov'è questo?
dove kwesto

Where is the tourist office?
Dov'è l'ufficio del turismo?
dove looffeecho del tooreezmo

Where is the post office?
Dov'è l'ufficio postale
dove looffeecho postale

Where is this office/this room?
Dov'è quest'ufficio/questa camera?
dove kwestooffeecho/kwesta kamera

Where are the toilets?
Dov'è la toilette?
dove la twalet

Is it far?
È lontano?
e lontano

Is the airport far away?
È lontano l'aeroporto?
e lontano liyroporto

How many kilometres?
Quanti chilometri?
kwantee keelometree

How long does it take (on
foot/by car)
**Quanto tempo ci vuole (a
piedi/in macchina)?**
*kwanto tempo chee vwole (a
pyedee/een makkeena)*

Is there a bus/train?
C'è un autobus/un treno?
che oon owtoboos/oon treno

Can I/we get there on foot?
Ci si può andare a piedi?
chee see pwo andare a pyedee

Can I/we get there by car?
Ci si può andare in macchina?
*chee see pwo andare een
makkeena*

Is there . . . ?
C'è . . . ?
che

Is there a bank around
here?
C'è una banca qui vicino?
*che oona banka kwee
veecheeno*

Is there a supermarket in
the village?
C'è un supermercato in paese?
che oon supermerkato een pa-eze

You may hear

Ha sbagliato strada
a sbalyato strada
You've gone the wrong way

Siamo qui
syamo kwee
We are here

Qui, qua
kwee, kwa
Here

Là
la
There

Di qua
dee kwa
This way

Di là
dee la
That way, Along there

A destra
a destra
(To the) right

A sinistra
a seeneestra
(To the) left

Dritto, sempre dritto
dreetto, sempre dreetto
Straight on

La prima a sinistra/destra
la preema a seeneestra/destra
The first on the left/right

La seconda a sinistra/destra
la sekonda a seeneestra/destra
The second on the left/right

La terza a sinistra/destra
la tertsa a seeneestra/destra
The third on the left/right

Alla fine della strada
alla feene della strada
At the end of the street

In fondo alla strada
een fondo alla strada
At the bottom of the street

Dalla parte opposta della piazza
dalla parte opposta della pyatsa
On the other side of the square

All'angolo
allangolo
On the corner

Giù
joo
Down; downstairs

Su
soo
Up; upstairs

Laggiù
lajjoo
Down there

Lassù
lassoo
Up there

Sotto
sotto
Under

Sopra
sopra
Over

Prima del semaforo
preema del semaforo
Before the traffic lights

Dopo la cattedrale
dopo la kattedrale
After/Past the cathedral

Di fronte a
dee fronte a
Opposite

Davanti a
davantee a
In front of

Dietro
dyetro
Behind

Vicino a
veecheeno a
Near, Close to

È nella piazza
e nella pyatsa
It's in the square

A Via Nazionale
a vee-a natsyonale
At (When you get to) Via
Nazionale

Verso la piazza
verso la pyatsa
Towards the square

Fino all' incrocio
feeno alleenkrocho
As far as the crossroads

(Non) è lontano
non e lontano
It's (not) far away

**Molto lontano. Abbastanza
lontano**
*molto lontano. Abbastantsa
lontano*
Very far. Quite far

È qui vicino
e kwee veecheeno
It's close by

Molto vicino. Abbastanza vicino
*molto veecheeno. Abbastantsa
veecheeno*
Very close. Quite close

È a cinque minuti
e a cheenkwe meenootee
It's five minutes away

È a venti chilometri
e a vayntee keelometree
It's twenty kilometres away

**Si deve prendere il treno/
l'autobus**
*see deve prendere eel treno/
lowtoboos*
You have to catch the train/
bus

È al terzo piano
e al tertso pyano
It's on the third floor

La prima/seconda porta
la preema/sekonda porta
The first/second door

Prenda l'ascensore
prenda lashensore
Take the lift

ROAD TRAVEL

● Consult motoring organisations for advice on taking your car to Italy.

● To take your car to Italy you need your registration document, a valid driving licence and valid insurance. You don't need a green card unless you are driving through Switzerland on the way down. You also need a translation of your driving licence, unless you already hold a pink EC licence.

● You drive on the right in Italy. Traffic from the right has priority at crossroads. On three-lane roads, the middle lane is reserved for overtaking. Wearing seatbelts is compulsory. Crash helmets are compulsory for both drivers and passengers of motorbikes and scooters.

● Speed limits are generally:
50 km per hour in towns, 90 km per hour on ordinary roads and on dual carriageways and 130 km per hour on motorways if your car is over 1100 cc.

● Main roads are labelled as follows:
A (Autostrada) Motorway
SS (Strada Statale) Trunk road
SP (Strada Provinciale) Provincial or secondary road.

● You have to pay a toll (**pedaggio**) on motorways.

● The main grades of petrol are **super** (4-star) and **normale** (2-star). Unleaded petrol (**senza piombo**) is becoming more widely available. Diesel (**gasolio**) is cheaper and available everywhere.

● Italian petrol is expensive. Tourists can save money on petrol and motorway tolls by buying petrol coupons, **buoni di benzina**, and motorway vouchers. These are available to owners of GB registered vehicles at London's **CIT (Compagnia**

Italiana del Turismo) office (*address p. 193*), motoring organisations or from the **ACI** (**Automobile Club d'Italia**) on the border. They are not available in Italy itself. Coupons cannot be paid for in Italian lire and are only issued to the owner of the car in person with his/her passport and car registration. Commercial or hired vehicles are not eligible. Special tourist packages with different combinations of petrol coupons and motorway vouchers are also available. Unused coupons can be refunded at the point of purchase.

Many petrol stations are not self-service, so you'll need a few words of Italian. They don't accept credit cards. The ones that take petrol coupons put out a sign (see **You may see**, page 34). Garages close for holidays on a rota system: look out for the sign **Chiuso per turno** or **per ferie**. Few garages stay open late at night, though on motorways a 24-hour service is guaranteed. You may see self-service garages where you pay by feeding L10,000 notes into a machine.

● Parking in towns and especially in the major cities is very restricted. Garages in cities and motoring organisations sell discs which will enable you to park in the **zona disco** in the centre of cities for a limited period. There are also blue zones, **zona blu**, often in historic city centres which are virtually closed to cars. If you park in a prohibited area your car may be towed away.

● The traffic police in Italy are the **Vigili Urbani**, easily recognised by their white helmets or caps. They can fine you on the spot for speeding and parking offences.

● You can arrange to hire a car in Britain with the large international car hire firms and can save money by doing it in advance. The large firms also have offices at airports and elsewhere in Italy (and there will often be someone who speaks English). There are local companies too in most towns and cities – look for the sign **Autonoleggio**. You may be able to hire mopeds and bicycles, especially in tourist areas. If you are between 21 and 70 with a valid driving licence and a credit card, you'll have no problem hiring a car.

Hired cars with chauffeurs are widely available but expensive.

● In case you have a breakdown make sure you take an emergency red triangle with you.

If you are near a telephone ring **116** and the **ACI** will arrange for your car to be towed to the nearest garage. This service is *free* if you pick up a fuel card, **carta carburante**, with your petrol coupons and motorway vouchers. If the repairs are likely to take more than 12 hours a **carta carburante** also entitles you to a replacement car provided by the **ACI**.

If you have to tell a mechanic what's wrong with your vehicle, the easiest way is to indicate the part affected and say 'this isn't working': **questo non funziona**. Otherwise, look up the word for the appropriate part.

● Accidents should be reported to the **Polizia stradale** by dialling **113** or to the **Vigili Urbani** in towns and cities.

You may see

Accendere i fari	Use headlights (in tunnel)
Allacciare le cinture	Seatbelt compulsory
Alt	Stop
A passo d'uomo	Dead slow
Aperto	Open
Attenzione	Caution
Autonoleggio	Car hire
Autostrada	Motorway
Buoni di benzina	Petrol coupons accepted
Centro città	Town/city centre
Centro storico	Historic centre
Chiuso	Closed
Chiuso per turno/ferie	(Garage) closed for weekly day off/holidays
Circonvallazione	Ring road

Coupons	Petrol coupons accepted
Curva pericolosa	Dangerous bend
Dare la precedenza	Give way
Dare la precedenza a destra	Priority to the right
Deviazione	Diversion
Divieto di sorpasso	No overtaking
Dogana	Customs
Fabbrica	Factory exit
Fine dell'autostrada	End of motorway
Fondo stradale irregolare	Uneven road surface
Incrocio pericoloso	Dangerous crossroads
Lavori in corso	Road works
Meccanico	Repair shop
Officina	Repair shop
Parcheggio (custodito/ sotterraneo)	(Supervised/underground) car park
Parcheggio libero	Free parking
P	Parking
Passaggio animali	Cattle track
Passaggio a livello	Level crossing
Passaggio pedonale	Pedestrian crossing
Passo carrabile	Allow free access
Passo chiuso	(Mountain) pass closed
Pedaggio	Toll
Pedoni	Pedestrians
Pericolo	Danger
Pista ciclabile	Bicycle path
Pronto soccorso	First-aid post
Rallentare	Slow down
Scuola	School
Senso vietato	No entry
Senso unico	One-way street
Sosta (vietata/limitata)	Parking (prohibited/limited)
Stazione di servizio	Service/petrol station
Strada chiusa	Road closed
Strada senza uscita	Cul-de-sac, no through road

Tenersi a destra	Keep right
Tenersi sulla sinistra/destra	Drive on the left/right
Uscita	Exit
Velocità limitata	Speed limit
Viadotto	Viaduct
Vietato il transito agli autocarri	Closed to heavy goods vehicles
Vietato l'ingresso	No entry
Vietato ingresso veicoli	No entry for vehicles
Zona blu	Blue zone (restricted parking)

You may want to say

Petrol

Is there a petrol station around here?
C'è una stazione di servizio qui vicino?
che oona statsyone dee serveetsee-o kwee veecheeno

4-star
Super
sooper

2-star
Normale
normale

Unleaded petrol
Benzina senza piombo
bendzeena sentsa pyombo

Diesel
Gasolio
gazolyo

20 litres of 4-star, please
Venti litri di super, per favore
vayntee leetree dee sooper per favore

40,000 lire's worth of unleaded, please
Quarantamila lire di benzina senza piombo, per favore
kwarantameela leere dee bendzeena sentsa pyombo per favore

Fill it up with 4-star/2-star, please
Il pieno di super/normale, per favore
eel pyeno dee sooper/normale per favore

A can of oil/petrol, please
Una lattina d'olio/di benzina, per favore
oona latteena dolyo/dee bendzeena per favore

Water, please
Acqua, per favore
akkwa per favore

Can you check (the pressure in) the tyres?
Può controllare la pressione delle gomme?
pwo kontrollare la pressyone delle gomme

Can you change the tyre?
Può cambiare la gomma?
pwo kambyare la gomma

Can you clean the windscreen?
Può pulire la parabrezza?
pwo pooleere la parabredza

Where is the air, please?
Dov'è posso gonfiare le gomme?
dove posso gonfyare le gomme

How does the car wash work?
Come funziona il lavaggio macchine?
kome foontsyona eel lavajo makkeene

How much is it?
Quant'è?
kwante

Do you take coupons?
Prende buoni di benzina?
prende bwonee dee bendzeena

Parking

Where can I/we park?
Dove si può parcheggiare?
dove see pwo parkejare

Can I/we park here?
Si può parcheggiare qua?
see pwo parkejare kwa

How long can I/we park here?
Per quanto tempo si può parcheggiare qua?
per kwanto tempo see pwo parkejare kwa

How much is it per hour?
Quanto è l'ora?
kwanto e lora

A parking disc, please
Un disco, per favore
oon deesko per favore

Hiring a car

(see Days, months, dates, page 177)

I want to hire a car
Voglio noleggiare una macchina
volyo nolejare oona makkeena

A small car, please
Una macchina piccola, per favore
oona makkeena peekola per favore

A medium-sized car, please
Una macchina media, per favore
oona makkeena medya per favore

A large car, please
Una macchina grande, per favore
oona makkeena grande per favore

An automatic car, please
Una macchina con il cambio automatico, per favore
oona makkeena kon eel kambyo owtomateeko per favore

A car with a chauffeur, please
Una macchina con autista, per favore
oona makkeena kon owteesta per favore

For three days
Per tre giorni
per tre jornee

For a week
Per una settimana
per oona setteemana

For two weeks
Per due settimane
per doo-e setteemane

From ... to ...
Da ... a ...
da ... a ...

From Monday to Friday
Da lunedì a venerdì
da loonedee a venerdee

From 10th August to 17th August
Dal dieci agosto al diciassette agosto
dal dyechee agosto al deechassette agosto

How much is it?
Quant'è?
kwante

Per day
Al giorno
al jorno

Per week
Alla settimana
alla setteemana

Per kilometre
Al chilometro
al keelometro

Is mileage (kilometrage) included?
È compreso il chilometraggio?
e kompreso eel keelometrajo

Is petrol included?
È compresa la benzina?
e kompreza la bendzeena

Is insurance included?
È compresa l'assicurazione?
e kompreza lasseekooratsyone

Comprehensive insurance cover
Auto assicurato con polizza casco
owto asseekoorato kon poleetsa kasko

My husband/wife is driving too
Anche mio marito/mia moglie guida
anke mee-o mareeto/mee-a molye gweeda

Do you take credit cards?
Si accettano le carte di credito?
see achettano le karte dee kredeeto

Do you take traveller's cheques?
Si accettano i travellers cheques?
see achettano ee travellers cheques

Can I leave the car in Florence?
Posso lasciare la macchina a Firenze?
posso lashare la makkeena a feerenze

Can I leave the car at the airport?
Posso lasciare la macchina all'aeroporto?
posso lashare la makkeena alliyroporto

How do the controls work?
Come funzionano i comandi?
kome foontsyonano ee komandee

Breakdowns and repairs

My car has broken down
La macchina si è rotta
la makkeena see e rotta

Is there a mechanic around here?
C'è un meccanico qui vicino?
che oon mekkaneeko kwee veecheeno

Can you telephone a mechanic?
Può chiamare un meccanico?
pwo kyamare oon mekkaneeko

Can you send a mechanic?
Può mandare un meccanico?
pwo mandare oon mekkaneeko

Can you tow me to the nearest mechanic?
Può trainarmi dal meccanico più vicino?
pwo triynarmee dal mekkaneeko pyoo veecheeno

Do you do repairs?
Fa riparazioni?
fa reeparatsyone

I don't know what's wrong
Non so cosa c'è che non va
non so koza che ke non va

I think . . .
Credo che . . .
kredo ke

It's the clutch
È la frizione
e la freetsyone

It's the radiator
È il radiatore
e eel radyatore

It's the brakes
Sono i freni
sono ee frenee

The car won't start
La macchina non parte
la makkeena non parte

The battery is flat
La batteria è scarica
la batteree-a e skareeka

The engine is overheating
Il motore si riscalda troppo
eel motore see reeskalda troppo

It's losing water/oil
Perde acqua/olio
perde akkwa/olyo

I have a puncture
Ho una gomma a forata
o oona gomma a forata

The . . . doesn't work
Il/La . . . non funziona
eel/la . . . non foontsyona

I need a . . . (for other car parts, see page 43)
Ho bisogno di un/una
o beezonyo dee oon/oona . . .

Is it serious?
È grave?
e grave

Can you repair it (today)?
Può ripararlo (oggi)?
pwo reepararlo ojee

When will it be ready?
Quando sarà pronta?
kwando sara pronta

How much will it cost?
Quanto costerà?
kwanto kostera

You may hear

Petrol

Che cosa desidera?
ke koza dezeedera
What would you like?

Quanta ne vuole?
kwanta ne vwole
How much do you want?

La chiave, per favore
la kyave per favore
The key, please

Parking

Non si può parcheggiare qua
non see pwo parkejare kwa
You can't park here

Sono cinquemila lire l'ora
sono cheenkwemeela leere lora
It's 5,000 lire an hour

Non si paga
non see paga
You don't pay

È gratuito
e gratweeto
It's free

C'è un parcheggio da quella parte
che oon parkejo da kwella parte
There's a car park over there

Hiring a car

Che tipo di macchina vuole?
ke teepo dee makkeena vwole
What kind of car do you want?

Per quanto tempo?
per kwanto tempo
For how long?

Per quanti giorni?
per kwantee jornee
For how many days?

Chi guida?
kee gweeda
Who is driving?

Chi guida principalmente?
kee gweeda preencheepalmente
Who is the main driver?

C'è qualcun altro che guida?
che kwalkoon altro ke gweeda
Is anyone else driving?

(Il prezzo/la tariffa) è sessanta/quattrocento-cinquantamila
eel pretso/la tareeffa e sessanta/kwattrochento-cheenkwantameela
(The price) is sixty/four hundred and fifty thousand lire

Per un giorno
per oon jorno
Per day

Per una settimana
per oona setteemana
Per week

La sua patente, per favore
la soo-a patente per favore
Your driving licence, please

Qual è il suo indirizzo?
kwal e eel soo-o eendeereetso
What is your address?

Ecco le chiavi
ekko le kyavee
Here are the keys

Per cortesia, restituisca la macchina con il pieno
per kortezeeya resteetoo-eeska la makkeena kon eel pyeno
Please return the car with a full tank

Per cortesia, restituisca la macchina prima delle sei
per kortezeeya resteetoo-eeska la makkeena preema delle say
Please return the car before six o'clock

Se l'ufficio è chiuso, può lasciare le chiavi nella cassetta delle lettere
se looffeecho e kyoozo pwo lashare le kyavee nella kassetta delle lettere
If the office is closed, you can leave the keys in the letterbox

Breakdowns and repairs

Cosa c'è che non va?
koza che ke non va
What's wrong with it?

Non ho i pezzi necessari
non o i petsee nechessaree
I don't have the necessary parts

Bisogna ordinare i pezzi
beezonya ordeenare ee petsee
I will have to order the parts

Sarà pronta il martedì prossimo
sara pronta eel martedee prosseemo
It will be ready next Tuesday

Costerà sessantamila lire
kostera sessantameela leere
It will cost 60,000 lire

Car and bicycle parts

Accelerator	**L'acceleratore**	*lacheleratore*
Air filter	**Il filtro aria**	*feeltro aree-a*
Alternator	**L'alternatore**	*lalternatore*
Battery	**La batteria**	*batteree-a*
Bonnet	**Il cofano**	*cofano*
Boot	**Il baule**	*bowle*
Brakes (front rear)	**I freni (davanti/ dietro)**	*frenee (davantee/ dyetro)*
Brake cable	**Il cavetto freno**	*kavetto freno*
Brake fluid	**L'olio dei freni**	*lolyo de-ee frenee*
Brake hose	**Il tubo freno**	*toobo freno*
Disc brakes	**I freni a disco**	*frenee a deesko*
Carburettor	**Il carburatore**	*karbooratore*
Chain	**La catena**	*katena*
Choke	**La valvola dell'aria**	*valvola dellaree-a*
Clutch	**La frizione**	*freetsyone*
Cooling system	**Il sistema di raffreddamento**	*seestema dee raffredamento*
Distributor	**Il distributore**	*deestreebootore*
Electrical system	**L'impianto elettrico**	*leempyanto elettreeko*
Engine	**Il motore**	*motore*

Exhaust pipe	Lo scappamento	scappamento
Fanbelt	La cinghia del ventilatore	cheengya del venteelatore
Frame (bicycle)	Il telaio	teliyo
Front fork	La forcella davanti	forchella davantee
Fuel gauge	L'indicatore della benzina	leendeekatore della bendzeena
Fuel pump	La pompa benzina	pompa bendzeena
Fuses	I fusibili	fooseebeelee
Gears	Le marce	marche
Gearbox	La scatola del cambio	skatola del kambyo
Gear lever	La leva cambio	leva kambyo
Handbrake	Il freno a mano	freno a mano
Handlebars	Il manubrio	manoobree-o
Headlights	I fari	faree
Heater	Il riscaldamento	reeskaldamento
Horn	Il clacson	klakson
Ignition	L'accensione	lachensyone
Ignition key	La chiave d'accensione	kyave dachensyone
Indicators	I lampeggiatori	lampejatoree
Inner tube	La camera d'aria	kamera daree-a
Lights (front/rear)	Le luci (davanti/dietro)	loochee (davantee/dyetro)
Lock	La serratura	serratoora
Oil filter	Il filtro olio	feeltro olyo
Oil gauge	L'indicatore livello olio	leendeekatore leevello olyo
Pedal	Il pedale	pedale
Points	Le puntine	poonteenee
Pump	La pompa	pompa
Radiator	Il radiatore	radyatore
Radiator hose (top/bottom)	Il tubo radiatore (superiore/inferiore)	toobo radyatore (sooperyore/eenferyore)

Reversing lights	**Le luci della retromarcia**	*loochee della retromarcha*
Rotor arm	**Il rotore**	*rotore*
Saddle	**Il sellino**	*selleeno*
Silencer	**Il silenziatore**	*seelentsyatore*
Spare wheel	**La ruota di scorta**	*roo-ota dee skorta*
Spark plugs	**Le candele**	*kandele*
Speedometer	**Il tachimetro**	*takeemetro*
Spokes	**I raggi**	*rajjee*
Starter motor	**Il motorino d'avviamento**	*motoreeno davvyamento*
Steering	**Lo sterzo**	*stertso*
Steering wheel	**Il volante**	*volante*
Transmission (automatic)	**La trasmissione (automatica)**	*trasmeessyone (owtomateeka)*
Tyre (front/rear)	**La gomma (davanti/ dietro)**	*gomma (davantee/ dyetro)*
Valve	**La valvola**	*valvola*
Warning lights	**Le luci hazard**	*loochee azard*
Wheel (front/rear)	**La ruota (davanti/ dietro)**	*roo-ota (davantee/ dyetro)*
Wheel rim	**Il cerchione**	*cherkyone*
Window	**Il finestrino**	*feenestreeno*
Windscreen	**La parabrezza**	*parabredza*
Windscreen washer	**Il lavacristallo**	*lavacreestallo*
Windscreen wiper	**Il tergicristallo**	*terjeecreestallo*

TAXIS

- You can hail taxis in the street, or find them at a taxi rank.

- Taxis have meters, but it's a good idea to ask what the fare will be approximately, especially if you are going some distance. There is a fixed starting charge. There are extra charges at night and on Sundays and public holidays. Extras for luggage, airport pick-ups etc. may not be shown on the meter. A tip of 10% or so is usual.

- Write down clearly the address of your destination if it's at all complicated so that you can show it to the taxi driver.

- It's always best to stick to official taxis. These are usually yellow in cities and have a little 'Taxi' sign on the roof or possibly the name of the city and their taxi number on the door, e.g. **Napoli 20, Milan 15**.

You may want to say

(*see also* Directions, *page 26*)

Is there a taxi rank around
  here?
**C'è una stazione di taxi qui
  vicino?**
*che oona statsyone dee taksee
  kwee veecheeno*

I need a taxi
Ho bisogno di un taxi
o beezonyo dee oon taksee

Can you call me a taxi,
  please?
**Può chiamarmi un taxi, per
  favore?**
*pwo kyamarmee oon taksee
  per favore*

Immediately
Subito
soobeeto

For tomorrow at nine o'clock
Per domani alle nove
per domanee alle nove

To go to the airport
Per andare all'aeroporto
per andare alliyroporto

The airport, please
All'aeroporto, per favore
alliyroporto per favore

The station, please
Alla stazione, per favore
alla statsyone per favore

The Hotel Vittoria, please
All'Hotel Vittoria, per favore
allotel veettoree-a per favore

To this address, please
A questo indirizzo, per favore
a kwesto eendeereetso per favore

Is it far?
È lontano?
e lontano

How much will it cost?
Quanto costerà?
kwanto kostera

I am in a hurry
Ho fretta
o fretta

Stop here, please
Fermi qui, per favore
fermee kwee per favore

That's fine here, thanks
Va bene qui, grazie
va bene kwee gratsye

Can you wait (a few minutes), please?
Può aspettare (qualche minuto), per favore?
pwo aspettare kwalke meenooto per favore

How much is it?
Quant'è?
kwante

There is a mistake
Ha sbagliato
a sbalyato

On the meter it's 7,500
Sul tassametro è settemilacinquecento
sool tassametro e settemeelacheenkwechento

Keep the change
Tenga il resto
tenga eel resto

That's all right
Va bene
va bene

Can you give me a receipt?
Può darmi una ricevuta?
pwo darmee oona reechevoota

For 9,000 lire
Per novemila lire
per novemeela leere

È a dieci chilometri
e a dyechee keelometree
It's ten kilometres away

**Costerà più o meno
quindicimila lire**
*kostera pyoo o meno
kweendeecheemeela leere*
It will cost approximately
15,000 lire

Sono diciottomila lire
sono deechottomeela leere
(It's) 18,000 lire

C'è un supplemento
che oon soopplemento
There is a supplement

Per i bagagli
per ee bagalyee
For the luggage

Per ogni valigia
per onyee valeeja
For each suitcase

Per l'aeroporto
per liyroporto
For the airport

AIR TRAVEL

- There are regular shuttle services between the big cities.

- At airports and airline offices, you'll generally find someone who speaks English, but be prepared to say a few things in Italian.

- Signs at major airports will be in English and Italian.

- Approximate flight times from Rome to some other main cities:

Pisa – 45 minutes	Naples – 45 minutes
Milan – 65 minutes	Venice – 65 minutes
Palermo – 65 minutes	

- The flight from London to Rome takes 1 hour 50 minutes.

- Approximate distances from main airports to city centres:
Rome (Fiumicino) – 35 km (22 miles)
Milan (Linate) – 10 km (6 miles)
   (Malpensa) – 46 km (30 miles)
Florence – 4 km (3 miles)
Venice – 13 km (8 miles)
Genoa – 6 km (4 miles)
Palermo – 32 km (20 miles)
Naples – 6 km (4 miles)
Turin – 16 km (10 miles)
Rimini – 6 km (4 miles)

- Children under two pay 10% of the fare and from two to twelve, 50%.

- There are reductions on domestic flights for families travelling together and if you travel at night.

- The international car hire firms have offices at major airports where you can arrange to hire or pick up cars.

You may see

Allacciare le cinture di sicurezza	Fasten seatbelts
Altri passaporti	Other passports
Arrivi	Arrivals
Articoli da dichiarare	Goods to declare
Autobus (al centro città)	Buses (to the town/city centre)
Autonoleggio	Car hire
Cambio	Bureau de change
CE	EC
Controllo passaporti	Passport control
Dogana	Customs
Entrata	Entrance
Informazioni	Information
Nienti da dichiarare	Nothing to declare
Partenze	Departures
Partenze internazionali	International departures
Partenze nazionali	Domestic departures
Ritardo	Delay
Ritiro bagagli	Luggage reclaim
Sala partenze	Departure lounge
Sciopero	Strike
Tassì	Taxis
Toilette	Toilets
Uscita	Exit, gate
Vietato fumare	No smoking

You may want to say

(see also Numbers, page 195; Days, months, dates, page 177; and Time, page 181)

Is there a flight (from Rome) to Palermo?
C'è un volo (da Roma) a Palermo?
che oon volo da roma a palermo

Today
Oggi
ojee

This morning/afternoon
Stamattina/oggi pomeriggio
stamatteena/ojee pomereejo

Tomorrow (morning/afternoon)
Domani (mattina/pomeriggio)
domanee matteena/pomereejo

Do you have a timetable of flights to Venice?
Ha l'orario dei voli per Venezia?
a loraryo de-ee volee per venetsya

What time is the first flight to Venice?
A che ora parte il primo volo per Venezia?
a ke ora parte eel preemo volo per venetsya

The next flight
Il prossimo volo
eel prosseemo volo

The last flight
L'ultimo volo
loolteemo volo

What time does it arrive (in Venice)?
A che ora arriva (a Venezia)?
a ke ora arreeva a venetsya

A ticket/Two tickets to Pisa, please
Un biglietto/Due biglietti per Pisa, per favore
oon beelyetto/doo-e beelyettee per peeza per favore

Single
Andata
andata

Return
Andata e ritorno
andata e reetorno

1st class/Business class
In prima classe/in business class
een preema klasse/een beezness class

For the eleven o'clock flight
Per il volo delle undici
per eel volo delle oondeechee

I want to change/cancel my reservation
Vorrei cambiare/annullare la mia prenotazione
vorray kambyare/annoollare la mee-a prenotatsyone

What is the number of my flight?
Che numero è il mio volo?
ke noomero e eel mee-o volo

What time do I/we have to check in?
A che ora si deve fare il check in?
a ke ora see deve fare eel check in

Which gate is it?
Che uscita è?
ke oosheeta e

Is there a delay?
C'è un ritardo?
che oon reetardo

Where is the luggage from the flight from London?
Dove sono i bagagli del volo da Londra?
dove sono ee bagalyee del volo da Londra

My luggage is not here
I miei bagagli non ci sono
ee mee-e-ee bagalyee non chee sono

Is there a bus to the centre of town?
C'è un autobus per il centro?
che oon owtoboos per eel chentro

You may hear

Vuole un posto vicino al finestrino?
vwole oon posto veecheeno al feenestreeno
Would you like a seat by the window?

Vuole un posto al corridoio?
vwole oon posto al korreedoyo
Would you like a seat on the aisle?

Fumatori o non fumatori?
foomatoree o non foomatoree
Smoking or non-smoking?

L'ora di imbarco è . . .
lora dee eembarko e . . .
The flight will be called/
  Board at . . . (time)

Uscita numero sette
oosheeta noomero sette
Gate number seven

Il suo biglietto, per favore
eel soo-o beelyetto per favore
Your ticket, please

Il suo passaporto, per favore
eel soo-o passaporto per favore
Your passport, please

**La sua carta di imbarco, per
  favore**
*la soo-a karta dee eembarko
  per favore*
Your boarding card, please

Com'è il suo bagaglio?
kome eel soo-o bagalyo
What does your luggage
  look like?

Ha l'etichetta?
a leteeketta
Do you have the reclaim tag?

Words to listen out for:

Il volo	*eel volo*	Flight
Chiamata finale	*kyamata feenale*	Final call
Ritardo	*reetardo*	Delay
Uscita	*oosheeta*	Gate

TRAVELLING BY TRAIN

● The Italian State railway company, **FS (Ferrovie dello Stato)**, is relatively inexpensive and well run.

● There are also a few non-FS lines in some towns and parts of the country. Inter Rail and Eurail tickets may not be valid on these lines.

● There are various types of trains, including, in reverse order of speed:

Locale (Accelerato) – very slow, stops at every station
Diretto – slightly faster, local train
Espresso – stops at main stations
Rapido/Inter City – travels between major towns. A supplement of roughly 30% of the ticket price is payable on all **Rapido** trains. Seat reservation may be compulsory and some may only have first class accommodation.
Super Rapido Inter City – Travel between the big cities. Part of the TEE (Trans European Express) network. First class accommodation only: seat reservation and supplement compulsory.

● Sleepers and couchettes must be booked in advance. Check that all tickets are stamped with the actual date you want to travel on.

● You can take bicycles on most trains, but only where there's a luggage van.

● When you buy your ticket you can book a hired car to be at your destination. The service is called **Treno più auto**.

● There are some Motorail trains on the longer routes.

● There are various types of ticket available to tourists:

Biglietto turistico libera circolazione Recommended to tourists who are planning extensive rail travel in Italy. It's best to buy these tickets from the **CIT** office in London (*address, page 193*) as they are only available from major railway stations in Italy. They give unlimited travel, for periods of 8, 15, 21 or 30 days, and entitle the holder to travel on **Rapido** trains without paying the supplement. Children get a 50% discount.

Chilometrico A special reduced ticket, valid for 3,000 kilometres, which can be used by up to five people on a maximum of 20 separate journeys.

Other discounts include:
Reductions for families travelling in Europe on Rail Europe family card. Details from British Rail Travel Centres.
A 15% reduction on day return tickets for journeys up to 50 kilometres or three-day returns for journeys up to 250 kilometres.

Children under four (not occupying a seat) travel free on the Italian railways and children between four and twelve travel for half price. (Supplements are always charged at the full rate.)

● Refreshments are available (at an inflated price) from a buffet car or trolley on long journeys. There is no drinking water on trains, so stock up with mineral water from station refreshment stands.

● The **Alberghi diurni**, day hotels, at large stations come into their own at the end of a long overnight journey. They provide facilities for washing and shaving.

● Beware of theft on trains, particularly on well-travelled tourist routes. Keep hold of your valuables while you sleep.

● Information centres at large stations may be able to book accommodation for you. You can also change money at large stations, though the exchange rate may not be as good as in a bank.

You may see

Ai binari	To the platforms
Allarme	Alarm
Arrivi	Arrivals
Bagagliaio	Luggage van
Biglietti	Tickets
Binario	Platform
Cambio	Bureau de change
Cappella	Chapel
Carrozza cuccette	Couchette
Cuccette	Couchettes
Deposito (bagagli)	Left luggage
Destinazione	Destination
Entrata	Entrance
Ferrovie dello Stato (FS)	Italian State Railways
Gabinetti	Toilets
Giorni feriali	Mondays to Saturdays
Giorni festivi	Sundays and holidays
Informazioni	Information
Locale	Local train
Orario	Train timetables
Partenze	Departures
Prenotazione	Reservations
Proibito-Vietato	No Access
Quotidiano	Daily
Sala d'Attesa/d'Aspetto	Waiting room
Self-Service	Buffet
Signori/Uomini	Gentlemen
Signore/Donne	Ladies
Stazione Ferroviaria	Railway Station
Tassi	Taxis
Ufficio oggetti smarriti	Lost property office
Ufficio prenotazioni	Booking office
Uscita	Exit
Vagone letto	Sleeping Car
Vagone ristorante	Dining Car
Vietato sporgersi	Do not lean out

You may want to say

Information

(*see* Time, *page 181*)

Is there a train to Brindisi?
C'è un treno per Brindisi?
che oon treno per breendeezee

Do you have a timetable of
trains to Rimini?
**Ha un orario dei treni per
Rimini?**
*a oon oraree-o de-ee trenee per
reemeenee*

What time . . . ?
A che ora . . . ?
a ke ora

What time is the train to
Genoa?
**A che ora parte il treno per
Genova?**
*a ke ora parte eel treno per
jenova*

What time is the first train
to Verona?
**A che ora parte il primo
treno per Verona?**
*a ke ora parte eel preemo
treno per verona*

The next train
Il prossimo treno
eel prosseemo treno

The last train
L'ultimo treno
loolteemo treno

What time does it arrive (at
Genoa)?
A che ora arriva (a Genova)?
a ke ora arreeva a jenova

What time does the train
from Rome arrive?
**A che ora arriva il treno da
Roma?**
*a ke ora arreeva eel treno da
roma*

The train to Mantua,
please?
**Il treno per Mantova, per
favore?**
*eel treno per mantova per
favore*

Which platform (for Mantua)?
Quale binario (per Mantova)?
kwale beenaryo per mantova

Does this train go to Trento?
Questo treno va a Trento?
kwesto treno va a trento

Is this right for Brennero?
È giusto per il Brennero?
e joosto per eel brennero

Do I/we have to change trains? Where?
Si deve cambiare? **Dove?**
see deve kambyare *dove*

Tickets

(*see* Time, *page 181;* Numbers, *page 195*)

One/two tickets to Florence, please
Un biglietto/Due biglietti per Firenze, per favore
oon beelyetto/doo-e beelyettee per feerenze per favore

Single
Solo andata
solo andata

Return
Andata e ritorno
andata e reetorno

For one adult/two adults
Per un adulto/due adulti
per oon adoolto/doo-e adooltee

(And) one child/two children
(E) un bambino/due bambini
e oon bambeeno/doo-e bambeenee

First/second class
Prima classe/seconda classe
preema klasse/sekonda klasse

For the 10.00 train to Milan
Per il treno delle dieci per Milano
per eel treno delle dyechee per meelano

For the Super Rapido to Naples
Per il super rapido per Napoli
per eel sooper rapeedo per napolee

I want to reserve a seat/two seats
Vorrei prenotare un posto/due posti
vorray prenotare oon posto/doo-e postee

I want to reserve a sleeper
Vorrei prenotare un posto sul vagone letto
vorray prenotare oon posto sool vagone letto

I want to reserve a couchette
Vorrei prenotare una cuccetta
vorray prenotare oona koochetta

I want to book tickets on the car-train to Geneva
Vorrei prenotare biglietti per il treno col auto seguito a Ginevra
vorray prenotare beelyettee per eel treno kol owto segweeto a jeenevra

For the car and two passengers
Per la macchina e due passeggeri
per la makkeena e doo-e passejeree

This car is a Fiat Uno
La macchina è un Fiat Uno
la makkeena e oon fee-at oono

Can I take my bicycle on the train?
Posso portare la mia bicicletta sul treno?
posso portare la mee-a beecheekletta sool treno

How much is it?
Quant'è?
kwante

Is there a supplement?
C'è un supplemento?
che oon sooplemento

Left luggage

Can I leave this?
Posso lasciare questo?
posso lashare kwesto

Can I leave these two suitcases?
Posso lasciare queste due valigie?
posso lashare kweste doo-e valeeje

Until three o'clock
Fino alle tre
feeno alle tre

What time do you close?
A che ora chiudete?
a ke ora kyoodete

On the train

I have reserved a seat
Ho prenotato un posto
o prenotato oon posto

I have reserved a couchette
Ho prenotato una cuccetta
o prenotato oona koochetta

I have reserved a sleeper
Ho prenotato un posto sul vagone letto
o prenotato oon posto sool vagone letto

Is this seat taken?
È libero questo posto?
e leebero kwesto posto

Excuse me, may I get by?
Permesso!
permesso

Where is the dining-car?
Dov'è il vagone-ristorante?
dove eel vagone reestorante

Where is the sleeping-car?
Dov'è il vagone letto?
dove eel vagone letto

Where is the buffet?
Dov'è il buffet?
dove eel booffe

May I open the window?
Posso aprire il finestrino?
posso apreere eel feenestreeno

May I smoke?
Posso fumare?
posso foomare

Where are we?
Dove siamo?
dove syamo

Are we at Como?
Siamo a Como?
syamo a komo

How long does the train
  stop here?
**Quanto tempo si ferma il
  treno qui?**
*kwanto tempo see ferma eel
  treno kwee*

Can you tell me when we
  get to Brescia?
**Può dirmi quando arriviamo
  a Brescia?**
*pwo deermee kwando
  arreevyamo a bresha*

You may hear

Information

(*see* Time, *page 181*)

Parte alle dieci e mezza
parte alle dyechee e medza
It leaves at 10.30

**Arriva alle quattro meno
  dieci minuti**
*arreeva alle kwattro meno
  dyechee meenootee*
It arrives at ten to four

Si deve cambiare a Padova
see deve kambyare a padova
You have to change trains
  at Padua

È al binario quattro
e al beenaryo kwattro
It's platform number four

61

Tickets

(*see* Time, *page 181;* Numbers, *page 195*)

Per quando vuole il biglietto?
per kwando vwole eel beelyetto
When do you want the
  ticket for?

Quando vuole viaggiare?
kwando vwole vyajare
When do you want to travel?

Andata o andata e ritorno?
andata o andata e reetorno
Single or return?

Quando vuole tornare?
kwando vwole tornare
When do you want to return?

Fumatori o non fumatori?
foomatoree o non foomatoree
Smoking or non-smoking?

(Sono) dodicimila lire
sono dodeecheemeela leere
(It's) 12,000 lire

**C'è un supplemento di
  cinquemila lire**
*che oon supplemento dee
  cheenkwemeela leere*
There is a supplement of
5,000 lire

**Quel treno è soltanto di
  prima classe**
*kwel treno e soltanto dee
  preema klasse*
That train's first class only

BUSES AND COACHES

● As well as town and city bus services, there are many buses between towns and villages. On long-distance buses, you either pay the driver as you get on or buy your ticket at the bus station. In big towns you must buy your ticket beforehand and stamp it in the machine as you get on. There are on-the-spot fines for travelling without a valid ticket. Tickets are available from kiosks, bars and tobacconists.

● If people get on the bus without a ticket, they usually ask the other passengers if they've got one that they can buy then and there.

● If you're using the buses extensively in towns and cities, it's worth buying a book of ten tickets or even a season ticket, **una tessera**.

● A coach is known as **un pullman**.

● In Venice there are special water buses, **vaporetti**, which run along the Grand Canal and the other main canals between the different tourist spots. You can buy tickets at a flat rate from authorised sellers.

● In Rome the **Romapass** is valid for three days on public transport and also gives free admission to public museums.

You may see

Entrata	Entrance
Fermata (di autobus)	Bus stop
Fermata di richiesta	Stops on request
Non parlare all'autista	Do not talk to the driver
Non salite senza biglietto; acquistatelo prima	Buy your ticket before boarding the bus
Obliterare il biglietto non appena siete saliti a bordo	Stamp your ticket on boarding
Salire dalla porta anteriore	Enter by the front door
Scendere dalla porta centrale	Alight by the centre door

You may want to say

(for sightseeing bus tours see Sightseeing, *page 134)*

Where is the bus stop?
Dov'è la fermata (di autobus)?
dove la fermata dee owtoboos

Where is the bus station?
Dov'è la stazione di autobus?
dove la statsyone dee owtoboos

Is there a bus to the beach?
C'è un autobus per la spiaggia?
che oon owtoboos per la spyaja

What number is the bus to the station?
Che numero è l'autobus per la stazione?
ke noomero e lowtoboos per la statsyone

Do they go often?
Partono spesso?
partono spesso

What time is the coach to Civitavecchia?
A che ora parte il pullman per Civitavecchia?
a ke ora parte eel poolman per cheeveetavekkya

What time is the first bus to Hadrian's Villa?
A che ora parte il primo autobus per Villa Adriana?
a ke ora parte eel preemo owtoboos per veella adree-ana

The next bus
Il prossimo autobus
eel prosseemo owtoboos

The last bus
L'ultimo autobus
loolteemo owtoboos

What time does it arrive?
A che ora arriva?
a ke ora arreeva

Where can I buy tickets?
Dove posso comprare i biglietti?
dove posso komprare ee beelyettee

Where does the bus to the town centre leave from?
Da dove parte l'autobus per il centro della città?
da dove parte lowtoboos per eel chentro della cheetta

Does the bus to the airport leave from here?
L'autobus per l'aeroporto parte da qua?
lowtoboos per liyroporto parte da kwa

Does this bus go to Circus Maximus?
Questo autobus va al Circo Massimo?
kwesto owtoboos va al cheerko masseemo

Is this right for the Colosseum?
È giusto per il Colosseo?
e joosto per eel kolosse-o

Can you tell me where to get off?
Può dirmi quando devo scendere?
pwo deermee kwando devo shendere

The next stop, please
La prossima fermata, per favore
la prosseema fermata per favore

Are you getting off at the next stop?
Scende alla prossima?
shende alla prosseema

Open the door, please!
Apra, per favore!
apra per favore

Excuse me, may I get by?
Permesso!
permesso

Ten tickets, please
Dieci biglietti, per favore
dyechee beelyettee per favore

Five tickets, please
Cinque biglietti, per favore
cheenkwe beelyettee, per favore

How much is it?
Quant'è?
kwante

A return to Frascati, please
Andata e ritorno per Frascati, per favore
andata e reetorno per fraskatee per favore

You may hear

L'autobus per il centro parte da quella fermata là
lowtoboos per eel chentro parte da kwella fermata la
The bus to the centre leaves from that stop there

Il cinquantasette va alla stazione
eel cheenkwantasette va alla statsyone
The 57 goes to the station

Può comprare i biglietti dal tabaccaio
pwo komprare ee beelyettee dal tabakkiy-o
You can buy tickets at a tobacconist's

Ha biglietti?
a beelyettee
Have you got any tickets?

Si paga all'autista
see paga allowteesta
You pay the driver

Andata o andata e ritorno?
andata o andata e reetorno
Single or return?

Scende?
shende
Are you getting off?

Deve scendere alla prossima
deve shendere alla prosseema
You have to get off at the next stop

Ha saltato la fermata
a saltato la fermata
You've missed the stop

UNDERGROUND TRAVEL

● The underground is called **la metropolitana**, and there are systems in Rome and Milan. There is a fixed fare for any distance so you only need to say how many tickets you want. You can buy tickets at any **metro** ticket office or from bars and tobacconists near the **metro** station.

● You can use the same tickets for the bus and **metro** in Milan but not in Rome where you have to buy different tickets for the **metro**.

● Children under a metre tall travel free.

You may see

Entrata	Entrance
Linea A	Line A
Metropolitana	Underground
M	Underground
Vietato fumare	No smoking
Uscita	Exit

You may want to say

Do you have a map of the underground?
Ha una piantina della metropolitana?
a oona pyanteena della metropoleetana

One/Two, please
Uno/Due, per favore
oono/doo-e per favore

Which line is it for the Pyramid?
Che linea è per la Piramide?
ke leenya e per la peerameede

Which stop is it for La Scala?
Che fermata è per La Scala?
ke fermata e per la skala

Where are we?
Dove siamo?
dove syamo

Is this the stop for Luna Park?
**È questa la fermata per il
    Luna Park?**
*e kwesta la fermata per eel
    loona park*

Does this train go to Ostia?
Questo treno va a Ostia?
kwesto treno va a ostya

You may hear

È la Linea B
e la leenya bee
It's line B

È la prossima fermata
e la prosseema fermata
It's the next stop

È stata la fermata scorsa
e stata la fermata skorsa
It was the last stop

Ha saltato la fermata
a saltato la fermata
You've missed the stop

BOATS AND FERRIES

● There are long-distance ferry services between Italy and Greece (mainly leaving from Brindisi and Bari), Yugoslavia, Turkey, North Africa, Spain, Majorca, the Canary Islands, Turkey, Malta and Corsica. Ferries also go from the mainland to Sicily and Sardinia and to the other islands in the Tyrrenhian Sea.

● Hydrofoils operate in the Bay of Naples, taking tourists to the islands of Capri and Ischia.

● There are plenty of pleasure boats and ferries on the Italian lakes in the north.

● If you go on a gondola trip in Venice, make sure you negotiate a price with the **gondoliere** before you set off.

You may see

Aliscafo	Hovercraft (Hydrofoil)
Barche	Boats
Battelli	Boats
Cabine	Cabins
Cintura di salvataggio	Lifebelt
Gite alla baia	Trips round the bay
Imbarcadero	Pier
Navi	Boats
Ponte macchine	Car deck
Porto	Port, harbour
Traghetto	Ferry

You may want to say

(see Time, page 181)

Is there a boat to Sicily (today)?
C'è una nave per la Sicilia (oggi)?
che oona nave per la seecheelya ojee

Is there a car ferry to Sardinia?
C'è un traghetto per la Sardegna?
che oon tragetto per la sardenya

Are there any boat trips?
Ci sono degli escursioni in battello?
chee sono delyee eskoorsyonee een battello

What time is the boat to Corfu?
A che ora parte la nave per Corfù?
a ke ora parte la nave per korfu

What time is the first boat?
A che ora parte la prima nave?
a ke ora parte la preema nave

The next boat
La prossima nave
la prosseema nave

The last boat
L'ultima nave
loolteema nave

What time does it arrive?
A che ora arriva?
a ke ora arreeva

What time does it return?
A che ora torna?
a ke ora torna

How long is the crossing?
Quanto tempo dura la traversata?
kwanto tempo doora la traversata

Where is the ferry for Sirmione?
Dov'è il traghetto per Sirmione?
dove eel tragetto per seermyone

Where does the hydrofoil for Capri leave from?
Da dove parte l'aliscafo per Capri?
da dove parte laleeskafo per kapree

Where can I buy tickets?
Dove posso comprare i biglietti?
dove posso komprare ee beelyettee

What is the sea like today?
Com'è il mare oggi?
kome eel mare ojee

71

Tickets

(*see* Numbers, *page 195*)

Four tickets to Ischia, please
Quattro biglietti per Ischia, per favore
kwattro beelyettee per eeskya per favore

Two adults and two children
Due adulti e due bambini
doo-ee adooltee e doo-e bambeenee

Single
Andata
andata

Return
Andata e ritorno
andata e reetorno

I want to book tickets for the ferry to Elba
Vorrei prenotare biglietti per il traghetto per l'isola d'Elba
vorray prenotare beelyettee per eel tragetto per leezola delba

For a car and two passengers
Per una macchina e due passeggeri
per oona makkeena e doo-e passejeree

I want to book a cabin
Vorrei prenotare una cabina
vorray prenotare oona kabeena

For one person
Per una persona
per oona persona

For two people
Per due persone
per doo-e persone

How much is it?
Quant'è?
kwante

On board

I have reserved a cabin
Ho prenotato una cabina
o prenotato oona kabeena

I have reserved two berths
Ho prenotato due cuccette
o prenotato doo-e koochette

Where are the cabins?
Dove sono le cabine?
dove sono le kabeene

Where is cabin number 20?
Dov'è la cabina numero venti?
dove la kabeena noomero vayntee

Can I/we go out on deck?
Si può uscire sul ponte?
see pwo oosheere sool ponte

You may hear

Ci sono navi lunedì e giovedì
chee sono navee loonedee e jovedee
There are boats on Mondays and Thursdays

Il traghetto per Ischia parte alle nove
eel tragetto per eeskya parte alle nove
The ferry to Ischia leaves at nine o'clock

Torna alle quattro e mezza
torna alle kwattro e medza
It returns at half past four

La nave per Corfù parte dall'imbarcadero numero due
la nave per korfu parte dalleembarkadero noomero doo-e
The boat to Corfu leaves from pier number two

Il mare è tranquillo
eel mare e trankweello
The sea is calm

Il mare è mosso
eel mare e mosso
The sea is rough

AT THE TOURIST OFFICE

● There are tourist board offices in each regional capital, **Ente Provinciale Turismo**. Look for the sign **E.P.T.** or alternatively **A.P.T. (Azienda di Promozione Turistica)**. There will often be someone who speaks English.

● Other towns, especially holiday centres, have their own offices, **Aziende Autonome di Cura e Soggiorno e Turismo (AACST)**.

● At local level unofficial tourist offices may be called **Pro loco**.

● Tourist offices have leaflets about sights worth seeing, lists of hotels, town plans and regional maps, and can supply information about opening times and local transport. They can also book hotel rooms for you.

You may want to say

(see Directions, page 26; Sightseeing, page 134; Time, page 181)

Where is the tourist office?
Dov'è l'ufficio di turismo?
dove looffeecho dee tooreezmo

Do you have . . . ?
Ha . . . ?
a

Do you have a plan of the town?
Ha una pianta della città?
a oona pyanta della cheetta

Do you have a map of the area?
Ha una pianta della zona?
a oona pyanta della dzona

Do you have a list of hotels and restaurants?
Ha un elenco di alberghi e ristoranti?
a oon elenko dee albergee e reestorantee

Do you have a list of campsites?
Ha un elenco di campeggi?
a oon elenko dee kampejee

Can you recommend a cheap hotel?
Può consigliarmi un albergo economico?
pwo konseelyarmee oon albergo ekonomeeko

Can you recommend a traditional restaurant, please?
Può consigliarmi un ristorante tipico, per favore?
pwo konseelyarmee oon reestorante teepeeko per favore

Can you book a hotel for me, please?
Può prenotarmi un albergo, per favore?
pwo prenotarmee oon albergo per favore

Where can I/we hire a car?
Dove si può noleggiare una macchina?
dove see pwo nolejare oona makkeena

Have you got information about . . . ?
Ha informazioni su . . . ?
a eenformatsyone soo

Have you got information about the festival?
Ha informazioni sulla festa?
a eenformatsyone soolla festa

Have you got information in English?
Ha informazioni in inglese?
a eenformatsyonee een eengleze

What is there to see here?
Che cosa c'è da vedere qui?
ke koza che da vedere kwee

Do you have any leaflets?
Ha dei dépliants?
a de-ee deplee-onz

Where is the archaeological museum?
Dov'è il museo archeologico?
dove eel mooze-o arke-olojeeko

Can you show me on the map?
Può mostrarmelo sulla pianta?
pwo mostrarmelo soolla pyanta

When is the Colosseum open?
Quando è aperto il Colosseo?
kwando e aperto eel kolosse-o

Are there any excursions?
Ci sono escursioni?
chee sono eskoorsyonee

You may hear

Dica?
deeka
Can I help you?

È inglese?
e eengleze
Are you English?

Tedesco?
tedesko
German?

Di dove è?
di dove e
Where are you from?

Quanto tempo rimane qui?
kwanto tempo reemane kwee
How long are you going to be here?

Dove si alloggia?
dove see alloja
Where are you staying?

Che tipo di albergo vuole?
ke teepo dee albergo vwole
What kind of hotel do you want?

È nel centro storico
e nel chentro storeeko
It's in the old part of town

ACCOMMODATION

- There is a wide range of hotels and guest houses in Italy.

- Hotels, **Alberghi**, are graded from one to five stars. Each hotel has fixed charges agreed with the provincial tourist board. Charges may vary with season and locality. Taxes and service charges are included in the given rate. Once a deposit has been paid, a booking is considered valid, so don't expect to get your deposit back if you have to cancel a booking – unless you have come to some previous arrangement.

- **Motels** Most of the motels along the major motorways are operated by **AGIP**, the petrol company. You can pick up a leaflet with further details from the Italian State Tourist Office. Most have a restaurant.

- If you're looking for a cheaper bed for the night, go to a **Pensione** or a **Locanda**. **Pensioni** are graded into three categories. You can always ask to look at the room. Meals may be provided. Make sure you check when you book exactly what is included in the price.

- Monasteries and convents often rent out rooms to tourists, especially in places like Assisi, Rome and Florence. A list of these and other historic buildings that offer accommodation is available from the Italian State Tourist Office.

- **Alberghi diurni**, 'day hotels', often located in the centre of large cities or at railway stations, offer facilities for washing and brushing up, but no sleeping accommodation. They are open from 6 a.m. to midnight.

- **Ostelli della Gioventù** The Italian Youth Hostels Association has hostels throughout Italy. You need to be a member of the IYHF to stay in one. Booking information and a list of hostels can be obtained from the Italian State Tourist Office. There are many other hostels open to all students.

• There are plenty of campsites all over Italy, especially along the coasts. Further information is available from the Italian State Tourist Office. In Italy local tourist offices will give information about the nearest sites. It is best to book first in popular coastal areas. Wild camping is allowed, except in state forests and national parks; it's always best to ask landowners first, though.

• When you book in somewhere, you will usually be asked for your passport. In a hotel, you may have to fill in a registration card. You may also have to leave your passport at reception overnight.

• There are plenty of self-catering cottages and farmhouses and there are also villas, flats and chalets to rent at many seaside resorts. Information is available at the local tourist offices; a list of these can be obtained from the Italian State Tourist Office, where you can also get information about **Rifugi Alpini**, mountain huts.

Information requested on a registration card

Nome	First name
Cognome	Surname
Indirizzo	Address
Nationalità	Nationality
Professione	Occupation
Data di nascita	Date of birth
Luogo di nascita	Place of birth
Numero passaporto	Passport number
Prossima destinazione	Further destination
Rilasciato a	Issued at
Data	Date
Firma	Signature

You may see

Acqua potabile	Drinking water
Albergo	Hotel
Albergo di lusso	Five star, luxury hotel
Albergo diurno	Day hotel
Ascensore	Lift
Camping/Campeggio	Campsite
Completo	Full up
Corrente	Electricity
Divieto di campeggio	No camping
Divieto di sosta alle roulottes	No caravans
Doccia	Showers
Camere (libere)	Rooms (vacant)
Gabinetto	WC
Gabinetti	Toilets
Garage	Garage
Lavanderia	Laundry
Letti	Beds
Locanda	Country restaurant/hotel
Mezza pensione	Half board
Non gettare rifiuti	Do not dump rubbish
Ostello della gioventù	Youth hostel
Pensione	Guest house
Pensione completa	Full board
1⁰ piano	1st floor
Pianterreno	Ground floor
Ricevimento	Reception
Rifugio	Mountain shelter
Ristorante	Restaurant
Roulotte vietate	No caravans
Sala	Lounge
Sala da pranzo	Dining-room
Sala della televisione	Television room
2⁰ piano	2nd floor
Servizio ai piani	Room service
Spazzatura	Rubbish

Suonare per il servizio	Ring for service
Toilette	Toilets
Toilette chimiche	Empty chemical toilets here
Uscita (di sicurezza)	(Emergency) exit
Vietato accendere fuochi	Do not light fires

You may want to say

Booking in and out

I've reserved a room
Ho prenotato una camera
o prenotato oona kamera

I've reserved two rooms
Ho prenotato due camere
o prenotato doo-e kamere

I've reserved a place
Ho prenotato un posto
o prenotato oon posto

My name is . . .
Mi chiamo . . .
mee kyamo

Do you have a room?
Ha una camera?
a oona kamera

A single room
Una camera singola
oona kamera seengola

A double room
Una camera matrimoniale
oona kamera matreemonyale

A twin-bedded room
Una camera doppia
oona kamera doppya

For one night
Per una notte
per oona notte

For two nights
Per due notti
per doo-e nottee

With bath/shower
Con bagno/doccia
kon banyo/docha

Do you have space for a tent?
Ha posto per una tenda?
a posto per oona tenda

Do you have space for a caravan?
Ha posto per una roulotte?
a posto per oona roolot

How much is it?
Quant'è?
kwante

Per night
Per una notte
per oona notte

Per week
Per la settimana
per la setteemana

Is there a reduction for
children?
**C'è uno sconto per i
bambini?**
*che oono skonto per ee
bambeenee*

Is breakfast included?
È inclusa la prima colazione?
e eenklooza la preema kolatsyone

It's too expensive
È troppo caro
e troppo karo

Do you have anything
cheaper?
Ha qualcosa di meno caro?
a kwalkoza dee meno karo

Do you have anything
bigger/smaller?
**Ha qualcosa più grande/
piccolo?**
*a kwalkoza pyoo grande/
peekkolo*

I'd like to stay another night
Vorrei rimanere un'altra notte
vorray reemanere oon altra notte

I am leaving tomorrow
morning
Parto domani mattina
parto domanee matteena

The bill, please
Il conto, per favore
eel konto per favore

Do you take credit cards?
Si accettano le carte di credito?
see achettano le karte dee kredeeto

Do you take traveller's cheques?
Si accettano i travellers cheques?
see achettano ee travellers cheques?

Can you recommend a hotel
in Pisa?
**Può consigliarmi un albergo
a Pisa?**
*pwo konseelyarmee oon
albergo a peeza*

Can you phone them to
make a booking, please?
**Può chiarmarle per
prenotare, per favore?**
*pwo kyamarle per prenotare
per favore*

In hotels

(see Problems and complaints, page 159; Time, page 181)

Where can I/we park?
Dove si può parcheggiare?
dove see pwo parkejare

Do you have a cot for the baby?
C'è un lettino per il bambino?
che oon letteeno per eel bambeeno

Is there room service?
C'è servizio ai piani?
che serveetsyo a-ee pyanee

Do you have facilities for
the disabled?
**Avete facilitazione per gli
handicappati?**
*avete facheeleetatsyone per
lyee andeecappatee*

A room at the back, please
**Una camera sul dietro, per
favore**
*oona kamera sool dyetro per
favore*

A room with a view, please
**Una camera con una vista,
per favore**
*oona kamera kon oona veesta
per favore*

Can I/we see the room?
Si può vedere la camera?
see pwo vedere la kamera

Can I/we have breakfast in
the room?
**Si può prendere la prima
colazione in camera?**
*see pwo prendere la preema
kolatsyone een kamera*

What time is breakfast?
A che ora è la prima colazione?
a ke ora e la preema kolatsyone

What time is dinner?
A che ora è la cena?
a ke ora e la chena

What time does the hotel close?
A che ora chiude l'albergo?
a ke ora kyoode lalbergo

I'll be back very late
Torno molto tardi
torno molto tardee

(Key) number 42, please
**(La chiave) numero
quarantadue, per favore**
*la kyave noomero
kwarantadoo-e per favore*

Are there any messages for me?
Ci sono messaggi per me?
chee sono messajee per me

Where is the bathroom?
Dov'è il bagno?
dove eel banyo

Where is the dining-room?
Dov'è la sala da pranzo?
dove la sala da prantso

Can I leave this in the safe?
Posso lasciare questo nella cassaforte?
posso lashare kwesto nella cassaforte

Can you give me my things from the safe?
Può darmi le mie cose dalla cassaforte?
pwo darmee le mee-e koze dalla cassaforte

Can you call me at eight o'clock?
Può chiamarmi alle otto?
pwo kyamarmee alle otto

Can you order me a taxi?
Può chiamarmi un tassi?
pwo kyamarmee oon tassee

For right now
Subito
soobeeto

For tomorrow at nine o'clock
Per domani alle nove
per domanee alle nove

Can you clean this jacket for me?
Può farmi lavare a secco questa giacca?
pwo farmee lavare a sekko kwesta jakka

Can you find me a babysitter?
Può trovarmi una babysitter?
pwo trovarmee oona babeeseeter

Can you put it on the bill?
Può metterlo sul conto?
pwo metterlo sool konto

Room number 21
Camera numero ventuno
kamera noomero ventoono

I need another pillow
Ho bisogno di un guanciale in più
o beezonyo dee oon gwanchale een pyoo

I need a towel
Ho bisogno di un asciugamano
o beezonyo dee oon ashoogamano

At campsites

Where can I/we park?
Dove si può parcheggiare?
dove see pwo parkejare

Is there a campsite around here?
C'è un campeggio qui vicino?
che oon kampejo kwee veecheeno

Can I/we camp here?
Ci si può accampare qui?
chee see pwo akkampare kwee

Where are the showers?
Dove sono le docce?
dove sono le doche

Where are the toilets?
Dove sono i gabinetti?
dove sono ee gabeenettee

Where are the dustbins?
Dove sono le pattumiere?
dove sono le pattoomyere

Where is the laundry-room?
Dov'è la lavanderia?
dove la lavanderee-a

Where is there an electric point?
Dov'è la presa della corrente?
dove la presa della korrente

Do we pay extra for the showers?
Si paga in più per le docce?
see paga een pyoo per le doche

Is the water drinkable?
È potabile l'acqua?
e potabeele lakkwa

Self-catering accommodation

(*see* Directions, *page 26;* Problems and complaints, *page 159*)

I have rented a villa
Ho affittato una villa
o affeettato oona veella

It's called Villa Leonardo
Si chiama Villa Leonardo
see kyama veella le-onardo

I have rented an apartment
Ho affittato un appartamento
o affeettato oon appartamento

We're in number 11
Siamo in numero undici
syamo een noomero oondeechee

My name is . . .
Mi chiamo . . .
mee kyamo

What is the address?
Qual è l'indirizzo?
kwal e leendereetso

How do I/we get there?
Come ci arrivo/ci arriviamo?
kome chee arreevo/chee arreevyamo

Can you give me the key, please?
Può darmi la chiave, per favore?
pwo darmee la kyave per favore

Where is . . . ?
Dov'è . . . ?
dove

Where is the stopcock?
Dov'è il rubinetto principale?
dove eel roobeenetto preencheepale

Where is the fusebox?
Dov'è la scatola dei fusibili?
dove la skatola de-ee foozeebeelee

How does the cooker work?
Come funziona il fornello?
kome foontsyona eel fornello

How does the water-heater work?
Come funziona lo scaldobagno?
kome foontsyona lo skaldobanyo

Is there air conditioning?
C'è l'aria condizionata?
che larya kondeetsyonata

Is there a spare gas bottle?
C'è un'altra bombola di gas?
che oonaltra bombola dee gas

Are there any more blankets?
Ci sono coperte in più?
chee sono koperte een pyoo

What day do they come to clean?
Quando vengono a fare le pulizie?
kwando vengono a fare le pooleetsye

Where do I/we put the rubbish?
Dove si mettono i rifiuti?
dove see mettono ee reefyootee

When do they collect the rubbish?
Quando raccolgono i rifiuti?
kwando rakkolgono ee reefyootee

Where can I contact you?
Dove posso trovarla?
dove posso trovarla

Are there any shops round here?
Ci sono negozi qui vicino?
chee sono negotsee kwee veecheeno

You may hear

Dica!
deeka
Can I help you?

Come si chiama, per favore?
kome see kyama per favore
What's your name, please?

Per quante notti?
per kwante nottee
For how many nights?

Per quante persone?
per kwante persone
For how many people?

Con bagno o senza bagno?
kon banyo o sentsa banyo
With bath or without bath?

Ha una tenda grande o una piccola?
a oona tenda grande o oona peekkola
Have you got a big or a small tent?

Mi dispiace, siamo al completo
mee deespyache syamo al kompleto
I'm sorry, we're full

Il passaporto, per favore
eel passaporto per favore
Your passport, please

La sua tessera, per favore
la soo-a tessera per favore
Your membership card, please

La sua firma qua, per favore
la soo-a feerma kwa per favore
Can you sign here, please

La domestica viene ogni giorno
la domesteeka vyene onyee jorno
The maid comes every day

Posso venire venerdì
posso veneere venerdee
I can come on Friday

Vengono un giorno sì e uno no
vengono oon jorno see e oono no
They come every other day

Raccolgono i rifiuti al martedì
rakkolgono ee reefyootee al martedee
They collect the rubbish on Tuesdays

86

TELEPHONES

● Telephone boxes are grey or yellow.

● Telephone boxes in the street have the signs **Interurbane** (for long-distance calls) and/or **Internazionale**. You can also find public telephones in many bars.

● For some payphones you need a special token, **un gettone**. Otherwise payphones take L100, L200 and L500 coins. Insert your money or **gettoni** before you dial and be ready to feed more in if necessary.

● You can also buy phone cards at different prices. Both phone cards and **gettoni** are sold in bars, tobacconists' and some newsagents.

● In large towns and cities and some railway stations, you can also make long-distance calls from telephone exchanges, usually operated by **SIP (Società Idroelettrica Prealpina)** or **ASST (Azienda di Stato per i Servizi Telefonici)**. The operator will put you through to the number you want. Some bars have metered phones.

● Rates are lower at the weekends and in the evenings.

● To call abroad, first dial **00**, then the code for the country – for the UK it's **44**. Follow this with the town code minus the **0**, and then the number you want. For example: for a central London number, dial **00 44 71**, then the number.

● The numbers for directory enquiries are:
12 Informazioni Italia (for numbers within Italy)
184 Informazioni internazionali Europa (for European numbers)
170 Informazioni intercontinentali (for international numbers).

● Emergency numbers are:

113 – for the police; this is the number to dial in any emergency situation

112 – for the **Carabinieri** (military police who act as a second police force)

115 – for the **Vigili del fuoco** (fire brigade).

You may see

Chiamate urbane e interurbane	Local and long-distance calls
Gettone	Telephone token
Internazionale	International calls
Nazionale	National calls
Società Telefonica	Telephone company
Telefono	Telephone
Inserire le monete e sganciare	Insert coins and lift the receiver
Comporre il numero	Dial the number
Monete in esaurimento	The money is running out
Riagganciare per la restitutzione	Hang up to retrieve unused coins
Per una nuova comunicazione premere il tasto senza riagganciare	Press the button to make another call – do not hang up
112-113-115- non occorrono monete	Emergency calls free of charge

You may want to say

Is there a telephone?
C'è un telefono?
che oon telefono

Where is the telephone?
Dov'è il telefono?
dove eel telefono

Can I make a phone call, please?
Posso telefonare, per favore?
posso telefonare per favore

Do you have change for the telephone, please?
Ha spiccioli per il telefono, per favore?
a speecholee per eel telefono per favore

A phone card, please
Una carta telefonica, per favore
oona karta telefoneeka per favore

Do you have the Rome telephone directory?
Ha l'elenco telefonico di Roma?
a lelenko telefoneeko dee roma

I want to call England
Vorrei telefonare in Inghilterra
vorray telefonare een eengeelterra

I want to make a reverse charge call
Vorrei fare una chiamata in 'erre'
vorray fare oona kyamata een erre

Mr Barberini, please
Il signor barberini, per favore
eel seenyor barbereenee per favore

Extension number 121, please
Interno centoventuno, per favore
eenterno chentoventoono per favore

It's Mrs Stanley speaking
Sono la signora Stanley
sono la seenyora stanley

It's Robert speaking
Sono Robert
sono robert

My name is . . .
Mi chiamo . . .
mee kyamo

When will he/she be back?
Quando torna?
kwando torna

I'll call later
Chiamerò più tardi
kyamero pyoo tardee

Can I leave a message?
Posso lasciare un messaggio?
posso lashare oon messajo

Please tell him/her that (your name) called
Per favore, gli/le dica che . . . ha chiamato
per favore lee/le deeka ke . . . a kyamato

I am in the Hotel Vittoria
Sto all'albergo Vittoria
sto allalbergo veettoree-a

My telephone number is . . .
Il mio numero di telefono è . . .
eel mee-o noomero dee telefono e

Can he/she call me?
Può farmi chiamare?
pwo farmee kyamare

Can you repeat that, please?
Può ripetere, per favore?
pwo reepetere per favore

Slowly
Lentamente
lentamente

We were cut off
È caduta la linea
e kadoota la leenya

How much is the call?
Quant'è la telefonata?
kwante la telefonata

Can you give me a number
to call a taxi?
**Può darmi il numero per un
tassi?**
*pwo darmee eel noomero per
un tassee*

You may hear

Pronto?
pronto
Hello?

Sono io
sono yo
Speaking

Chi parla?
kee parla
Who's calling?

Un attimo, per favore
oon atteemo per favore
One moment, please

Aspetti, per favore
aspettee per favore
Please wait

Glielo passo subito
lyee-elo passo soobeeto
I'm putting you straight
through

È occupato
e okkoopato
The line's engaged

Vuole aspettare
vwole aspettare
Do you want to hold on?

Non risponde nessuno
non reesponde nessoono
There's no answer

Non c'è
non che
He/She is not in

Ha sbagliato numero
a sbalyato noomero
You've got the wrong
number

CHANGING MONEY

• The Italian unit of currency is the **lira** (abbreviated as **L**). There are coins of 5, 10, 20, 50, 100, 200 and 500 lire, and banknotes of 1,000, 2,000, 5,000, 10,000, 50,000 and 100,000 lire.

• You can change money, traveller's cheques or Eurocheques into lire at banks, and other places (hotels, travel agencies, main railway stations and airports) where you see a **cambio** sign. You'll probably get the best rate in a bank.

• Banks are open from 8.30a.m. to 1.20p.m. Mondays to Fridays, and for an hour in the afternoon, usually from 3.00p.m. to 4.00p.m., but check locally. Banks are not open at weekends or on other national holidays. Savings banks (**cassa di risparmio**) may not have exchange facilities. Privately run **uffici cambio** are open longer hours and on Saturdays and Sundays.

• In banks, you go first to the **cambio** desk where a form is filled in for you to sign. You then get your money from the cashier (**cassa**). You'll need your passport to change money.

• You can get money from banks and from some cash dispensers by using the major credit cards.

You may see

Aperto	Open
Banca	Bank
Cassa automatica	Cash dispenser
Cassa di risparmio	Savings bank
Cambio	Exchange, Bureau de change
Chiuso	Closed
Entrata	Entrance
Istituto bancario	Bank
Uscita	Exit

You may want to say

I'd like to change some pounds sterling
Vorrei cambiare delle sterline
vorray kambyare delle sterleene

I'd like to change some traveller's cheques
Vorrei cambiare dei travellers cheques
vorray kambyare de-ee travellers cheques

I'd like to change a Eurocheque
Vorrei cambiare un Eurocheque
vorray kambyare oon oirochek

I'd like to get some money with this credit card
Vorrei prendere dei soldi con questa carta di credito
vorray prendere de-ee soldee kon kwesta karta dee kredeeto

What's the exchange rate today?
Com'è il cambio oggi?
kome eel kambyo ojee

Can you give me some change, please?
Può darmi degli spiccioli, per favore?
pwo darmee delyee speecholee per favore

Can you give me five thousand-lire notes?
Può darmi cinque banconote da mille lire
pwo darmee cheenkwe bankonote da meelle leere

I'm at the Hotel Michelangelo
Sto all'albergo Michelangelo
sto allalbergo meekelanjelo

I'm staying with friends
Sto presso degli amici
sto presso delyee ameechee

The address is Viale Manzoni, 25
L'indirizzo è Viale Manzoni, venticinque
leendeereetzo e vyale mantsonee vaynteecheenkwe

You may hear

Il suo passaporto, per favore
*eel **soo**-o passa**por**to per favore*
Your passport, please

Quanto vuole cambiare?
kwanto vwole kambyare
How much do you want to change?

Il suo indirizzo, per favore?
*eel **soo**-e eendee**reet**so per favore*
Your address, please?

Il nome del suo albergo, per favore?
*eel **no**me del **soo**-o al**ber**go per favore*
The name of your hotel, please?

Firmi qui, per favore
*feer**mee** kwee per favore*
Sign here, please

Si accomodi alla cassa, per favore
*see ak**ko**modee **al**la **kas**sa per favore*
Please go to the cashier

EATING AND DRINKING

● To order something, all you need do is name it, and say 'please', adding 'for me', 'for him' or 'for her' if you're ordering for several people to show who wants what.

● In bars you pay for all your drinks and so on first at the cash desk, unless you are sitting down. It's usual to leave some small change in a saucer on the bar itself as a tip. It costs a lot more to sit at a table than to stand up at the bar, especially on a terrace or pavement outside a bar or café. In restaurants the bill will say if service is included, **servizio compreso** (it usually is); however it's usual to leave a tip of 10% anyway.

● There will also be a cover charge, **pane e coperto**, added to your bill in restaurants. Look on the menu to see how much it is.

● Bars tend to open early in the morning (for breakfast) and stay open till around midnight. Meal times in Italy are roughly the same as in Britain. Lunch, **il pranzo**, is around 1p.m. and the largest meal of the day. Dinner/supper, **la cena**, is usually eaten around 8p.m.

● Bars and cafés serve all kinds of drinks – alcohol, soft drinks, coffee and tea, etc. Most also serve food, which may be sandwiches, rolls or pastries. There will often be a menu on the wall, but you may have to ask what's available. There are no age restrictions.

● **Tavola Calda, Pizzeria, Rosticceria** are usually the cheapest places to eat. A **Tavola Calda** will usually offer a few hot dishes, pizza and sandwiches. You may find pasta dishes as well as pizzas at a **Pizzeria**. Some pizzerias sell pizza by slice and weight, **al taglio**, to take away.

● Generally a **Ristorante** will be more expensive than a **Trattoria**. Many restaurants offer a tourist menu, **il menù**

turistico, at a fixed price. This usually includes two courses plus wine. By law a restaurant should give you a receipt, **una ricevuta fiscale**.

● **Un espresso** is strong, black coffee served in a small cup. **Un caffè lungo** is a longer, weaker espresso. **Un caffelatte** is white coffee, usually only drunk at breakfast time, **la prima colazione**. **Cappuccino** is a milky expresso often served with grated chocolate on top of the froth. You can also drink **caffè freddo**, iced coffee, or **caffè corretto**, coffee with brandy or **grappa**. Tea (made with tea-bags) comes on its own – you have to ask for milk or lemon. Ask for **una camomilla** if you want a herbal tea.

● Milk-shake, **frullato**, is delicious. You can choose your flavour. **Granite** are crushed-ice drinks and **una spremuta** is fresh fruit juice prepared on the spot.

● Italians are fond of liqueurs, **digestivi**, and there is a wide range in bars and restaurants. Try **amaretto**, almond liqueur, if you have a sweet tooth.

● Many of the 21 regions in Italy produce their own excellent wines. The best known include **Chianti**, which comes from Tuscany, **Soave** and **Valpolicella** from the Lake Garda area, **Frascati** from the hills near Rome and **Marsala** from Sicily. **Classico** on a label means that the wine comes from the oldest part of that particular wine-producing area. **D.O.C. (Denominazione d'origine controllata)** on the label is a guarantee of quality.

● Italian beer is the light lager type. It comes in bottles, **in bottiglia**, or in cans, **in lattina**, unless you ask for it on draught, **alla spina**.

● Cider is virtually unknown in Italy.

● Sandwiches, **tramezzini**, are usually made with sliced white bread and a savoury filling and are sold in bars and cafés. **Panini**, or rolls, are also available in bars and cafés; common fillings include **prosciutto crudo** (raw ham) and cheese – **formaggio**. You could also ask for **un toast**, a toasted sandwich.

● If you want something sweeter in a bar or café, especially at breakfast time, try **un cornetto** or **una brioche**, both are croissant-type rolls.

● Italian ice-cream, **gelato**, shouldn't be missed. If you're buying it to take away you can usually choose between a cornet, **un cono**, and a tub, **una coppetta**, with two or three different flavours topped with cream. Or you can go the whole hog and sit down in a **Gelateria**, an ice-cream parlour, which will probably sell cakes, pastries and drinks as well as ice-creams.

● Regional variations are an important feature of the legendary Italian cuisine. Bologna is traditionally the gastronomic capital and has given its name to the meat and tomato sauce served with spaghetti to make **spaghetti alla bolognese**. The region around Bologna, Emilia Romagna, is also home to Parma ham and Parmesan (**Parmigiano**) cheese.

Pizza is served all over Italy but is the special pride of Naples and the Campania region. **Pizza Napoletana** with mozzarella cheese, tomatoes and anchovies is delicious and usually one of the cheaper pizzas on the menu.

You may see

Alcolici e bibite	Alcoholic and soft drinks
Bar	Bar
Bar all'aperto	Open-air snack bar; picnic area
Birreria	Bar, pub
Bottiglieria	Wine cellar; off-licence
Caffè	Café
Gelateria	Ice-cream parlour
Guardaroba	Cloakroom
Locanda	Inn
Menù turistico	Tourist menu
Menù turistico serale	Evening tourist menu
Osteria	Inn, tavern

Paninoteca	Sandwich bar
Pizzeria	Pizzeria, eat in or take away
Ristorante	Restaurant
Rosticceria	Snack bar
Self service	Self-service
Si accettano le carte di credito	We accept credit cards
Tavola calda	Snack bar
Toilettes	Toilets
Trattoria	Restaurant

You may want to say

General Phrases

Are there any inexpensive restaurants around here?
Ci sono i ristoranti economici qui vicino?
chee sono ee reestorantee ekonomeechee kwee veecheeno
(see Directions, page 26)

A (one) . . . , please
Un/Una . . . , per favore
oon/oona . . . per favore

Another . . . . please
Un altro/un'altra . . . , per favore
oon altro/oon altra . . . per favore

More . . . , please
Ancora di . . . , per favore
ankora dee . . . per favore

More bread, please
Ancora di pane, per favore
ankora dee pane per favore

A little more, please
Un po' di più, per favore
oon po dee pyoo per favore

A little less, please
Un po' di meno, per favore
oon po dee meno per favore

For me
Per me
per me

For him
Per lui
per loo-ee

For her
Per lei
per le-ee

For them
Per loro
per loro

This, please
Questo, per favore
kwesto per favore

Two of these, please
Due di questi, per favore
doo-e dee kwestee per favore

Do you have . . . ?
Ha . . . ?
a

Is/Are there any . . . ?
C'è/Ci sono . . . ?
che/chee sono

What is there to eat?
Cosa c'è da mangiare?
koza che da manjare

What is there for dessert?
Che dolci ci sono?
ke dolchee chee sono

What do you recommend?
Cosa consiglia?
koza konseelya

Do you have any typical
  local dishes?
Ha piatti tipici della zona?
a pyattee teepeechee della dzona

What is this?
Che cosa è questo?
ke koza e kwesto

How do you eat this?
Come si mangia questo?
kome see manja kwesto

Cheers!
Cin Cin!
cheen cheen

Enjoy your meal!
Buon appetito!
bwon appeteeto

Thank you, same to you
Grazie, altrettanto
gratsye altrettanto

Where are the toilets?
Dov'è la toilette?
dove la twalett

Nothing else, thanks
Nient'altro, grazie
nyentaltro gratsye

The bill, please
Il conto, per favore
eel konto per favore

Bars and cafés

A black coffee, please
Un espresso, per favore
oon espresso per favore

Two cappuccinos, please
Due cappuccini, per favore
doo-e kappoocheenee per favore

A tea with milk/lemon, please
Un tè al latte/limone, per favore
oon te al latte/leemone per favore

A coffee with brandy, please
Un caffè corretto, per favore
oon kaffe korretto per favore

A hot chocolate, please
Un cioccolato caldo, per favore
oon chokkolato kaldo per favore

Mineral water, please
Acqua minerale, per favore
akkwa meenerale per favore

Fizzy/Still
Gassata/Non gassata
gassata/non gassata

A fizzy orange, please
Un'aranciata, per favore
oon aranchata per favore

What fruit juices do you have?
Che succhi di frutta ha?
ke sookkee dee frootta a

An orange juice, please
Un succo di arancia, per favore
oon sookko dee arancha per favore

A milk-shake, please
Un frullato, per favore
oon froollato per favore

A beer, please
Una birra, per favore
oona beerra per favore

A glass of red wine, please
Un vino rosso, per favore
oon veeno rosso per favore

A gin and tonic, please
Un gin tonico, per favore
oon jeen toneeko per favore

With ice
Con ghiaccio
kon gyacho

A glass of water, please
Un bicchiere d'acqua, per favore
oon beekkyere dakkwa per favore

A cake, please
Una pasta, per favore
oona pasta per favore

A brioche, please
Una brioche, per favore
oona breeosh per favore

Some pizza, please
Un po' di pizza, per favore
oon po dee peetsa per favore

A toasted sandwich, please
Un toast, per favore
oon toast per favore

What rolls do you have?
Che panini ha?
ke paneenee a

A ham roll, please
Un panino al prosciutto, per favore
oon paneeno al proshootto per favore

Two cheese rolls, please
Due panini al formaggio, per favore
doo-e paneenee al formajo per favore

Do you have ice-creams?
Ha gelati?
a jelatee

Chocolate, coffee and banana, please
Cioccolato, caffè e banana, per favore
chokkolato, kaffe e banana per favore

A little of this
Un po' di questo
oon po dee kwesto

With cream
Con panna
kon panna

Booking a table

I want to reserve a table for two people
Vorrei riservare un tavolo per due persone
vorray reeservare oon tavolo per doo-e persone

For nine o'clock
Per le nove
per le nove

For tomorrow at half past eight
Per domani alle otto e mezza
per domanee alle otto e medza

I have booked a table
Ho riservato un tavolo
o reeservato oon tavolo

My name is . . .
Mi chiamo . . .
mee kyamo

In restaurants

A table for four, please
Un tavolo per quattro, per favore
oon tavolo per kwattro per favore

Outside/On the terrace, if possible
Fuori/Sulla terrazza, se è possibile
fworee/soolla terratsa se e posseebeele

Excuse me!
Scusi!
skoozee

The menu, please
Il menù, per favore
eel menoo per favore

The wine list, please
La lista di vini, per favore
la leesta dee veenee per favore

Do you have a set price menu?
Ha un menù a prezzo fisso?
a oon menoo a pretso feesso

Do you have vegetarian dishes?
Ha piatti vegetariani?
a pyattee vejetaryanee

The tourist menu (at L12,000), please
Il menù turistico (a dodici mila lire), per favore
eel menoo tooreesteeko (a dodeechee meela leere) per favore

For the starter . . .
Per antipasto . . .
per anteepasto

Ham and melon, please
Prosciutto e melone, per favore
proshootto e melone per favore

Tuna and beans, please
Tonno e fagioli, per favore
tonno e fajolee per favore

For the first course . . .
Per primo . . .
per preemo

The fish soup, please
La zuppa di pesce, per favore
la tsooppa dee peshe per favore

101

Spaghetti with sauce, please
Spaghetti al sugo, per favore
spagettee al soogo per favore

For the second course . . .
Per secondo . . .
per sekondo

The roast chicken, please
Il pollo arrosto, per favore
eel pollo arrosto per favore

The trout, please
La trota, per favore
la trota per favore

Are vegetables included?
È con contorno?
e kon kontorno

With chips
Con patate fritte
kon patate freette

And a mixed/green salad
E un'insalata mista/verde
e oon eensalata meesta/verde

For dessert . . .
Per dolce . . .
per dolche

Fruit salad, please
Macedonia di frutta, per favore
machedonee-a dee frootta per favore

A peach, please
Una pesca, per favore
oona peska per favore

What cheeses are there?
Che formaggi ci sono?
ke formajee chee sono

Excuse me, where is my steak?
Scusi, dov'è la mia bistecca?
skoozee dove la mee-a beestekka

More bread, please
Ancora di pane, per favore
ankora dee pane per favore

More chips, please
Ancora di patate fritte, per favore
ankora dee patate freette per favore

A glass/A jug of water
Un bicchiere/Una caraffa di acqua
oon beekkyere/oona karaffa dee akkwa

A bottle of red house wine
Una bottiglia di vino rosso della casa
oona botteelya dee veeno rosso della kaza

A litre of white house wine
Un litro di vino bianco della casa
ooon leetro dee veeno byanko della kaza

Half a litre of white wine
Mezzo litro di vino bianco
medzo leetro dee veeno byanko

(for ordering coffee, see page 99)

It's very good
È molto buono
e molto bwono

It's really delicious
È ottimo
e otteemo

This is burnt
È bruciato
e broochato

This is not cooked
Questo non è cotto
kwesto non e kotto

No, I ordered the chicken
No, ho ordinato il pollo
no o ordeenato eel pollo

The bill, please
Il conto, per favore
eel konto per favore

Do you accept credit cards?
Si accettano le carte di credito?
see achettano le karte dee kredeeto

Do you accept traveller's cheques?
Si accettano i travellers cheques?
see achettano ee travellers cheques

Excuse me, there is a mistake here
Scusi, c'è un errore qui
skoozee che oon errore kwee

You may hear

Bars and cafés

Dica?
deeka
What can I do for you?

Cosa desidera?
koza dezeedera
What would you like?

Cosa prende?
koza prende
What will you have?

Con ghiaccio?
kon gyacho
Would you like ice?

Gassato/a o non gassato/a?
gassato/a o non gassato/a
Fizzy or still?

Grande o piccolo/a?
grande o peekkolo/a
Large or small?

Subito
soobeeto
Right away

C'è/abbiamo . . .
che/abbyamo
We have . . .

Quale?/Cosa preferisce?
kwale/koza prefereeshe
Which one?

Restaurants

Quanti siete?
kwantee syete
How many are you?

Per quante persone?
per kwante persone
For how many people?

Un attimo
oon atteemo
Just a moment

Ha riservato un tavolo?
a reezervato oon tavolo
Have you booked a table?

Deve aspettare dieci minuti
deve aspettare dyechee meenootee
You will have to wait ten minutes

Vuole aspettare?
vwole aspettare
Would you like to wait?

Cosa desidera/desiderano?
koza dezeedera/deezeederano
What would you like?

Cosa preferisce/ preferiscono?
koza prefereeshe/prefereeskono
What would you like?

Ha/hanno deciso?
a/anno decheezo
Have you decided?

Consigliamo . . .
konseelyamo
We recommend . . .

Per antipasto
per anteepasto
For the starter

Per primo
per preemo
For the first course

Per secondo
per sekondo
For the second course

Da bere?
da bere
To drink?

Chi prende . . . ?
kee prende
Who is the . . . for?

Vorrebbe/vorrebbero un dolce, o un caffè?
vorrebbe/vorrebbero oon dolche o oon kaffe
Would you like dessert, or coffee?

Vorrebbe/vorrebbero un digestivo?
verrebbe/vorrebbero oon deejesteevo
Would you like a liqueur?

Ha/hanno finito?
a/anno feeneeto
Have you finished?

Qualcos'altro?
kwalkozaltro
Anything else?

MENU READER

General phrases

Antipasti	hors d'oeuvres
Aperitivi	aperitifs
Bevande	drinks
Bibite	soft drinks
Carne	meat
Cena	dinner
Contorni	vegetable dishes
Dolci	desserts
Digestivi	liqueurs
Formaggi	cheeses
Frutta	fruit
Gelati	ice-creams
IVA incluso	VAT included
Listino prezzi	price list
Menù turistico	tourist menu
Menù alla carta	à la carte menu
Minestre	soups
Pane e coperto	cover charge
Pesce	fish
Piatti del giorno	menu of the day
Pietanze	main courses
Pizze	pizzas
Pollame	fowl
Pranzo	lunch
Prima colazione	breakfast
Primi piatti	first courses
Secondi piatti	second courses
Servizio compreso	service included
Uova	egg dishes
Vini	wines

Drinks

Acqua	water
di seltz	soda-water
minerale	mineral water
tonica	tonic water
Acquavite	brandy, liqueur
Amaretto	almond liqueur
Americano	vermouth with bitters, brandy and lemon peel
Aranciata	fizzy orange
Barattolo	canned soft drinks
Bibite	soft drinks
Birra	beer
alla spina	draught
estera	imported
in bottiglia	bottled
in lattina	in a can
nazionale	Italian (like lager)
Caffè	coffee
corretto	laced with brandy
espresso	strong, black coffee
freddo	iced
latte	with milk
lungo	longer, weaker black coffee
macchiato	with a dash of milk
Cappuccino	frothy, white coffee, often with grated chocolate on top
Cioccolata	hot chocolate
Frullato di latte	milk-shake
Gassato/a	sparkling, fizzy
Gin tonico	gin and tonic
Granita	crushed-ice drink
all'arancia	with orange
al limone	with lemon
Grappa	strong grape liqueur
Latte	milk
macchiato	with a splash of coffee

Limonata	lemonade
Marsala	light, Sicilian dessert wine
Non gassato/a	still
Sambuca	aniseed liqueur
Sidro	cider
Spremuta	fresh fruit juice
d'arancia	fresh orange juice
di limone	fresh lemon juice
di pompelmo	fresh grapefruit juice
Spumante	sparkling wine
Strega	strong herb liqueur
Succo di frutta	fruit juice
d'ananas	pineapple juice
di pesca	peach juice
Tè	tea
al latte	with milk
al limone	with lemon
freddo	iced
Vino	wine
bianco	white
da tavola	table wine, in a carafe
dolce	sweet
in bottiglia	in the bottle
leggero	light
ordinario	table wine, in a carafe
pieno	full bodied
rosato	rosé
rosso	red
secco	dry

Food

Acciughe	anchovies
Aglio	garlic
all'aglio e olio	with oil and garlic
Agnello	lamb
rustico	roast leg of lamb with cheese and lemon

Agnolotti	pasta envelopes filled with meat or cheese
Agro: all'agro	with a dressing of lemon juice and oil
Albicocca	apricot
Alici	anchovies
Amarena	wild cherry
Ananas	pineapple
Anguilla	eel
Anitra	duck
Antipasto	starter
misto	selection of cold meats, usually ham and salami
Aragosta	lobster
Arancia	orange
Aranci caramellizzati	caramel oranges
Arancini di riso	deep fried rice balls with mozzarella cheese
Arrabbiata: all'arrabbiata	hot tomato sauce with chillies
Arrosto	roast
di manzo	roast beef
Baccalà	salt cod
Bagna cauda	hot anchovy and garlic dip served with crisp, raw vegetables
Banana	banana
Bel paese	mild, creamy cheese
Ben cotto	(steak) well done
Besciamella	béchamel (white) sauce
Bianco: in bianco	served with butter and Parmesan cheese
Bistecca	steak (usually beef)
(di) manzo	braised beef with wine
di vitello	veal steak
Bollito	boiled
Bollito misto	mixed boiled meats

Brace: alla brace	grilled. *Lit: 'over an open fire'*
Braciola	rib steak
Braciola di maiale	pork chop
Broccoli	broccoli
Brodo	broth
Brodo lungo	thin broth
in brodo	in broth
Bruschetta al pomodoro	garlic bread with olive oil and fresh tomatoes
Burrida	fish soup, fish stew
Burro	butter
al burro	cooked in butter
Cacciatora: alla cacciatora	'hunter's style': cooked with onions, tomatoes, mushrooms, peppers and red or white wine
Calamari	squid
alla veneziana	squid cooked in its own ink
Calzone	pizza rolled up and stuffed with ham and mozzarella cheese
Cannelloni	rolls of pasta
Cannelloni al forno	rolls of pasta stuffed with meat sauce, baked and served with melted cheese
Cappelletti	'little hats' of stuffed pasta
Carbonara: alla carbonara	cooked with smoked bacon, egg and black pepper
Carciofi	artichokes
Carne	meat
Carote	carrots
Casalinga: alla casalinga	home made
Cassata	ice-cream cake with candied fruit
alla siciliana	sponge cake with chocolate and cream cheese
Castagne	chestnuts

Cavolfiore	cauliflower
Cavolo	cabbage
Ceci	chick peas
Ciliegie	cherries
Cinghiale	wild boar
Cioccolato	chocolate
Cipolle	onions
Cocomero	water melon
Conchiglie	pasta shells
Coniglio	rabbit
all'agro	stewed in red wine
alla molisana	rabbit and sausage on skewers
Costoletta	cutlet
alla milanese	in breadcrumbs and cheese
Cotto	cooked
a puntino	(steak) medium
Cozze	mussels
Crema	cream, custard
Crostini	toast, croutons
di fegatini di pollo	fried chicken livers on toast
Dente: al dente	not over-cooked
Dolce	cake or sweet
Dolcelatte	soft, sharp cheese
Entrecote	steak
barolo	with mushrooms and red wine
Fagioli	haricot or butter beans
Fagiolini	French beans
Farfalle	butterfly-shaped pasta
Fegato	liver
alla veneziana	calf's liver fried with onion
Fettucine	long, ribbon pasta
Fichi	figs
Finocchi: di finocchi	with fennel
Fonduta	melted cheese with egg yolk, white wine, milk and truffles

Formaggio	cheese
Forno: al forno	baked
Fragole	strawberries
di bosco	wild strawberries
Frittata	omelette
Fritto/a	fried
misto di mare	deep fried sea food
Frutta	fruit
di stagione	seasonal fresh fruit
Frutti di mare	seafood
Funghi	mushrooms
Fusilli	pasta spirals
Gamberi	prawns
Gamberetti	shrimps
Gelato	ice-cream
Gelati assortiti	assorted ice-cream
Ghiacciato	iced, chilled
Gnocchi	little dumplings
alla romana	potato dumplings
di semolino	dumplings made with semolina
verdi	spinach dumplings
Gorgonzola	blue-veined, sharp-tasting cheese
Granchi	crabs
Gratinato/a	sprinkled with breadcrumbs and cheese and grilled
Griglia: alla griglia	grilled
Grissini	crispy bread sticks
Insalata	salad
mista	mixed salad
russa	cold diced vegetables in mayonnaise
verde	green salad
Lamponi	raspberries
Lasagne	wide strips of pasta
verdi	'green', spinach lasagne
Lattuga	lettuce

111

Lenticchie	lentils
Limone	lemon
Linguine	flattened spaghetti
Lombata di vitello	loin of veal
Maccheroni	macaroni
Macedonia di frutta fresca	fresh fruit salad
Maiale	pork
ubriaco	pork cooked in red wine
Malaga	sweet, alcoholic flavour, usually of ice-cream
Mandorle	almonds
Marroni	chestnuts
Mascarpone	cream cheese
Mela	apple
Melanzane	aubergines
sott'olio	pickled aubergines
Melone	melon
Merluzzo	cod
Miele	honey
Minestra	soup
Minestrone	thick vegetable soup
More	blackberries
Mortadella	mild spiced salami
Mozzarella	moist, white buffalo milk cheese
in carrozza	mozzarella sandwiches dipped in egg and fried
Nocciola	hazelnut
Noci	walnuts
Olivi	olives
Ossobuco	knuckle of veal stewed in wine with onion, tomatoes and parsley
Ostriche	oysters
Paglia e fieno	mixed green and white pasta, usually spaghetti or tagliatelli. *Lit: 'hay and straw'*

Pagliarda di vitella	thin veal chop with ham
Pagliata	sweetbreads
Panettone	light, candied fruit cake, often eaten at Christmas
Panforte di Siena	cake with honey, candied fruits, almonds and cloves
Panna	cream
alla panna	cream sauce usually with mushrooms or ham
Parmigiano	Parmesan cheese, usually grated
Pasta	
asciutta	plain pasta
e fagioli	with beans
in brodo	pasta in broth
Patate fritte	chips
Pecorino	hard, white sheep's or goat's cheese
fresco	fresh
Penne	small tubes of pasta
Pera	pear
Pesca	peach
Pesce	fish
spada	swordfish
Pesto: al pesto	sauce of basil and garlic
alla genovese	sauce of basil, garlic, herbs, cheese and pine nuts
Petti di pollo	chicken breast
alla bolognese	with ham and cheese
Piccata	escalope (usually veal)
alla lombarda	with butter, parsley and lemon juice
milanese	veal escalope in breadcrumbs
di pollo	chicken escalope with pimento and wine sauce
Piselli	peas
Pistacchio	pistacchio

Pizza	pizza
capricciosa	pizza with tomatoes, mozzarella and mushrooms
margherita	pizza with tomatoes and mozzarella
napoletana	pizza with mozzarella, tomatoes and anchovies
quattro stagioni	'four seasons' pizza with a bit of everything and a fried egg
salsiccia	pizza with sausage, tomatoes and mozzarella
siciliana	pizza with anchovies, tomatoes and olives
Pizzaiola: alla pizzaiola	with tomatoes, garlic and basil
Polenta	porridge-like mixture made from maize, sometimes made into dumplings
napoletana	polenta with spiced sausages
Pollo	chicken
arrosto	roast chicken
(alla) diavola	grilled with pepper, pimento and mustard
cacciatore	with mushroom sauce
principessa	with asparagus tips
sorpresa	rolled breast of chicken filled with butter and garlic
Polpettone	meatballs
Polpo	octopus
in purgatorio	'in purgatory' with tomatoes, garlic, parsley and peppers
Pomodoro	tomato
al pomodoro	with tomato sauce
Pompelmo	grapefruit
Porchetta	roast pork stuffed with cheese and herbs
Prezzemolo: al prezzemolo	with parsley

Prosciutto	ham
affumicato	smoked
crudo	raw, cured ham
cotto	cooked ham
di Parma	cured, raw ham from Parma
di San Daniele	raw ham
Provolone	delicate, creamy, firm white cheese
Prugne	plums
Radicchio	wild red chicory
Ragù	bolognese sauce (meat, cheese and tomato)
Ravioli	cushions of pasta filled with meat or cheese
di magro	ravioli stuffed with fish
Ricotta	white, soft cheese
Rigatoni	'ribbed' tubes of pasta
Ripieno	stuffed
Riso	rice
Risi e bisi	rice and peas
Risotto	rice dish
alla milanese	rice cooked with saffron and beef marrow stock
Robiola	mild white sheep's cheese
Rognoni	kidneys
Rollè di vitella	roast veal
Salame	salami
Salmone	salmon
Salsa	sauce
bolognese	meat, cheese and tomato sauce
Salsicce	spicy sausages
Saltimbocca alla romana	veal with ham, sage and wine sauce
Salvia: alla salvia	with sage
Scaloppine	small slices of veal

Scampi	scampi
alla romana	scampi with pimento, tomato and mushroom sauce
provinciale	scampi with garlic and tomato sauce
Scamorza alla brace	melted scamorza cheese
Semifreddo	ice-cream with biscuits
Sgombro	mackerel
Sogliola	sole
Spaghetti	spaghetti
all'amatriciana	with bacon, pepper and tomatoes
alla carbonara	with egg and bacon
alla siciliana	with fennel and sardines
marinara	with garlic, basil, anchovies and tomatoes
Spezzatino	stew, goulash
Spigola	sea bass
Spinaci	spinach
Stracciatella	clear soup with egg beaten into it
Sugo	sauce
al sugo	with sauce
Supplì	rice croquettes filled with tomato sauce
Tacchino	turkey
Tagliatelli	ribbon pasta
Tartufi	truffles
Tiramisù	type of trifle
Tonno	tuna
e fagioli	tuna and butter (haricot) bean salad
Tornedo rossini	fillet steak on toast with pâté and sherry sauce
Torta	flan, tart
pasqualina	with artichokes, eggs, mushrooms and Parmesan cheese

Tortellini	'hats' of pasta filled with meat or cheese
Trippa	tripe
Trota	trout
meunière	with butter, lemon and parsley
Uova	egg
alla fiorentina	poached eggs served in a béchamel sauce with spinach
Uva	grapes
Vaniglia	vanilla
Verdura	vegetables
mista	mixed vegetables
Vermicelli	long, very thin pasta
Vitello	veal
alla bolognese	veal cutlet cooked with parma ham and cheese
tonnato	cold braised veal with tuna mayonnaise
valdostana	veal chops stuffed with soft cheese
Vongole	clams
Zabaglione (zabaione)	light fluffy egg dessert made with Marsala wine
Zampa di vitello alla toscana	Calf's feet or pig's trotters cooked with vegetables and Parmesan cheese
Zucchini	courgettes
Zuppa	soup
inglese	trifle
pavese	egg soup

SHOPPING

● Shop opening hours vary a bit, but in general shops are open from 9 a.m. (food shops 8 a.m.) to 1 p.m. and from 4 p.m. to 7.30 p.m., or 4.30 to 8 p.m. in summer. In Northern Italy, lunch hours may be shorter and closing times earlier.

● There are some chains of department stores, such as **La Rinascente**, **Upim** and **Standa**, with branches mainly in large towns and cities. They usually don't close for lunch. There are also large self-service supermarkets, especially in tourist areas. On the whole, though, Italian shops are smaller, individual ones. In villages and small towns, it's sometimes hard to tell where shops are. There are often no signs or shop windows, just an open door with a plastic strip curtain.

● If you go to the large towns and cities during July and August, you will frequently come across the sign **Chiuso per ferie** (closed for the holidays) on shop doors and windows, especially those of smaller shops.

● Many places have markets – some permanent, some only one day a week, some outdoor, some indoor. Some sell only fruit and vegetables, others sell almost anything.

● Chemists (**farmacia**) have a red cross in a circle outside. They sell mainly medicines and baby foods. There should be a list in the window with names and times of chemists in the area who stay open late. Cosmetics and toiletries are sold at a **profumeria** or **drogheria**. Lists of duty chemists that are open late are displayed on the shop doors and are printed in newspapers.

● **Tabacchi**, the sign for which is a white **T** on a black background, are the best place to buy stamps.

● Post offices (**L'ufficio postale**) are usually open only in the mornings. Postboxes are red, and they may have separate slots for mail within the city (**per la città**) and other destinations (**tutte le altre destinazioni**).

If you want to receive mail at a *poste restante*, have it addressed to **Fermo Posta** at the town or village you're staying in. Take your passport along when you go to pick it up.

● To ask for something in a shop, all you need do is name it and add 'please' – or just point and say 'some of this, please' or 'two of those, please'.

● Before you go shopping, try to make a list of what you need – in Italian. If you're looking for clothes or shoes, work out what size to ask for and other things like colour, material and so on.

● Shopkeepers and customers always exchange greetings and goodbyes, so check up on the correct phrases for the time of day (see inside front cover).

You may see

Abbigliamento (donne/uomini/bambini)	Clothes (women/men/children)
Alimentari	Groceries
Antiquario	Antiques
Aperto	Open
Articoli sportivi	Sports goods
Bottiglieria	Wine cellar; off-licence
Calzature	Shoe shop
Calzoleria	Shoe repairs
Cartoleria	Stationer's
Cassa	Cashier
Chiuso (per ferie)	Closed (for holidays)
Cibi macrobiotici	Health foods
Confetteria	Confectioner's
Confezioni	Clothes/Fashions
Copisteria	Photo-copy shop
Dischi	Records
Drogheria	Drugstore; grocer's

Elettrodomestici	Electrical goods
Entrata	Entrance
Erboristeria/Cibi macrobiotici	Health foods
Farmacia	Chemist's
Farmacie di turno	Duty chemists
Ferramenta	Ironmonger's/Hardware
Foto-ottica	Photo shop
Frutteria, Fruttivendolo	Fruiterer's
Giocattoli	Toy shop
Gioielleria	Jeweller's
Ingresso libero	Free admission (no obligation to buy)
Ipermercato	Hypermarket
Latteria	Dairy
Lavanderia	Launderette
Libreria	Bookshop
Macelleria	Butcher's
Mobili	Furniture
Moda	Clothes
Orologeria	Watchmaker's
Ottico	Optician's
Panetteria, Panificio	Baker's
Parrucchiere/a	Hairdresser's
Pasticceria	Cake shop
Pelletteria	Leather goods
Pescheria	Fishmonger's
Posta, l'Ufficio postale	Post office
Prezzo di vendita al dettaglio	Retail price
Profumeria	Drugstore/Perfumery
Regali	Gifts
Saldi	Sales/Reductions
Salottini di prova	Fitting rooms
Salumeria	Cooked-meat shop
Scarpe	Shoes
Sconti	Reductions
Servizio notturno	Night service (for chemists)
Si prega di non toccare	Please do not touch

Souvenirs	Souvenirs
Supermercato	Supermarket
Tabacchi	Tobacconist`s
Tintoria	Dry-cleaner`s
Uscita (di sicurezza)	(Emergency) exit
Vinaio	Wine shop

You may want to say

General phrases

(*see also* Directions, *page 26;* Problems and complaints, *page 159;* Numbers, *page 195*)

Where is the main shopping area?
Dov'è il centro commerciale?
dove eel chentro kommerchale

Where is the chemist`s?
Dov'è la farmacia?
dove la farmachee-a

Is there a food shop around here?
C'è un alimentario qui vicino?
che oon aleementareeo kwee veecheeno

Where can I buy batteries?
Dove posso comprare delle pile?
dove posso komprare delle peele

Have you got . . . ?
Ha . . . ?
a . . .

Have you got stamps?
Ha francobolli?
a frankobollee

How much is it . . . ?
Quant'è . . . ?
kwante . . .

How much does it cost?
Quanto costa?
kwanto kosta

How much do they cost?
Quanto costano?
kwanto kostano

I don't understand
Non capisco
non kapeesko

Can you write it down, please?
Può scriverlo, per favore?
pwo skreeverlo per favore

It's too expensive
È troppo caro
e troppo karo

Have you got anything
  cheaper?
Ha qualcosa di meno caro?
a kwalkoza dee meno karo

I don't have enough money
Non ho abbastanza soldi
non o abbastantsa soldee

Can you keep it for me?
Può tenermelo da parte?
pwo tenermelo da parte

When do you open in the
  morning?
A che ora aprite di mattino?
a ke ora apreete dee matteeno

When do you close?
A che ora chiudete?
a ke ora kyoodete

What time does the post
  office open?
A che ora apre l'ufficio postale
a ke ora apre looffeecho postale

Do you close for lunch?
Chiudete a mezzogiorno?
kyoodete a medzojorno

I'm just looking
Sto solo guardando
sto solo gwardando

I'll think about it
Ci penserò
chee pensero

That one there, please
Quello lì, per favore
kwello lee per favore

This one here, please
Questo qua, per favore
kwesto kwa per favore

Two of those, please
Due di quelle, per favore
doo-e dee kwelle per favore

Some of these, please
Alcuni di questi, per favore
alkoonee dee kwestee per favore

A bit of that, please
Un po' di questo, per favore
oon po dee kwesto per favore

What is this?
Che cosa è?
ke koza e

Can I try it?
Posso provarlo?
posso provarlo

It's a gift
È un regalo
e oon regalo

I'm taking it to England
Lo porto in Inghilterra
lo porto een eengeelterra

Can you wrap it, please
Può incartarlo, per favore?
pwo eenkartarlo per favore

With lots of paper, please
Con molta carta, per favore
kon molta karta per favore

A bag, please
Una borsa, per favore
oona borsa per favore

The receipt, please
La ricevuta, per favore
la reechevoota per favore

Where do I pay?
Dove si paga?
dove see paga

Do you take credit cards?
Si accettano le carte di credito?
see achettano le karte dee kredeeto

Do you take traveller's cheques?
Si accettano i travellers cheques?
see achettano ee travellers cheques

I'm sorry, I don't have any change
Mi dispiace, non ho spiccioli
mee deespyache non o speecholee

I'll take it
Lo prendo
lo prendo

That's fine
Va bene
va bene

Nothing else, thank you
Nient'altro, grazie
nyentaltro gratsye

Buying food and drink

A kilo of . . . ., please
Un chilo di . . . , per favore
oon keelo dee . . . per favore

A kilo of cherries, please
Un chilo di ciliegie, per favore
oon keelo dee cheelee-ejye per favore

2 kilos of apples, please
Due chili di mele, per favore
doo-e keelee dee mele per favore

Half a kilo of courgettes, please
Mezzo chilo di zucchini, per favore
medzo keelo dee tsookeenee per favore

A hundred grams of . . . .
please
Un etto di . . . , per favore
oon etto dee . . . per favore

A hundred grams of olives,
please
Un etto di olive, per favore
oon etto dee oleeve per favore

Two hundred grams of
salami, please
Due etti di salame, per favore
doo-e ettee dee salame per favore

A piece of cheese, please
**Un pezzo di formaggio, per
favore**
oon petso dee formajo per favore

Five slices of ham, please
**Cinque fette di prosciutto
crudo, per favore**
*cheenkwe fette dee proshootto
kroodo per favore*

A bottle of water, please
**Una bottiglia d'acqua, per
favore**
*oona botteelya dakkwa per
favore*

A litre of red wine, please
**Un litro di vino rosso, per
favore**
*oon leetro dee veeno rosso per
favore*

Half a litre of milk, please
Mezzo litro di latte, per favore
medzo leetro dee latte per favore

Two cans of beer, please
Due lattine di birra, per favore
*doo-e latteene dee beerra per
favore*

A bit more, please
Un po' di più, per favore
oon po dee pyoo per favore

A bit less, please
Un po' di meno, per favore
oon po dee meno per favore

What's this like?
Com'è questo?
kome kwesto

What's it made of?
Di che cosa è fatto?
dee ke koza e fatto

That's enough, thank you
Basta così
basta kozee

At the Chemist's

Aspirins, please
Delle aspirine, per favore
delle aspeereene per favore

Plasters, please
Dei cerotti, per favore
de-ee cherottee per favore

Have you got something for
. . . ?
Ha qualcosa per . . . ?
a kwalkoza per . . .

Have you got something for
sunburn?
Ha qualcosa per le scottature?
a kwalkoza per le skottatoore

Have you got something for
diarrhoea?
Ha qualcosa per la diarrea?
a kwalkoza per la dee-arre-a

Have you got something for
insect bites?
**Ha qualcosa per le punture di
insetti?**
*a kwalkoza per le poontoore
dee eensettee*

Have you got something for
period pains?
**Ha qualcosa per i dolori
mestruali?**
*a kwalkoza per ee doloree
mestroo-alee*

Buying clothes and shoes

I want . . .
Voglio . . .
volyo . . .

I want a skirt
Voglio una gonna
volyo oona gonna

My size is . . .
La mia taglia è . . .
la mee-a talya e . . .

Can I try it on?
Posso provarlo?
posso provarlo

Can I try them on? (*shoes*)
Posso provarle?
posso provarle

Is there a mirror?
C'è uno specchio?
che oono spekkyo

I like it
Mi piace
mee pyache

I don't like it
Non mi piace
non mee pyache

It's very nice
È molto bello
e molto bello

They're very nice
Sono molto belli
sono molto bellee

Fine, very good
Molto bene
molto bene

It's too big
È troppo grande
e troppo grande

They're too big
Sono troppo grandi
sono troppo grandee

It's too small
È troppo piccolo
e troppo peekkolo

They're too small
Sono troppo piccoli
sono troppo peekkolee

What size is it?
Che taglia è?
ke talya e

Have you got size 42?
Ha una quarantadue?
a oona kwarantadoo-e

Have you got a smaller size?
Ha una taglia più piccola?
a oona talya pyoo peekkola

Have you got a bigger size?
Ha una taglia più grande?
a oona talya pyoo grande

Have you got another colour?
Ha un altro colore?
a oon altro kolore

Can you measure me?
Può prendermi la misura, per favore?
pwo prendermee la meezoora per favore

Miscellaneous

Five stamps for England, please
Cinque francobolli per l'Inghilterra, per favore
cheenkwe frankobollee per leengeelterra per favore

... for postcards/letters
... per cartoline/lettere
... per kartoleene/lettere

Three postcards, please
Tre cartoline, per favore
tre kartoleene per favore

Matches, please
Una scatola di cerini, per favore
oona skatola dee chereenee per favore

A film for my camera, please
Una pellicola per la mia macchina fotografica, per favore
oona pelleekola per la mee-a makkeena fotografeeka per favore

Have you got an English newspaper?
Ha un giornale inglese?
a oon jornale eengleze

You may hear

Dica!
deeka
May I help you?

Che cosa desidera?
ke koza dezeedera
What would you like?

Quanto ne vuole?
kwanto ne vwole
How much would you like?

Quanti ne vuole?
kwantee ne vwole
How many would you like?

Nient'altro?
nyentaltro
Anything else?

Basta così?
basta kozee
Is that enough?

Mi dispiace, non ce n'è più
mee deespyache non che ne pyoo
I'm sorry, we're sold out

Mi dispiace, siamo chiusi adesso
mee deespyache syamo kyoozee adesso
I'm sorry, we're closed now

Glielo incarto?
lyee-elo eenkarto
Shall I wrap it?

Ha spiccioli?
a speecholee
Have you got any change?

Ci vuole una ricetta
chee vwole oona reechetta
You need a prescription

Che taglia ha?
ke talya a
What size are you?

Cartolina o lettera?
kartoleena o lettera
Postcard or letter?

Che tipo di . . . ?
ke teepo dee
What sort of . . . ?

Che tipo di macchina fotografica ha?
ke teepo dee makkeena fotografeeka a
What sort of camera do you have?

Che tipo di pellicola vuole?
ke teepo dee pelleekola vwole
What sort of film do you want?

BUSINESS TRIPS

● You'll probably be doing business with the help of inter-preters or in a language everyone speaks, but you may need a few Italian phrases to cope at a company's reception desk.

● When you arrive for an appointment, all you need do is say who you've come to see and give your name or hand over your business card. However, if you're not expected, you may need to make an appointment or leave a message.

You may see

Ascensore	Lift
Ditta	Firm, company
Entrata	Entrance
Guasto	Out of order
Informazioni	Information/Reception
Pianterreno	Ground floor
1º piano	1st floor
2º piano	2nd floor
Scala	Stairs
Società	Company
Spingere	Push
S.r.l.=Società da responsabilità limitata	Limited company
Tirare	Pull
Uscita (di sicurezza)	(Emergency) exit
Vietato fumare	No smoking
Vietato l'ingresso	No entry
Vietato l'ingresso alle persone non autorizzate	No entry to unauthorised persons

You may want to say

(see also Days, months, dates, page 177; Time, page 181)

Mr Barberini, please
Il signor Barberini, per favore
eel seenyor barbereenee per favore

Mrs de Mattia, please
La signora de Mattia, per favore
la seenyora de mattee-a per favore

Miss Ferrari, please
La signorina Ferrari, per favore
la seenyoreena ferraree per favore

The manager, please
Il direttore, per favore
eel deerettore per favore

My name is ...
Mi chiamo ...
mee kyamo ...

I work for ...
Lavoro per ...
lavoro per ...

I have an appointment with
Mr Paolo Barberini
**Ho un appuntamento con il
Signor Paolo Barberini**
*o oon appoontamento kon eel
seenyor powlo barbereenee*

I don't have an appointment
Non ho un appuntamento
non o oon appoontamento

I'd like ...
Vorrei ...
vorray ...

I'd like to make an
appointment with Miss
Bedoni
**Vorrei fissare un
appuntamento con la
Signorina Bedoni**
*vorray feessare oon
appoontamento kon la
seenyoreena bedonee*

I'd like to talk to the export
manager
**Vorrei parlare con il direttore
alle esportazioni**
*vorray parlare kon eel
deerettore alle esportatsyonee*

What is his/her name?
Qual è il suo nome?
kwal e eel soo-o nome

When will he/she be back?
Quando torna?
kwando torna

I am free this afternoon at
five o'clock
**Sono libero/a questo
pomeriggio alle cinque**
*sono leebero/a kwesto
pomereejo alle cheenkwe*

Can I leave a message?
Posso lasciare un messaggio?
posso lashare oon messajo

Can he/she call me?
Può farmi chiamare?
pwo farmee kyamare

My telephone number is . . .
Il mio numero di telefono è . . .
eel mee-o noomero dee telefono e . . .

I am staying at the Hotel Excelsior
Sto all'Hotel Excelsior
sto allotel exchelsyor

Where is his/her office?
Dov'è il suo ufficio?
dove eel soo-o ooffeecho

I am here for the exhibition
Sono qui per l'esposizione
sono kwee per lesposeetsyone

I am here for the trade fair
Sono qui per la fiera campionaria
sono kwee per la fyera kampyonarya

I am attending the conference
Sono qui per il congresso
sono kwee per eel kongresso

I need to make a phone call (to Britain)
Dovrei telefonare (in Gran Bretagna)
dovray telefonare een gran bretanya

I need to send a telex
Dovrei mandare un telex
dovray mandare oon telex

I need to send this by fax
Dovrei mandare questo per fax
dovray mandare kwesto per fax

I need to send this by post
Dovrei mandare questo per posta
dovray mandare kwesto per posta

I need to send this by courier
Dovrei mandare questo con un fattorino
dovray mandare kwesto kon oon fattoreeno

I need someone to type a letter for me
Ho bisogno di qualcuno che mi scriva questo a macchina
o beezonyo dee kwalkoono ke mee skreeva kwesto a makkeena

I need a photocopy (of this)
Ho bisogno di una fotocopia (di questo)
o beezonyo dee oona fotocopee-a dee kwesto

I need an interpreter
Mi serve un interprete
mee serve oon eenterprete

You may hear

Il suo nome, per favore?
eel soo-o nome per favore
Your name, please?

Come si chiama?
kome see kyama
What is your name?

Il nome della sua società, per favore?
eel nome della soo-a socheta per favore
The name of your company, please?

Ha un appuntamento?
a oon appoontamento
Do you have an appointment?

Ha un biglietto della ditta?
a oon beelyetto della deetta
Do you have a card?

La sta aspettando?
la sta aspettando
Is he/she expecting you?

(Aspetti) un attimo, per favore
aspettee oon atteemo per favore
(Wait) one moment, please

Gli/le dico che lei è qui
lyee/le deeko ke lay e kwee
I'll tell him/her you're here

Viene subito
vyene soobeeto
He/she's just coming

Si accommodi, prego
see akkommodee prego
Please sit down

Vuole sedersi?
vwole sedersee
Would you like to sit down?

Entri, per favore
entree per favore
Go in, please

Da questa parte, prego
da kwesta parte prego
Come this way, please

Il signor Barberini non c'è
eel seenyor barbereenee non che
Mr Barberini isn't in

La signora de Mattia torna alle undici
la seenyora de mattee-a torna alle oondeechee
Mrs de Mattia will be back at eleven o'clock

Tra una mezz'ora/un'ora
tra oona medzora/oonora
in half an hour/an hour

Prenda l'ascensore al terzo piano
prenda lashensore al tertso pyano
Take the lift to the third floor

Vada lungo il corridoio
vada loongo eel korreedoyo
Go along the corridor

È la prima/seconda porta
e la preema/sekonda porta
It's the first/second door

A sinistra/a destra
a seeneestra/a destra
On the left/right

È la camera numero trecentoventi
e la kamera noomero trechentoventee
It's room number 320

Avanti!
avantee
Come in!

SIGHTSEEING

● Opening hours vary for historic buildings, museums, galleries and so on, but most are shut on Mondays. The Italian State Tourist Office has a useful list with opening times of the major galleries and museums.

● Some churches are only open for services.

● Sightseeing tours by coach with English-speaking guides are available in many cities and tourist areas.

● Italy has five national parks with picnic areas and there are plans to establish more in the next few years.

● General audiences with the Pope are usually held every Wednesday. If you would like to join in, apply to the **Prefettura della Casa Pontificia** (address page 194).

You may see

Aperto	Open
Chiuso (per restauri)	Closed (for restoration)
Non toccare	Do not touch
Orario visite	Visiting hours
Privato	Private
Vietato fotografare	No photographs
Visite guidate	Guided tours

You may want to say

(see At the tourist office, *page 74, for asking for information, brochures, etc.)*

Opening times

(see Time, *page 181)*

When is the museum open?
Quando è aperto il museo?
kwando e aperto eel mooze-o

What time does the church open?
A che ora apre la chiesa?
a ke ora apre la kyeza

What time does the castle close?
A che ora chiude il castello?
a ke ora kyoode eel kastello

Is it open on Sundays?
È aperto la domenica?
e aperto la domeneeka

Can I/we visit the monastery?
Si può visitare il monastero?
see pwo veezeetare eel monastero

Is it open to the public?
È aperto al pubblico?
e aperto al poobbleeko

Visiting places

One/Two, please
Uno/Due, per favore
oono/doo-e per favore

Two adults and one child
Due adulti e un bambino
doo-e adooltee e oon bambeeno

Are there reductions for children?
Ci sono sconti per i bambini?
chee sono skontee per ee bambeenee

For students
Per studenti
per stoodentee

For pensioners
Per pensionati
per pensyonatee

For the disabled
Per handicappati
per andeekappatee

For groups
Per gruppi
per grooppee

Are there guided tours (in English)?
Ci sono visite guidate (in inglese)?
chee sono veezeete gweedate een eengleze

Can I/we take photos?
Si possono fare fotografie?
see possono fare fotografee-e

Could you take a photo of me/us, please?
Potrebbe fare una foto di me/noi, per cortesia?
potrebbe fare oona foto dee me/noy per kortezee-a

When was this built?
Quando è stato costruito questo?
kwando e stato kostroo-eeto kwesto

Who was the painter?
Chi è il pittore?
kee e eel peettore

In what year?
In che anno?
een ke anno
(see Days, page 177)

What time is mass?
A che ora è la messa?
a ke ora e la messa

Is there a priest who speaks English?
C'è un prete che parla inglese?
che oon prete ke parla eengleze

What is this flower called?
Come si chiama questa fiore?
kome see kyama kwesta fyore

What is that bird called?
Come si chiama questo uccello?
kome see kyama kwesto oochello

Sightseeing excursions

What tourist excursions are there?
Che escursioni ci sono?
ke eskoorsyonee chee sono

Are there any excursions to Tivoli?
Ci sono escursioni a Tivoli?
chee sono eskoorsyonee a teevolee

What time does it leave?
A che ora parte?
a ke ora parte

How long does it take to get there?
Quanto tempo ci vuole per arrivarci?
kwanto tempo chee vwole per arreevarchee

How long does it last?
Quanto tempo dura?
kwanto tempo doora

What time does it get back?
A che ora torna?
a ke ora torna

Where does it leave from?	How much is it?
Da dove parte?	**Quant'è?**
da dove parte	*kwante*

Does the guide speak English?
Parla inglese la guida?
parla eengleze la gweeda

You may hear

Il museo è aperto tutti i giorni a parte il lunedì
eel mooze-o e aperto toottee ee jornee a parte eel loonedee
The museum is open every day except Mondays

È chiuso la domenica
e kyoozo la domeneeka
It's closed on Sundays

Il castello è stato costruito nell'undicesimo secolo
eel kastello e stato kostroo-eeto nelloondeechezeemo sekolo
The castle was built in the eleventh century

È una pittura da Rafaello
e oona peettoora da rafiy-ello
It's a painting by Raphael

Ci sono escursioni il giovedì e il sabato
chee sono eskoorsyone eel jovedee e eel sabato
There are excursions every Thursday and Saturday

Il pullman parte alle dieci dalla Piazza della Repubblica
eel poolman parte alle dyechee dalla pyatsa della repoobbleeka
The coach leaves at ten o'clock from Piazza della Repubblica

ENTERTAINMENTS

- Italy's most popular spectator sport is football. This and other sports are usually played on Sundays.

- Cinemas usually open at 4 p.m. and have a continuous programme. Films are categorised as suitable for people over certain ages, e.g. **18 anni** or **14 anni**. It is usual to give a small tip to theatre and cinema ushers.

- Many American and British films are shown in Italian cinemas, most of them dubbed. In the big cities there are English language cinemas, like **Pasquino** in Rome.

- Smoking is forbidden in cinemas and theatres unless otherwise specified.

- Opera is performed all over Italy and Milan is home to one of the world's great opera houses, **La Scala**. The opera season begins in December. In the summer, operas are performed in the open air.

- You can find out about events taking place at particular times of year from the Italian State Tourist Office. For example, **il Palio**, Siena's famous horserace, in August or the Venice Carnival in February.

- In most cities, you can find out what's on by buying the English language paper *This week in . . .*

You may see

Biglietti per oggi

Tickets for today's performance

Cineclub	Film club
Cinema	Cinema
Circo	Circus
Discoteca	Discothèque
Fila	Row, tier
Galleria	Circle
Ingresso	Entrance
Ingresso vietato dopo l'inizio dello spettacolo	No entry once the performance has begun
Ippodromo	Racecourse
Non c'è intervallo	No interval
Palchi	Boxes
Parcheggio	Parking
Platea	Stalls
Poltrone di Platea	Orchestra stalls
Porta	Door
Prenotazioni	Advance booking
Sala da concerti	Concert hall
Sala da ballo	Dance hall
Spettacolo continuato	Continuous performance (at the cinema)
Spettacolo pomeridiano	Matinee
Spettacolo serale	Evening performance
Stadio	Stadium
Teatro	Theatre
Teatro dell'Opera	Opera house
Tribuna	Stand, grandstand
Tutto esaurito	Sold out
Vietato ai minori di 18 anni	Under-18s not allowed

139

You may want to say

(see Time, page 181)

What is there to do in the evenings?
Cosa c'è da fare la sera?
koza che da fare la sera

Is there a disco around here?
C'è una discoteca qui vicino?
che oona deeskoteka kwee veecheeno

Is there any entertainment for children?
Ci sono divertimenti per bambini?
chee sono deeverteementee per bambeenee

What's on tonight?
Cosa danno stasera?
koza danno stasera

What's on tomorrow?
Cosa danno domani?
koza danno domanee

At the cinema
Al cinema
al cheenema

At the theatre
Al teatro
al te-atro

Who is playing? (*music*)
Chi suona?
kee swona

Who is singing?
Chi canta?
kee kanta

Who is dancing?
Chi balla?
kee balla

Does the film have subtitles?
Il film è con sottotitoli?
eel feelm e kon sottoteetolee

Is there a football match on Sunday?
C'è una partita di calcio domenica?
che oona parteeta dee kalcho domeneeka

Who's playing? (*sport*)
Chi gioca?
kee joka

Where can I/we get tickets?
Dove si può comprare i biglietti?
dove see pwo komprare ee beelyettee

What time does the show start?
A che ora comincia lo spettacolo?
a ke ora komeencha lo spettakolo

What time does the concert start?
A che ora comincia il concerto?
a ke ora komeencha eel koncherto

When does it end?
A che ora termina?
a ke ora termeena

How long does the performance last?
Quanto tempo dura lo spettacolo?
kwanto tempo doora lo spettakolo

Tickets

Can you get me tickets for the opera?
Può comprarmi biglietti per l'opera?
pwo komprarmee beelyettee per lopera

For the football match
Per la partita di calcio
per la parteeta dee kalcho

For the theatre
Per il teatro
per eel te-atro

Two, please
Due, per favore
doo-e per favore

Two for tonight, please
Due per stasera, per favore
doo-e per stasera per favore

Two for the 11 o'clock screening, please
Due per lo spettacolo delle undici, per favore
doo-e per lo spettakolo delle oondeechee per favore

Are there any seats left for Saturday?
Ci sono biglietti per sabato?
chee sono beelyettee per sabato

I want to book a box for four people
Vorrei prenotare un palco per quattro persone
vorray prenotare oon palko per kwattro persone

I want to book two seats
Vorrei prenotare due posti
vorray prenotare doo-e postee

For Friday
Per venerdì
per venerdee

In the stalls
In platea
een plate-a

In the circle
In galleria
een galleree-a

How much are the seats?
Quanto costano i biglietti?
kwanto kostano ee beelyettee

Do you have anything cheaper?
Ha qualcosa di meno caro?
a kwalkoza dee meno karo

That's fine
Va bene
va bene

At the show/game

Where is this, please?
  (*showing your ticket*)
Dov'è questo, per favore?
dove kwesto per favore

Where is the cloakroom?
Dov'è il guardaroba?
dove eel gwardaroba

Where is the bar?
Dov'è il bar?
dove eel bar

Where are the toilets?
Dov'è la toilette?
dove la twalett

A programme, please
Una programma, per favore
oona programma per favore

Where can I/we get a
  programme?
**Dove si può comprare una
  programma?**
*dove see pwo komprare oona
  programma*

Is there an interval?
C'è un intervallo?
che oon eentervallo

You may hear

Può comprare i biglietti qui nell'albergo
pwo komprare ee beelyettee kwee nellalbergo
You can get tickets here in the hotel

Al teatro dell'opera
al te-atro dellopera
At the opera house

Allo stadio
allo stadyo
At the stadium

Comincia alle sette
komeencha alle sette
It begins at seven o'clock

Dura due ore e un quarto
doora doo-e ore e oon kwarto
It lasts two and a quarter hours

Termina alle nove e mezza
termeena alle nove e medza
It ends at half past nine

C'è un intervallo di quindici minuti
che oon intervallo dee kweendeechee meenootee
There is a fifteen-minute interval

Per quando li vuole?
per kwando lee vwole
When would you like them for?

In platea o galleria?
een plate-a o galleree-a
In the stalls or in the circle?

Ce ne sono due qui, in platea *(indicating on seating plan)*
che ne sono doo-e kwee een plate-a
There are two here, in the stalls

Mi dispiace, è tutto esaurito
mee deespyache e tootto esowreeto
I'm sorry, we're sold out

Posso vedere il suo biglietto?
posso vedere eel soo-o beelyetto
May I see your ticket?

SPORTS AND ACTIVITIES

● There are good facilities in many parts of Italy for skiing, golf, tennis, horseriding and watersports – information about locations from the Italian State Tourist Office or travel agents.

● **Fishing** You need a permit for freshwater fishing. This is obtainable from the **Federazione Italiana della Pesca Sportiva** along with information on local restrictions. There should be an office in every provincial capital. Sea fishing (without an aqualung) is possible without a permit.

● **Hiking and Climbing** The **CAI (Club Alpino Italiano)** or the Italian State Tourist Office can provide information about trails, scenic walks and mountain refuges.

● **Sailing** Italy has a long and beautiful coastline and with its many natural harbours is ideal for sailing. Contact the State Tourist Office for information on the regulations for bringing your boat to Italy.

● **Beaches** Some beach space in holiday resorts is reserved for guests of nearby hotels or is private, **spiaggia privata**. Look for the free beach, **spiaggia libera**.
At the beach, a red flag flying means it is dangerous to swim, either because the sea is too rough, or because it is too polluted.

You may see

Abbonamenti	Season tickets
Affito sci	Ski hire
Bagnino	Beach attendant
Barche	Boats
Cabine	Huts
Campo di calcio	Football pitch
Campo di golf	Golf course
Campo da tennis	Tennis court

Centro sportivo	Sports centre
Divieto di balneazione	No swimming
Divieto di pesca	No fishing
Funivia	Cable car
Lettini	Sunbeds
Noleggio	For hire
Ombrelloni	Umbrellas
Pedalò	Pedal boats
Pericolo	Danger
Pericolo di valanghe	Danger of avalanches
Piscina	Swimming pool
Pista di sci	Ski run
Poltroncine	Chairs
Pronto soccorso	First Aid
Riserva di caccia (privata)	(Private) hunting reserve
Sciovia	Ski-lift
Scuola di sci	Ski school
Sedie a Sdraio	Deckchairs
Seggiovia	Chair-lift
Spiaggia	Beach
Spiaggia libera con servizi	Free beach with facilities
Spiaggia privata	Private beach
Valanghe	Avalanches
Zona Slavine	Avalanche area

You may want to say

Can I/we . . . ?
Si può . . . ?
see pwo . . .

Can I/we go fishing?
Si può pescare?
see pwo peskare

Can I/we hire a bike?
Si può noleggiare una bicicletta?
see pwo nolejare oona beecheekletta

Can I/we go riding?
Si può andare a cavallo?
see pwo andare a cavallo

Where can I/we . . . ?
Dove si può . . . ?
dove see pwo . . .

Where can I/we play tennis?
Dove si può giocare a tennis?
dove see pwo jokare a tennees

Where can I/we go climbing?
Dove si può fare alpinismo?
dove see pwo fare alpeeneezmo

I don't know how to . . .
Non so . . .
non so . . .

I don't know how to ski
Non so sciare
non so shee-are

Is it possible to have lessons?
Si possono prendere lezioni?
see possono prendere letsyonee

I'm a beginner
Sono un principiante
sono oon preencheepyante

I'm quite experienced
Sono abbastanza esperto (*male*)/**esperta** (*female*)
sono abbastantsa esperto/ esperta

How much is it per hour?
Quanto costa all'ora?
kwanto kosta allora

How much is it for the whole day?
Quanto costa per tutto il giorno?
kwanto kosta per tootto eel jorno

How much is it per game?
Quanto costa a partita?
kwanto kosta a parteeta

Is there a reduction for children?
C'è uno sconto per i bambini?
che oono skonto per ee bambeenee

Can I/we hire equipment?
Si può noleggiare l'equipaggiamento?
see pwo nolejare lekipajamento

Can I/we hire rackets?
Si possono noleggiare rachette?
see possono nolejare rakette

Can I/we hire clubs?
Si possono noleggiare mazze?
see possono nolejare mattse

Do I/we need a licence?
C'è bisogno di un permesso?
che beezonyo dee oon permesso

Where can I get one?
Dove posso otterne uno?
dove posso otterne oono

Is it necessary to be a member?
Bisogna essere un socio?
beezonya essere oon socho

Beach and pool

Can I/we swim here?
Si può nuotare qui?
see pwo nwotare kwee

Can I/we swim in the river?
Si può nuotare nel fiume?
see pwo nwotare nel fyoome

Is it dangerous?
È pericoloso?
e pereekolozo

Is it safe for children?
È sicuro per i bambini?
e seekooro per ee bambeenee

When is high tide?
A che ora è l'alta marea?
a ke ora e lalta mare-a

Where is the free beach?
Dov'è la spiaggia libera?
dove la spyaja leebera

Is the water clean?
È pulita l'acqua?
e pooleeta lakkwa

Skiing

What is the snow like?
Com'è la neve?
kome la neve

How much is the lift pass?
Quanto costa lo skipass?
kwanto kosta lo skeepass

Per day
Al giorno
al jorno

Per week
Alla settimana
alla setteemana

Is there a nursery slope?
C'è una pista per i principianti?
che oona peesta per ee preencheepyantee

What time is the last ascent?
A che ora è l'ultima corsa?
a ke ora e loolteema korsa

Is it steep?
È ripido?
e reepeedo

Is it icy?
È ghiacciato?
e gee-achato

Is the run wide?
È larga la pista?
e larga la peesta

You may hear

È un principiante?
e oon preencheepyante
Are you a beginner?

Sa sciare?
sa shee-are
Do you know how to ski?

Sa fare il windsurf?
sa fare eel weendsurf
Do you know how to
  windsurf?

Costa ventimila lire all'ora
*kosta vaynteemeela leere
  allora*
It's 20,000 lire per hour

**C'è un deposito di
  quindicimila lire**
*che oon depozeeto dee
  kweendeecheemeela leere*
There's a deposit of 15,000
  lire

Mi dispiace, siamo impegnati
*mee deespyache syamo
  eempenyatee*
I'm sorry, we're booked up

Torni un po' più tardi
tornee oon po pyoo tardee
Come back later

Che taglia ha?
ke talya a
What size are you?

C'è bisogno di una foto
che beezonyo dee oona foto
You need a photo

Che tipo di sci vuole?
ke teepo dee shee vwole
What kind of skis do you want?

La neve è profonda
la neve e profonda
The snow is deep

La neve è molle/farinosa
la neve e molle/fareenoza
The snow is soft/powdery

Non c'è molto neve
non che molto neve
There isn't much snow

HEALTH

Medical record – to show a doctor

(Tick where appropriate, or fill in details)

	Self Io	Other members of family/party (names)		
Blood group **Gruppo sanguigno**				
Asthmatic **Asmatico/a**				
Blind **Cieco/a**				
Deaf **Sordo/a**				
Diabetic **Diabetico/a**				
Epileptic **Epilettico/a**				
Handicapped **Handicappato/a**				
Heart condition **Mal di cuore**				
High blood pressure **Pressione alta**				
Pregnant **Incinta**				

Allergic to **Allergico/a a**				
Antibiotics **Antibiotichi**				
Penicillin **Penicillina**				
Cortisone **Cortisona**				

Medicines **Medicine**

Self **Io** _____

Others **altri** _____

● Your local Department of Health office can provide information about medical and dental care abroad. Within the EC you can obtain the local equivalent of NHS treatment by producing the required form – you may have to pay first and reclaim the payment when you return to Britain.

● Italian chemists are highly trained and can often help with minor disorders and injuries.

● To indicate where the pain is, you can simply point and say 'it hurts here' (**mi fa male qua**). Otherwise you'll need to look up the Italian for the appropriate part of the body. Notice that in Italian you refer to 'the arm', 'the stomach', etc. rather than '*my* arm, *my* stomach' (**il braccio, lo stomaco**).

You may see

Ambulanze	Ambulance station
Ambulatorio	Surgery, Out-patients
Clinica	Clinic, hospital
H	Hospital
Orario visite	Surgery/visiting hours
Ospedale	Hospital
Pronto soccorso	First aid post, Casualty
Servizi d'Emergenza	Emergency services

You may want to say

At the doctor

I need a doctor
Ho bisogno di un medico
o beezonyo dee oon medeeko

Please call a doctor
Per favore, chiami un medico
per favore kyamee oon medeeko

It's my husband
È mio marito
e mee-o mareeto

It's my wife
È mia moglie
e mee-a molye

It's my friend
È mio amico (*male*)/**mia amica** (*female*)
*e **mee**-o a**mee**ko/**mee**-a a**mee**ka*

It's my daughter
È mia figlia
*e **mee**-a **feel**ya*

It's my son
È mio figlio
*e **mee**-o **feel**yo*

Your symptoms

I feel unwell
Mi sento male
*mee **sen**to **male***

It hurts here
Mi fa male qui
*mee fa **male** kwee*

My . . . hurts
Mi fa male . . .
*mee fa **male** . . .*

My stomach hurts
Mi fa male lo stomaco
*mee fa **male** lo **stoma**ko*

My back hurts
Mi fa male la schiena
*mee fa **male** la **skyena***

My . . . hurt
Mi fanno male . . .
*mee **fanno male** . . .*

My eyes hurt
Mi fanno male gli occhi
*mee **fanno male** lyee **okk**ee*

My feet hurt
Mi fanno male i piedi
*mee **fanno male** ee **pye**dee*

I have a sore throat
Ho mal di gola
*o mal dee **gola***

I have a temperature
Ho la febbre
*o la **febbre***

I have diarrhoea
Ho la diarrea
*o la dee-**arre**-a*

I feel dizzy
Ho le vertigini
*o le ver**teegee**nee*

I have been sick
Ho vomitato
*o vomee**tato***

I can't sleep
Non riesco a dormire
*non **ryes**ko a dor**meere***

I can't breathe
Non riesco a respirare
non ryesko a respeerare

My . . . is bleeding
Il/la . . . sanguina
eel/la . . . sangweena

I think that . . .
Credo che . . .
kredo ke

It's my . . .
È il/la . . .
e eel/la . . .

It's my arm
È il braccio
e eel bracho

It's my leg
È la gamba
e la gamba

It's my wrist
È il polso
e eel polso

It's broken
È rotto/a
e rotto/a

It's sprained
È storto/a
e storto/a

I have cut myself
Mi sono tagliato/a
mee sono talyato/a

I have burnt myself
Mi sono bruciato/a
mee sono broochato/a

I have been stung by an insect
Mi ho punto un insetto
mee o poonto oon insetto

I have been bitten by a dog
Mi ho morso un cane
mee o morso oon kane

Someone else's symptoms

He/She feels unwell
Si sente male
see sente male

He/She is unconscious
È svenuto/a
e svenooto/a

It hurts here
Gli (*male*)/**Le** (*female*) **fa male qui**
lyee/le fa male kwee

His/Her . . . hurts
Gli/Le fa male . . .
lyee/le fa male . . .

His/Her stomach hurts
Gli/Le fa male lo stomaco
lyee/le fa male lo stomako

His/Her back hurts
Gli/Le fa male la schiena
lyee/le fa male la skyena

His/Her ... hurt
Gli/Le fanno male ...
lyee/le fanno male ...

His/Her eyes hurt
Gli/Le fanno male gli occhi
lyee/le fanno male lyee okkee

His/Her feet hurt
Gli/Le fanno male i piedi
lyee/le fanno male ee pyedee

He/She has a sore throat
Ha mal di gola
a mal dee gola

He/She has a temperature
Ha la febbre
a la febbre

He/She has diarrhoea
Ha la diarrea
a la dee-arre-a

He/She feels dizzy
Ha le vertigini
a le verteegeenee

He/She has been sick
Ha vomitato
a vomeetato

He/She is bleeding
Sanguina
sangweena

He/She can't sleep
Non riesce a dormire
non ryeshe a dormeere

He/She can't breathe
Non riesce a respirare
non ryeshe a respeerare

He/She thinks that ...
Crede che ...
krede ke

It's his/her ...
È il/la ...
e eel/la ...

It's his/her ankle
È la caviglia
e la kaveelya

It's his/her leg
È la gamba
e la gamba

It's broken
È rotto/a
e rotto/a

It's sprained
È storto/a
e storto/a

He/She has cut himself/
  herself
Si è tagliato/a
see e talyato/a

He/She has burnt himself/
  herself
Si è bruciato/a
see e broochato/a

He/She has been stung by an insect
Le ha punto un insetto
*le a **poonto** oon insetto*

He/She has been bitten by a dog
Le ha morso un cane
*le a **morso** oon kane*

You may hear

Dove le fa male?
dove le fa male
Where does it hurt?

Le fa male qui?
le fa male kwee
Does it hurt here?

Molto? Poco?
molto? poko?
A lot? A little?

Da quanto tempo si sente così?
da kwanto tempo see sente kozee
How long have you been feeling like this?

Quanti anni ha?
kwantee annee a
How old are you? (*also* How old is he/she?)

Apra la bocca, per favore
apra la bokka per favore
Open your mouth, please

Si spogli, per favore
see spolyee per favore
Get undressed, please

Si sdrai lì, per favore
see sdryee lee per favore
Lie down over there, please

Prende delle medicine?
prende delle medeecheene
Are you taking any medicines?

È allergico/a alle medicine?
e allerjeeko/a alle medeecheene
Are you allergic to any medicine?

È vaccinato contro il tetano?
e vacheenato kontro eel tetano
Have you been vaccinated against tetanus?

Che cosa ha mangiato oggi?
ke koza a manjato ojee
What have you eaten today?

Le do una ricetta
le do oona reechetta
I am going to give you a prescription

Prenda una compressa tre volte al giorno
prenda oona kompressa tre volte al jorno
Take a tablet three times a day

Dopo i pasti
dopo ee pastee
After meals

Alla sera
alla sera
At night

C'è un'infezione
che ooneenfetsyone
There is an infection

Devo farle un'iniezione
devo farle ooneenyetsyone
I have to give you an injection

Devo metterle alcuni punti
devo metterle alkoonee poontee
I have to give you some stitches

Si deve fare una radiografia
see deve fare oona radyografee-a
It is necessary to do an X-ray

Bisogna prendere un campione del sangue/ dell'urina
beezonya prendere oon kampyone del sangwe/ dell'ooreena
I need to take a blood/urine sample

Ha l'intossicazione alimentare
a leentosseecatsyone aleementare
You have food poisoning

È un attacco cardiaco
e oon attakko kardee-ako
It's a heart attack

Deve riposare
deve reepozare
You must rest

Deve restare a letto per tre giorni
deve restare a letto per tre jornee
You must stay in bed for three days

Deve tornare fra cinque giorni
deve tornare fra cheenkwe jornee
You must come back in five days' time

Deve andare all'ospedale
deve andare allospedale
You will have to go to hospital

Non è nulla di grave
non e noolla dee grave
It is nothing serious

Non ha niente
non a nyente
There is nothing wrong with you

Può vestirsi
pwo vesteersee
You can get dressed again

You may want to say

At the dentist

I need a dentist
Ho bisogno di un dentista
o beezonyo dee oon denteesta

I have toothache
Ho mal di denti
o mal dee dentee

This tooth hurts
Mi fa male questo dente
mee fa male kwesto dente

I have broken a tooth
Mi si è rotto un dente
mee see e rotto oon dente

I have lost a filling
Ho perso un'otturazione
o perso oonottooratsyone

I have lost a crown/cap
Ho perso una càpsula
o perso oona kapsoola

He/She has toothache
Ha mal di denti
a mal dee dentee

He/She has broken a tooth
Gli/Le si è rotto un dente
lyee/le see e rotto oon dente

He/She has lost a filling
Ha perso un'otturazione
a perso oonottooratsyone

He/She has lost a crown/cap
Ha perso una càpsula
a perso oona kapsoola

Can you fix it temporarily?
Può curarlo provvisoriamente?
pwo koorarlo provveezoryamente

Can you give me an injection?
Può farmi un'iniezione?
pwo farmee ooneenyetsyone

Can you give him/her an injection?
Può fargli/farle un'iniezione?
pwo farlyee/farle ooneenyetsyone

This denture is broken
Questa dentiera è rotta
kwesta dentyera e rotta

Can you repair it?
Può ripararla?
pwo ripararla

How much will it cost?
Quanto costerà?
kwanto kostera

You may hear

Apra la bocca, per favore
apra la bokka per favore
Open your mouth, please

Le faccio un'iniezione
le facho ooneenyetsyone
I'll give you an injection

Ha bisogno di un'otturazione
a beezonyo dee oonottooratsyone
You need a filling

Parts of the body

ankle	la caviglia	kaveelya
appendix	l'appendice (f)	appendeeche
arm	il braccio	bracho
back	la schiena	skyena
bladder	la vescica	vesheeka
blood	il sangue	sangwe
body	il corpo	korpo
bone	l'osso (m)	osso
bottom	il sedere	sedere
bowels	l'intestino (m)	eentesteeno
breast	il seno	seno
buttocks	le natiche	nateeke
cartilage	la cartilagine	karteelajeene
chest	il torace	torache
chin	il mento	mento
ear	l'orecchio (m)	orrekkyo
elbow	il gomito	gomeeto
eye	l'occhio (m)	okkyo
face	la faccia	facha
finger	il dito	deeto
foot	il piede	pyede
genitals	i genitali	jeneetalee
gland	la ghiandola	gee-andola
hair	i capelli	kapellee
hand	il mano	mano
head	la testa	testa

heart	il cuore	*kwore*
heel	il calcagno	*kalkanyo*
hip	il fianco	*fyanko*
jaw	la mandibola	*mandeebola*
joint	l'articolazione (*f*)	*arteekolatsyone*
kidney	il rene	*rene*
knee	il ginocchio	*jeenokkyo*
leg	la gamba	*gamba*
ligament	il legamento	*legamento*
lip	il labbro	*labbro*
liver	il fegato	*fegato*
lung	il polmone	*polmone*
mouth	la bocca	*bokka*
muscle	il muscolo	*mooskolo*
nail	l'unghia (*f*)	*oongya*
neck	il collo	*kollo*
nerve	il nervo	*nervo*
nose	il naso	*naso*
penis	il pene	*pene*
private parts	gli organi sessuali	*organee sessoo-alee*
rectum	il retto	*retto*
rib	la costola	*kostola*
shoulder	la spalla	*spalla*
skin	la pelle	*pelle*
spine	la spina dorsale	*speena dorsale*
stomach	lo stomaco	*stomako*
tendon	il tendine	*tendeene*
testicles	i testicoli	*testeekoli*
thigh	la coscia	*kosha*
throat	la gola	*gola*
thumb	il pollice	*polleeche*
toe	il dito del piede	*deeto del pyede*
tongue	la lingua	*leengwa*
tonsils	le tonsille	*tonseelle*
tooth	il dente	*dente*
vagina	la vagina	*vajeena*
wrist	il polso	*polso*

PROBLEMS AND COMPLAINTS

● There are three kinds of police in Italy. **La Polizia** are the regular police force, recognisable by their pale blue uniforms. Accidents or crime should be reported to them. They are helped out by the military police, the **Carabinieri**, who wear black uniforms with a red stripe down the trousers. The **Vigili Urbani**, in their white helmets or caps, are the traffic police who have the power to impose on-the-spot fines for driving and parking offences.

● Beware of pickpockets and petty thieves, especially in cities. They have all sorts of ploys for stealing wallets and bags. If you do have something stolen, report it to the police within 24 hours so that you can make an insurance claim.

You may see

Guasto   Out of order

(*For* Car breakdowns, *see page 39;* Emergencies, *page 267*)

You may want to say

Can you help me?
Può aiutarmi?
pwo iyootarmee

Can you fix it
(immediately)?
Può ripararlo (subito)?
pwo reepararlo soobeeto

When can you fix it?
Quando può ripararlo?
kwando pwo reepararlo

Can I speak to the manager?
Posso parlare col direttore?
posso parlare col deerettore

There's a problem with . . .
C'è un problema con . . .
che oon problema kon

There isn't/aren't any . . .
Non c'è . . ./non ci sono . . .
non che . . ./non chee sono . . .

I need . . .
Ho bisogno di . . .
o beezonyo dee . . .

The . . . doesn't work
Non funziona il/la . . .
non foontsyona eel/la . . .

The . . . is broken
Il/Lo . . . è rotto
eel/lo . . . e rotto
or
La . . . è rotta
la . . . e rotta

I can't . . .
Non posso . . .
non posso . . .

It's not my fault
Non è colpa mia
non e kolpa mee-a

I have forgotten . . .
Ho dimenticato . . .
o deementeekato . . .

I have lost . . .
Ho perso . . .
o perso . . .

Someone has stolen my . . .
Qualcuno mi ha rubato . . .
kwalkoono mee a roobato . . .

My . . . has disappeared
Il mio . . ./La mia . . . è
sparito/a
eel mee-o . . ./la mee-a . . . e
spareeto/a

My passport has disappeared
Il mio passaporto è sparito
eel mee-o passaporto e spareeto

My . . . isn't here
Il mio/La mia . . . non c'è
eel mee-o . . ./la mee-a . . . non
che

My money isn't there
I miei soldi non ci sono
ee mee-e-ee soldee non chee sono

My traveller's cheques aren't
there
I miei travellers cheques non
ci sono
ee mee-e-ee travellers cheques
non chee sono

Something is missing
Manca qualcosa
manka kwalkoza

The . . . is missing
Manca il/la . . .
manka eel/la . . .

This isn't mine
Questo non è il mio
kewsto non e eel mee-o

Where you're staying

There isn't any (hot) water
Non c'è acqua (calda)
non che akkwa kalda

There isn't any toilet paper
Non c'è carta igienica
non che karta eejeneeka

There isn't any electricity
Non c'è elettricità
non che elettreecheeta

There aren't any towels
Non ci sono asciugamani
non chee sono ashoogamanee

I need another pillow
**Ho bisogno di un guanciale in
più**
*o beezonyo dee oon gwanchale
een pyoo*

I need another blanket
**Ho bisogno di una coperta in
più**
*o beezonyo dee oona koperta
een pyoo*

I need a light bulb
Ho bisogno di una lampadina
o beezonyo dee oona lampadeena

The light doesn't work
La luce non funziona
la looche non foontsyona

The shower doesn't work
La doccia non funziona
la docha non foontsyona

The lock is broken
La serratura è rotta
la serratoora e rotta

The bed is broken
Il letto è rotto
eel letto e rotto

I can't open the window
Non posso aprire la finestra
non posso apreere la feenestra

I can't turn the tap off
Non posso chiudere il robinetto
non posso kyoodere eel robeenetto

The toilet doesn't flush
Il water non funziona
eel vater non foontsyona

The drain is blocked
Lo scarico è bloccato
lo skareeko e blokkato

The wash-basin is dirty
Il lavandino è sporco
eel lavandeeno e sporko

The room is . . .
La camera è . . .
la kamera e . . .

The room is too hot
La camera è troppo calda
la kamera e troppo kalda

The room is too dark
La camera è troppo scura
la kamera e troppo skoora

The room is too small
La camera è troppo picola
la kamera e troppo peekkola

There's a lot of noise
C'è molto rumore
che molto roomore

The bed is uncomfortable
Il letto è scomodo
eel letto e skomodo

There's a smell of gas
C'è un odore di gas
che oon odore dee gas

In bars and restaurants

This isn't cooked
Non è cotto
non e kotto

This glass is cracked
Il bicchiere è rotto
eel beekkyere e rotto

This is burnt
È bruciato
e broochato

This is dirty
Questo è sporco
kwesto e sporko

This is cold
È freddo
e freddo

This smells bad
Questo ha cattivo odore
kwesto a katteevo odore

I didn't order this, I ordered the . . .
Non ho ordinato questo, ho ordinato il/la . . .
non o ordeenato kwesto, o ordeenato eel/la . . .

This tastes strange
Questo ha un sapore strano
kwesto a oon sapore strano

There is a mistake on the bill
C'è un errore nel conto
che oon errore nel konto

Shops

I bought this (yesterday)
Ho comprato questo (ieri)
o komprato kwesto yeree

I want to return this
Voglio restituire questo
volyo resteetoo-eere kwesto

Can you change this for me?
Può cambiarmi questo?
pwo kambyarmee kwesto

Can you refund me the money?
Mi può rimborsare?
mee pwo reemborsare

Here is the receipt
Ecco la ricevuta
ekko la reechevoota

It's no good
Non va bene
non va bene

It has a flaw
Ha un difetto
a oon deefetto

It has a hole
Ha un buco
a oon booko

There is a stain/mark
Ha una macchia
a oona makkya

This is off/rotten
Questo è marcio
kwesto e marcho

This isn't fresh
Questo non è fresco
kwesto non e fresko

The lid is missing
Manca il coperchio
manka eel koperkyo

Forgetting and losing things and theft

I have forgotten my ticket
Ho dimenticato il mio biglietto
o deementeekato eel mee-o beelyetto

I have forgotten the key
Ho dimenticato la chiave
o deementeekato la kyave

I have lost my bag
Ho perso la mia borsa
o perso la mee-a borsa

I have lost my wallet
Ho perso il mio portafoglio
o perso eel mee-o portafolyo

I have lost my driving licence
Ho perso la mia patente
o perso la mee-a patente

We've lost our rucksacks
Abbiamo perso i nostri zaini
abbyamo perso ee nostree tsiyeenee

Where is the lost property office?
Dov'è l'ufficio di oggetti smarriti?
dove looffeecho dee ojettee smarreetee

Where is the police station?
Dov'è la questura?
dove la kwestoora

Someone has stolen my bag
Mi hanno rubato la borsa
mee anno roobato la borsa

Someone has stolen the car
Mi hanno rubato la macchina
mee anno roobato la makkeena

Someone has stolen my money
Mi hanno rubato i soldi
mee anno roobato ee soldee

If someone is bothering you

Please leave me alone
Mi lasci in pace, per favore
mee lashee een pache per favore

Go away or I'll call the police
Se ne vada o chiamo la polizia
se ne vada o kyamo la poleetsee-a

There's someone following me
C'è qualcuno che mi sta seguendo
che kwalkoono ke mee sta segwendo

You may hear

Helpful and unhelpful replies

Un attimo, per favore
oon atteemo per favore
Just a moment, please

Certo
cherto
Of course

Eccolo
ekkolo
Here you are

Gliene porto un altro
lyee-e-ne porto oon altro
I'll bring you another one

Gliene porto uno subito
lyee-e-ne porto oono soobeeto
I'll bring you one immediately

Subito
soobeeto
Right away

Lo aggiusterò domani
lo ajoostero domanee
I'll fix it tomorrow

Mi dispiace, non è possibile
mee deespyache non e posseebeele
I'm sorry, it's not possible

Mi dispiace, non posso far niente
mee deespyache non posso far nyente
I'm sorry, there's nothing I can do

Non sono io il responsabile
non sono yo eel responsabeele
I am not the person responsible

Non siamo noi i responsabili
non syamo noy ee responsabeelee
We are not responsible

Dovrebbe ...
dovrebbe ...
You should ...

Dovrebbe dinunciarlo alla polizia
dovrebbe deenooncharlo alla poleetsee-a
You should report it to the police

Questions you may be asked

Quando l'ha comprato?
kwando la komprato
When did you buy it?

Ha la ricevuta?
ha la reechevoota
Do you have the receipt?

Quando è successo?
kwando e soochesso
When did it happen?

Dove l'ha perso/a?
dove la perso/a
Where did you lose it?

Dov'è stato rubato?
dove stato roobato
Where was it stolen?

Com'è la sua borsa?
kome la soo-a borsa
What does your bag look like?

Com'è la sua macchina?
kome la soo-a makkeena
What does your car look like?

Che marca è?
ke marka e
What make is it?

Qual è la targa della sua macchina?
kwal e la targa della soo-a makkeena
What is the registration number of your car?

Come si chiama?
kome see kyama
What's your name?

Dove sta?
dove sta
Where are you staying?

Qual è il suo indirizzo?
kwal e eel soo-o eendeereetso
What is your address?

Qual è il numero della sua camera?
kwal e eel noomero della soo-a kamera
What is your room number?

Qual è il numero del suo appartamento?
kwal e eel noomero del soo-o appartamento
What is the number of your apartment?

In quale villa abita?
een kwale veella abeeta
Which villa are you in?

Qual è il numero del suo passaporto?
kwal e eel noomero del soo-o passaporto
What is your passport number?

È assicurato?
e asseekoorato
Are you insured?

Riempia questo modulo per favore
ree-empya kwesto modoolo per favore
Please fill in this form.

BASIC GRAMMAR

Nouns

All Italian nouns have a gender – masculine or feminine.

Words for male people or animals are masculine; for females they are feminine. Otherwise, the word ending often shows the gender.

Most nouns ending in **-o** are masculine. The few exceptions include **la mano** (hand), and **la radio** (radio).

Most nouns ending in **-a** are feminine. Exceptions include **il cinemà**. Nouns ending in **-ione** are also generally feminine.

Words ending in **-e** can be masculine or feminine – the dictionary indicates which.

A masculine plural noun can refer to a mixture of masculine and feminine, e.g.:

i bambini (children, i.e. sons and daughters)
gli italiani (Italian men, *or* the Italians

Plurals

All masculine nouns ending in **-o** form their plural with **-i**.
e.g. **ragazzo** (boy) **ragazzi** (boys)

Most feminine nouns ending in **-a** form their plural with **-e**.
e.g. **ragazza** (girl) **ragazze** (girls)
The exceptions are feminine nouns with a stressed final vowel. These do not change in the plural.
e.g. **la città/le città** (town/towns)
la difficoltà/le difficoltà (difficulty/difficulties)

Most nouns ending in **-e** form their plural with **-i**.
e.g. **giornale** (newspaper) **giornali** (newspapers)

Many nouns ending in -co, -go, -ca and -ga form their plural in -chi, -ghi, -che and -ghe.

e.g.	**buco** (hole)	**buchi** (holes)
	mucca (cow)	**mucche** (cows)
	fungo (mushroom)	**funghi** (mushrooms)
	banca (bank)	**banche** (banks)

A notable exception to this is **amico** (male friend) which becomes **amici**.

Articles ('a'/'an', 'the')

The Italian indefinite article (the equivalent of 'a' or 'an') has different forms: **un** is used with masculine nouns, **una** with feminine ones.

e.g. **un giorno**　　　　　**una macchina**

Uno is used with masculine nouns beginning with a 'z' or with an 's' followed by a consonant (known as an impure 's').

e.g. **uno zio, uno specchio**

Un' is used with feminine nouns beginning with a vowel.

e.g. **un'aranciata**

The definite article ('the') has different forms for masculine and feminine, and also for singular and plural.

In the masculine singular, **il** is used for nouns beginning with a consonant. **Lo** is used for nouns beginning with 'z' or impure 's' and **l'** is used for nouns beginning with a vowel.
In the masculine plural, **i** is used for nouns beginning with a consonant and **gli** for nouns beginning with a vowel or an impure 's'.

e.g.	**il ragazzo**	**i ragazzi**
	l'amico	**gli amici**
	lo zio	**gli zii**

In the feminine singular, **la** is used for nouns beginning with a consonant and **l'** before nouns beginning with a vowel.
In the feminine plural, **le** is used in all cases.

e.g.	**la ragazza**	**le ragazze**
	l'amica	**le amiche**

Adjectives

Adjectives 'agree' with the nouns they are describing – they have different endings for masculine and feminine, singular and plural.

Many adjectives end in **-o** for masculine and **-a** for feminine and change the ending in the plural in the same way as nouns do:

un ragazzo stupido	**ragazzi stupidi**
una macchina rossa	**macchine rosse**

Some adjectives have only one ending for the singular, both masculine and feminine, and masculine and feminine plurals end in **-i**. They include adjectives ending in **-e**.

un ragazzo intelligente	**ragazzi intelligenti**
una ragazza intelligente	**ragazze intelligenti**

Adjectives ending in **-co**, **-go**, **-ca** and **-ga** behave in the same way as nouns with those endings when it comes to forming the plural (see above). Some **-co** endings are an exception to this rule e.g. **simpatico-simpatici**.

Position of adjectives

Most adjectives come after the nouns.
e.g. **vino bianco**   **escursioni turistiche**   **una macchina rossa**

Some common adjectives always come *before* the noun, including:

molto (much)	**poco** (little)	**pochi, poche** (few)
troppo (too much)	**tanto** (so much)	
questo (this)	**quello** (that)	

e.g.
troppo soldi (too much money)
questo ragazzo (this boy)
poche donne (few women)

Adjectives of nationality always follow the noun.

Comparatives and superlatives ('more', 'the most')

'More' is **più** and comes before the adjective. It also gives the equivalent of 'bigger', 'smaller'.

e.g. **più interessante** (more interesting)

   più grande (bigger)

   più vecchio (older)

'Less' is **meno**:

meno importante (less important)

meno complicato (less complicated)

The comparatives of 'good' and 'bad' are **meglio** (better) and **peggiore** (worse).

'Than', as in 'more than' and 'less than', is **di**, if you are comparing two different things.

e.g. **questa macchina è più grande di quest'altra** (this car is bigger than the other)

To say 'the most' or 'the least', put the definite article **il** or **la** before **più** or **meno**.

e.g. **la più bella città** (the most beautiful city)

   il/la più grande del mondo (the biggest in the world)

   il ristorante meno caro (the cheapest restaurant)

   Meno tends to come after the noun.

If you want to add emphasis to an adjective and say that something is 'very ...', add **-issimo**, **-issima**, **issimi**, **-issime** to the stem of the adjective (the endings depend on whether the adjective is masculine or feminine and singular or plural).

e.g. **L'Italia è bellissima** (Italy is very beautiful)

   L'uomo è gentilissimo (the man is very kind)

Possessives ('my', 'your', 'his', 'her', etc.)

Like other adjectives, possessive adjectives 'agree' with the nouns they are describing. The forms are:

	singular		*plural*
	masculine, feminine		*masculine, feminine*
my	mio, mia		miei, mie
your	tuo, tua	tuoi, tue	
his/her/your*	suo, sua	suoi, sue	
our	nostro, nostra		nostri, nostre
your	vostro, vostra		vostri, vostre
their/your*	loro		loro

(*'Your' when addressing someone as **Lei** or **Loro** – see below.)

e.g.
mio fratello (my brother)
la nostra casa (our house)

To indicate possession as in, for example, 'John's brother' (rather than 'his brother') or 'John and Susan's house' (rather than 'their house'), the word **di** (of) is used. There is no equivalent of the English apostrophe s.

e.g. **il fratello di John**   **la casa di John e Susan**

Prepositions

a	to, at
di	of
in	in
su	on

When these prepositions are followed by a definite article (**il**, **la**, **lo**, **l'** in the singular or **i**, **le**, **gli** in the plural), they combine with the article to make one word

e.g. at/to the shops	**ai negozi (a + i)**
at/to the supermarket	**al supermercato (a + il)**
at/to the hospital	**all'ospedale (a + l')**
of the boy	**del ragazzo (di + il)**

of the women	**delle donne (di + le)**	
in the water	**nell'acqua (in + l')**	
in the city	**nella città (in + la)**	
in the nineties	**negli anni novanta (in + gli)**	
on the train	**sul treno (su + il)**	

Demonstrative ('this', 'that')

	singular		*plural*	
	masculine	*feminine*	*masculine*	*feminine*
this, these	**questo**	**questa**	**questi**	**queste**
that, those	**quello**	**quella**	**quei/quegli**	**quelle**

All of these words are also used as demonstrative pronouns ('this one', 'that one', etc.).

Subject pronouns ('I', 'you', 'he', 'she', etc.)

I	**io**
you (informal)*	**tu**
you (formal)*	**lei**
he	**lui**
she	**lei**
we	**noi**
you (informal)*	**voi**
you (formal)*	**loro**
they	**loro**

(*see **'You'** below)

These pronouns are not used much. Italian verbs have different endings which show what the subject is (see **Verbs** below). **Lei** tends to be used slightly more to show politeness. In general the subject pronouns are used mainly for emphasis or to avoid confusion.

e.g. **lui è inglese, lei è scozzese** (he is English, she is Scottish)

'You'

In English there is only one way of addressing people – using the word 'you'. In Italian there are two ways – one is more polite/formal, the other more casual/informal.

The informal way is used between friends and family members, and people of the same age group. The part of the verb used is the second person (singular or plural as appropriate). The word for 'you' is **tu (voi** in the plural).

The formal way uses the third person of the verb (singular or plural). The word for 'you' is **lei (loro** in the plural). Most of the phrases in this book use the formal way of saying 'you'.

Verbs

Italian verbs have different endings according to (i) the subject of the verb, (ii) the tense. There are three main groups of verbs, with different sets of endings for each group.

In dictionaries, verbs are listed in the infinitive form which ends in **-are**, **-ere** or **-ire** (these are the three groups).

Below are the endings for the present tense of these three groups:

	-are	-ere	-ire
	parlare	vedere	partire
io	parlo	vedo	parto
tu	parli	vedi	parti
lui, lei	parla	vede	parte
noi	parliamo	vediamo	partiamo
voi	parlate	vedete	partite
loro	parlano	vedono	partono

The Italian present tense translates both the English 'I ...' and 'I am ...-ing' forms, e.g. **parlo** means both 'I speak' and 'I am speaking'.

There are some verbs in the third group which have different endings:

e.g. **capire** – to understand

io	capisco
tu	capisci
lui, lei	capisce
noi	capiamo
voi	capite
loro	capiscono

Other common verbs with the same endings are **finire** – to finish – and **preferire** – to prefer.

'To be' and 'to have'

Both of these verbs are irregular.

essere – to be

io	sono
tu	sei
lui, lei	è
noi	siamo
voi	siete
loro	sono

avere – to have

io	ho
tu	hai
lui, lei	ha
noi	abbiamo
voi	avete
loro	hanno

Other irregular verbs

Other common verbs that are also irregular include:

sapere	andare	potere	volere
so	vado	posso	voglio
sai	vai	puoi	vuoi
sa	va	può	vuole
sapiamo	andiamo	possiamo	vogliamo
sapete	andate	potete	volete
sanno	vanno	possono	vogliono

Other verb tenses

A few verbs in other tenses that you may find useful:

andare	I have been/I went	sono andato/a
	we have been/we went	siamo andati/e
	I went/I used to go	andavo
	we went/we used to go	andavamo
essere	I have been/I was	sono stato/a
	we have been/we were	siamo stati/e
	I was/I used to be	ero
	we were/we used to be	eravamo
avere	I have had/I had	ho avuto
	we have had/we had	abbiamo avuto
	I had/used to have	avevo
	we had/used to have	avevamo
venire	I have come/I came	sono venuto/a
	we have come/came	siamo venuti/e
	I came/I used to come	venivo
	we came/we used to come	venivamo

For talking about the future, you can often use the present tense.

e.g. **domani gioco al tennis** (tomorrow I am playing tennis)

Negatives

To make the verb negative, put **non** before it.

e.g. **non ho bambini** (I don't have any children)

non capisco (I don't understand)

il signor Bedoni non c'è (Mr Bedoni isn't in)

Italian has double negatives.

e.g. **non ho niente** (I don't have anything); **niente** literally means 'nothing'.

Questions

To ask a question, use a question word ('why', 'when', 'who' etc.) plus the verb. If there is no question word, simply put a question in your voice by making it go up at the beginning of the sentence.

e.g. **Quando viene?** When is he coming?

Chi parla? Who's speaking?

(Lei) Ha bambini? Have you got children?

DAYS, MONTHS, DATES

Names of days and months are not written with capital letters.

Days

Monday	**lunedì**	*loonedee*
Tuesday	**martedì**	*martedee*
Wednesday	**mercoledì**	*merkoledee*
Thursday	**giovedì**	*jovedee*
Friday	**venerdì**	*venerdee*
Saturday	**sabato**	*sabato*
Sunday	**domenica**	*domeneeka*

Months

January	**gennaio**	*jenniyo*
February	**febbraio**	*febbriyo*
March	**marzo**	*martso*
April	**aprile**	*apreele*
May	**maggio**	*majo*
June	**giugno**	*joonyo*
July	**luglio**	*loolyo*
August	**agosto**	*agosto*
September	**settembre**	*settembre*
October	**ottobre**	*ottobre*
November	**novembre**	*novembre*
December	**dicembre**	*deechembre*

Seasons

spring	**la primavera**	*la preemavera*
summer	**l'estate**	*lestate*
autumn	**l'autunno**	*lowtoonno*
winter	**l'inverno**	*leenverno*

General phrases

day	**il giorno**	*eel jorno*
week	**la settimana**	*la setteemana*
fortnight	**quindici giorni**	*kweendeechee jornee*
month	**il mese**	*eel meze*
year	**l'anno**	*lanno*

on Monday	**lunedì**	*loonedee*
on Thursdays	**il giovedì**	*eel jovedee*
	(di giovedì)	*(dee jovedee)*
every Wednesday	**ogni mercoledì**	*onyee merkoledee*

in August	**in agosto**	*een agosto*
at the beginning of March	**all'inizio di marzo**	*aleeneetsyo dee martso*
in the middle of June	**alla metà di giugno**	*alla meta dee joonyo*
at the end of September	**alla fine di settembre**	*alla feene dee settembre*
in six months' time	**fra sei mesi**	*fra say mezee*
during the summer	**durante l'estate**	*doorante lestate*

two years ago	**due anni fa**	*doo-e annee fa*
(in) the nineties	**negli anni novanta**	*nelyee annee novanta*

last ...	**... scorso/a**	*... skorso/a*
last Monday	**lunedì scorso**	*loonedee skorso*
last week	**la settimana scorsa**	*la setteemana skorsa*
last month	**il mese scorso**	*eel meze skorso*
last year	**l'anno scorso**	*lanno skorso*

next …	… prossimo/a	… *prosseemo*
next Tuesday	martedì prossimo	*martedee prosseemo*
next week	la settimana prossima	*la settimana prosseema*
next month	il mese prossimo	*eel meze prosseemo*
next year	l'anno prossimo	*lanno prosseemo*
What day is it today?	Che giorno è oggi?	*ke jorno e ojee*
What is the date today?	Quanti ne abbiamo oggi?	*kwantee ne abbyamo ojee*
When is your birthday?	Quando è il suo compleanno?	*kwando e eel soo-o komple-anno*
When is your saint's day?*	Quando è il suo onomastico?	*kwando e eel soo-o onomasteeko*

* Italians celebrate the saint's day corresponding to their Christian name

Today	oggi	*ojee*
This morning	questa mattina	*kwesta matteena*
This afternoon	questo pomeriggio	*kewsto pomereejo*
Yesterday	ieri	*yeree*
The day before yesterday	l'altro ieri	*laltro yeree*
Yesterday morning	ieri mattina	*yeree matteena*
Last night	ieri sera	*yeree sera*
Tomorrow	domani	*domanee*
The day after tomorrow	dopodomani	*dopodomanee*
Tomorrow afternoon	domani pomeriggio	*domanee pomereejo*
Before Saturday	prima di sabato	*preema dee sabato*
After Thursday	dopo giovedì	*dopo jovedee*
Until Friday	fino a venerdì	*feeno a venerdee*

(on) the first of January	il primo di gennaio	*eel preemo dee jenniyo*
(on) Tuesday 10th May	martedì il dieci di maggio	*martedee eel dyechee dee majo*
1990	mille novecento novanta	*meelle novechento novanta*
the 14th century	il quattrocento	*eel kwattroshento*

TIME

one o'clock	**l'una**	*loona*
two o'clock	**le due**	*le doo-e*
three o'clock etc	**le tre**	*le tre*
quarter past ...	**... e un quarto**	*e oon kwarto*
half past ...	**... e mezza**	*e medza*
five past ...	**... e cinque**	*e cheenkwe*
twenty-five past ...	**... e venticinque**	*e vaynteecheenkwe*
quarter to ...	**... meno un quarto**	*meno oon kwarto*
ten to ...	**... meno dieci**	*meno dyechee*
twenty to ...	**... meno venti**	*meno vayntee*
noon/midday	**mezzogiorno**	*medzojorno*
midnight	**mezzanotte**	*medzanotte*
in the morning (a.m.)	**di mattina**	*dee matteena*
in the afternoon (p.m.)	**di pomeriggio**	*dee pomereejo*
in the evening	**di sera**	*dee sera*
a quarter of an hour	**un quarto d'ora**	*oon kwarto dora*
three quarters of an hour	**tree quarti d'ora**	*tre kwartee dora*
half an hour	**mezz'ora**	*medzora*

24-hour clock

0045	**le zero e quarantincinque**	*la **dzero** e kwaranta**cheenk**we*
0900	**le nove**	*le **nove***
1300	**le tredici**	*le **tredee**chee*
1430	**le quattordici e trenta**	*le kwat**tor**deechee e **trenta***
2149	**le ventuno e quarantanove**	*le ven**toono** e kwaranta**nove***

General phrases

at...	**alla/alle...**	*alla/alle...*
exactly/precisely...	**le ... in punto**	*le... een **poonto***
about...	**circa le ...**	***cheerk**a le...*
nearly...	**quasi le ...**	*kwa**zee** le...*
soon	**fra poco**	*fra **poko***
early	**presto**	***presto***
(trains etc.)	**in anticipo**	*een antee**cheepo***
late	**tardi**	***tardee***
(trains etc.)	**in ritardo**	*een ree**tardo***
on time	**in tempo, puncuale**	*een **tempo**, poontoo-**ale***
earlier on	**prima**	***preema***
later on	**più tardi**	*pyoo **tardee***
half an hour ago	**mezz'ora fa**	***medzora** fa*
in ten minutes' time	**fra dieci minuti**	*fra **dyechee** mee**nootee***

What time is it?	**che ora è?**
	ke ora e
It's ...	**È .../Sono ...**
	e .../sono ...
It's one o'clock	**È l'una**
	e loona
It's six o'clock	**Sono le sei**
	sono le say
It's quarter past eight	**Sono le otto e un quarto**
	sono le otto e oon kwarto
(At) what time ...?	**A che ora ...?**
	a ke ora ...
At ...	**Alla .../Alle ...**
	alla .../alle ...
At half past one	**All'una e mezza**
	alloona a medza
At 2155	**Alle ventuna e cinquantacinque**
	alle ventoona e cheenkwantacheenkwe

COUNTRIES AND NATIONALITIES

Languages are the same as the masculine adjective.
Adjectives are written with a small letter.

Country	Nationality (masculine, feminine)
Africa **Africa**	**africano, africana**
Argentina **Argentina**	**argentino, argentina**
Asia **Asia**	**asiatico, asiatica**
Australia **Australia**	**australiano, australiana**
Austria **Austria**	**austriaco, austriaca**
Belgium **Belgio**	**belga, belga**
Bulgaria **Bulgaria**	**bulgaro, bulgara**
Canada **Canada**	**canadese, canadese**
Central America **America Centrale**	**centroamericano, centroamericana**
China **Cina**	**cinese, cinese**
Cuba **Cuba**	**cubano, cubana**
Czechoslovakia **Cecoslovachia**	**cecoslovaco, cecoslovaca**
Denmark **Danimarca**	**danese, danese**
Egypt **Egitto**	**egiziano, egiziana**
Eire **l'Eire**	**irlandese, irlandese**
England **Inghilterra**	**inglese, inglese**
Europe **Europa**	**europeo, europea**

Finland	**Finlandia**	**finlandese, finlandese**
France	**Francia**	**francese, francese**
Germany	**Germania**	**tedesco, tedesca**
Great Britain	**Gran Bretagna**	**britannico, britannica**
Greece	**Grecia**	**greco, greca**
Hungary	**Ungheria**	**ungherese, ungherese**
India	**India**	**indiano, indiana**
Ireland	**Irlanda**	**irlandese, irlandese**
Israel	**Israele**	**israelìano, israelìana**
Italy	**Italia**	**italiano, italiana**
Japan	**Giappone**	**giapponese, giapponese**
Luxembourg	**Lussemburgo**	**lussemburghese, lussemburghese**
Malta	**Malta**	**maltese, maltese**
Mexico	**Messico**	**messicano, messicana**
Netherlands	**I Paesi Bassi**	**olandese, olandese**
New Zealand	**Nuova Zelanda**	**neozelandese, neozelandese**
Northern Ireland **l'Irlanda del Nord**		**irlandese, irlandese**
Norway	**Norvegia**	**norvegese, norvegese**
Poland	**Polonia**	**polacco, polacca**
Portugal	**Portogallo**	**portoghese, portoghese**
Romania	**Romanìa**	**rumeno, rumena**
Russia	**Russia**	**russo, russa**
Scotland	**la Scozia**	**scozzese, scozzese**
South Africa	**Sudafrica**	**sudafricano, sudafricana**

South America	**Sudamerica**	sudamericano, sudamericana
Soviet Union **l'Unione Sovietica**		
Spain	**Spagna**	spagnolo, spagnola
Sweden	**Svezia**	svedese, svedese
Switzerland	**Svizzera**	svizzero, svizzera
Turkey	**Turchia**	turco, turca
United Kingdom **il Regno Unito**		
United States	**gli Stati Uniti**	americano, americana
Wales	**il Galles**	gallese, gallese
West Indies **le Indie Occidentali**		indiano occidentale, indiana occidentale
Yugoslavia	**Iugoslavia**	iugoslavo, iugoslava

GENERAL SIGNS AND NOTICES

Acqua potabile	Drinking water
Aperto	Open
Ascensore	Lift
Attenti al cane	Beware of the dog
Attenzione	Caution
Avanti	Go
Bibite fredde	Cold drinks
Caldo	Hot
Camere libere	Rooms to let
Cassa	Cashier
Cassa continua	24-hour safe
Chiuso	Closed
Completo	Full
Da affittare	To let, for hire
Divieto	Prohibited
Divieto transito	No thoroughfare
Donne	Ladies/Women
Eccetto (autobus)	Except for (buses)
Entrare senza bussare	Enter without knocking
Entrata	Entrance
Entrata libera	Free entry
Freddo	Cold
Giù	Down
Guasto	Out of order
I trasgressori saranno puniti a normi di legge	Trespassers will be prosecuted
Informazioni	Information
Ingresso libero	Admission free
In vendita	For sale
IVA	VAT
Libero	Free, vacant
Non disturbare	Do not disturb
Non potabile	Not for drinking

Occupato	Engaged
Offerta speciale	Special offer
Pericolo	Danger
Pericolo di morte	Danger of death
Pista per ciclisti	Cycle path
Polizia	Police
Privato	Private
Rimborsi non saranno effettuati	No refunds
Riservato	Reserved
Saldi	Sales
Scala mobile	Escalator
Signore	Ladies
Signori	Gentlemen
Spingere	Push
Su	Up
Suonare per favore	Please ring
Svendita	Sale
Tirare	Pull
Uomini	Men, gentlemen
Uscita	Exit
Uscita di sicurezza	Emergency exit
Veleno	Poison
Vietato fumare	No smoking
Vietato l'ingresso	No entrance
Vietato toccare	Do not touch
Vuoto	Empty

CONVERSION TABLES
(approximate equivalents)

Linear measurements

centimetres   **centimetri (cm)**
metres   **metri (m)**
kilometres   **chilometri (km)**

10 cm = 4 inches	1 inch = 2.54 cm
50 cm = 19.6 inches	1 foot = 30 cm
1 metre = 39.37 inches	1 yard = 0.91 m
(just over 1 yard)	
100 metres = 110 yards	
1 km = 0.62 miles	1 mile = 1.61 km

To convert
km to miles: divide by 8 and multiply by 5
miles to km: divide by 5 and multiply by 8

Miles		Kilometres
0.6	1	1.6
1.2	2	3.2
1.9	3	4.8
2.5	4	6.4
3	5	8
6	10	16
12	20	32
19	30	48
25	40	64
31	50	80
62	100	161
68	110	177
75	120	193
81	130	209

Liquid measures

litre   **litro (l)**

1 litre = 1.8 pints   1 pint = 0.57 litre
5 litres = 1.1 gallons   1 gallon = 4.55 litres
'A litre of water's a pint and three quarters'

Gallons   ## Litres

Gallons		Litres
0.2	1	4.5
0.4	2	9
0.7	3	13.6
0.9	4	18
1.1	5	23
2.2	10	45.5

Weights

gram   **grammo (g)**
100 grams   **un etto (cento grammi)**
200 grams   **due etti (duecento grammi)**
kilo   **chilo (kg)**

100 g = 3.5 oz   1 oz = 28 g
200 g = 7 oz   ¼ lb = 113 g
½ kilo = 1.1 lb   ½ lb = 225 g
1 kilo = 2.2 lb   1 lb = 450 g

Pounds   ## Kilos (Grams)

Pounds		Kilos (Grams)
2.2	1	0.45 (450)
4.4	2	0.9 (900)
6.6	3	1.4 (1400)
8.8	4	1.8 (1800)
11	5	2.3 (2300)
22	10	4.5 (4500)

Area

hectare	**ettaro**
1 hectare = 2.5 acres	1 acre = 0.4 hectare

To convert
hectares to acres: divide by 2 and multiply by 5
acres to hectares: divide by 5 and multiply by 2

Hectares		Acres
0.4	1	2.5
2.0	5	12
4	10	25
10	50	124
40.5	100	247

Clothing and shoe sizes

Women's dresses and suits

UK	10	12	14	16	18	20
Continent	36	38	40	42	44	46

Men's suits and coats

UK	36	38	40	42	44	46
Continent	46	48	50	52	54	56

Men's shirts

UK	14	14½	15	15½	16	16½	17
Continent	36	37	38	39	41	42	43

Shoes

UK	2	3	4	5	6	7	8	9	10	11
Continent	35	36	37	38	39	41	42	43	44	45

Waist and chest measurements

inches	28	30	32	34	36	38	40	42	44	46	48	50
centimetres	71	76	80	87	91	97	102	107	112	117	122	127

Tyre pressures

lb/sq in	15	18	20	22	24	26	28	30	33	35
kg/sq cm	1.1	1.3	1.4	1.5	1.7	1.8	2.0	2.1	2.3	2.5

NATIONAL HOLIDAYS

Capodanno/ Primo dell'anno	New Year's Day	1 January
La Befana/Epifania	Epiphany	6 January
Lunedì dell'Angelo	Easter Monday	
Anniversario della Liberazione	Liberation Day	25 April
Festa dei Lavoratori	Labour Day	1 May
Ferragosto/Assunzione	Assumption	15 August
Tutti i santi/I morti	All Saints' Day	1 November
Immacolata Concezione	Immaculate Conception	8 December
Natale	Christmas Day	25 December
Santo Stefano	St Stephen's Day	26 December

USEFUL ADDRESSES

In the UK and the Republic of Ireland

Italian State Tourist Office
1 Princes Street
London W1R 8AY
Tel: 071-408 1254

Italian Embassy
14 Three Kings Yard
Davies Street
London W1Y 2EH
Tel: 071-629 8200

Italian Institute of Culture (for information about cultural events and language courses)
39 Belgrave Square
London SW1X 8NX
Tel: 071-235 1461

Italian Chamber of Commerce
Walmar House
296 Regent Street
London W1R 6AE
Tel: 071-637 3153

Italian Trade Centre
37 Sackville Street
London W1X 2DQ
Tel: 071-734 2412
(Showroom: 46 Piccadilly, London W1)

CIT (Compagnia Italiana del Turismo)
(Italian State Railways)
50 Conduit Street
London W1R 9FB
Tel: 071-434 3844

Italian State Tourist Office
47 Merrion Square
Dublin 2
Tel: Dublin 76 63 97

Italian Embassy
63/65 Northumberland Road
Dublin 4
Tel: Dublin 60 17 44

Italian Cultural Institute
11 Fitzwilliam Square
Dublin 2
Tel: Dublin 76 66 62

Italian Trade Centre
16 St Stephen's Green
Dublin 2
Tel: Dublin 76 78 29 ·

In Italy

British Embassy and Consulate
Via XX Settembre 80A,
00187 Rome
Tel: 475 5441

There are also consulates in: Cagliari, Florence, Genoa, Milan, Naples, Turin, Trieste and Venice.

Irish Embassy
Largo del Nazareno 3
00187 Rome
Tel: 678 2541

Prefettura della Casa Pontificia
Biglietti per le udienze pontificie
(Tickets for papal audiences)
Città del Vaticano
00120 Rome

NUMBERS

0	**zero**	*dzero*
1	**uno**	*oono*
2	**due**	*doo-e*
3	**tre**	*tre*
4	**quattro**	*kwattro*
5	**cinque**	*cheenkwe*
6	**sei**	*se-ee*
7	**sette**	*sette*
8	**otto**	*otto*
9	**nove**	*nove*
10	**dieci**	*dyechee*
11	**undici**	*oondeechee*
12	**dodici**	*dodeechee*
13	**tredici**	*tredeechee*
14	**quattordici**	*kwattordeechee*
15	**quindici**	*kweendeechee*
16	**sedici**	*sedeechee*
17	**diciassette**	*deechassette*
18	**diciotto**	*deechotto*
19	**diciannove**	*deechanove*
20	**venti**	*vayntee*
21	**ventuno**	*ventoono*
22	**ventidue**	*venteedoo-e*
23	**ventitre**	*venteetre*
24	**ventiquattro**	*venteekwattro*
25	**venticinque**	*venteecheenkwe*
26	**ventisei**	*venteese-ee*
27	**ventisette**	*venteesette*
28	**ventotto**	*ventotto*
29	**ventinove**	*venteenove*

For numbers after **venti***, follow the same pattern: keep the final vowel except with one and eight.*

30	trenta	*trenta*
31	trentuno	*trentoono*
32 etc.	trentadue	*trentadoo-e*
40	quaranta	*kwaranta*
50	cinquanta	*cheenkwanta*
60	sessanta	*sessanta*
70	settanta	*settanta*
80	ottanta	*ottanta*
90	novanta	*novanta*
100	cento	**chento**
101 etc.	centouno	*chento-oono*
200	duecento	*doo-echento*
300	trecento	*trechento*
400	quattrocento	*kwattrochento*
500	cinquecento	*cheenkwechento*
600	seicento	*sechento*
700	settecento	*settechento*
800	ottocento	*ottochento*
900	novecento	*novechento*
1,000	mille	*meelle*
2,000 etc.	duemila	*doo-emeela*
100,000	centomila	*chentomeela*
1,000,000	un milione	*oon meelyone*
2,000,000 etc.	due milioni	*doo-e meelyonee*

● One: use **un**, **uno** or **una** with a noun to mean 'one' or 'a'.
e.g. **un caffè** (one/a coffee), **uno specchio** (one/a mirror), **una
birra** (one/a beer)

● The word for a hundred, **cento**, doesn't change in the plural
– duecento, trecento, etc. **Mille**, a thousand, becomes **mila** in the
plural – **duemila**, **tremila**, etc.

● For talking about millions of something, add **di**.
e.g. **due milioni di uomini** (2,000,000 men).

● Years:

| 1990 | mille novecento novanta |
| 1492 | mille quattrocento novantadue |

DICTIONARY

Italian nouns are given with the definite article ('the') to show their gender: **il** or **lo** for masculine, **la** for feminine (**i** or **gli** for masculine plural, **le** for feminine plural). Where the gender is not clear, the abbreviations *(m)* or *(f)* are added.

Adjectives which have different endings for masculine and feminine are shown like this: **bianco/a** (i.e. **bianco** for masculine, **bianca** for feminine). See Basic grammar, page 167, for notes on gender, plurals, etc.

Other abbreviations: *(pl)* – plural.

Words for food and drink are given in the Menu Reader, page 105.

See also General signs and notices, page 187, and the lists of **You may see** in the individual sections.

A

a to, at
abbastanza enough, plenty; quite, fairly
l'abbonamento (*m*) season ticket
abitare to live (*dwell*)
l'abito (*m*) suit (*for men*)
accanto/a nearby
accendere to light
l'accendino (*m*) lighter
acceso/a lit, on (*light etc.*)
accettare to accept
accomodarsi to make oneself at home
  si accomodi make yourself comfortable/at home
l'aceto (*m*) vinegar
l'acqua (*f*) water
  l'acqua distillata distilled water
acuto/a sharp (*pain*)
addomesticato/a tame
adesso now
l'adulto (*m*) adult
l'aeroplano (*m*) aeroplane
l'aeroporto (*m*) airport
gli affari business
  per affari on business
affilato/a sharp
affittare to let, rent out
l'affitto (*m*) rent

affollato/a crowded
affumicato smoked
l'agenzia (*f*) agency, branch office
  l'agenzia di viaggio travel agency
l'agnello (*m*) lamb
l'agricoltore (*m*) farmer
aiutare to help
aiuto! help!
l'aiuto (*m*) help
l'ala (*f*) wing
l'albergo (*m*) hotel
l'albero (*m*) tree
alcolico/a alcoholic
l'alcool (*m*) alcohol
alcuni/e (*a*) few, some
al di là di . . . beyond . . .
l'alimento (*m*) food
  gli alimenti per bambini baby food
l'aliscafo (*m*) hovercraft, hydrofoil
l'allarme (*m*) alarm
l'alloggio (*m*) accommodation
almeno at least
alto/a high, tall
gli altri the others
altro/a other
alzarsi to stand up, to get up
amare to love
l'ambasciata (*f*) embassy
ambedue both

198

l'ambiente (*m*) environment
l'ambulanza (*f*) ambulance
l'amica (*f*) friend (*female*)
l'amico (*m*) friend (*male*)
ammalato/a ill, sick
l'amministratore (*m*) delegato managing director
l'amore (*m*) love
analcolico/a non-alcoholic
l'anatra (*f*), l'anitra (*f*) duck
anche also, as well
ancora still
 ancora (una volta) again
andare to go
 andare a casa to go home
 andare in bicicletta to go for a bicycle ride
 andare in cavallo to go horse riding
 andare via to go away
(di) andata single (*ticket*)
(di) andata e ritorno return (*ticket*)
andiamo! let's go!
l'anello (*m*) ring
l'angolo (*m*) corner
l'animale (*m*) animal
l'anitra (*f*) *see* l'anatra
l'anno (*m*) year
annullare to cancel
anticipo: in anticipo in advance; early
l'antisettico (*m*) antiseptic
l'anziano/a senior citizen
aperto/a open
l'appartamento (*m*) appartment, flat
appartenere (a) to belong (to)
appiccicoso/a sticky
l'appuntamento (*m*) appointment, date

l'apribottiglie (*m*) bottle opener
aprire to open
l'apriscatole (*m*) tin opener
l'arachide (*f*) peanut
l'architetto/a architect
l'arco (*m*) arch
l'argento (*m*) silver
l'aria (*f*) air
l'aria condizionata air conditioning
l'armadio (*m*) cupboard
arrivederci goodbye
l'arte (*f*) art
l'articolo (*m*) article
artificiale artificial
l'artista (*m or f*) artist
l'ascensore (*m*) lift
l'asciugamano (*m*) towel
asciugare to dry
 asciugare con il föhn to blow dry (*hair*)
ascoltare to listen (to)
aspettare to wait (for), to expect
l'aspirapolvere (*m*) vacuum cleaner
aspro/a sour
l'assegno (*m*) cheque
assicurato/a insured
l'assicurazione (*f*) insurance
l'assistente sociale (*m or f*) social worker
assolato/a sunny
assomigliare to look like
gli assorbenti sanitary towels
l'atmosfera (*f*) atmosphere
attaccare to attack
attento/a careful
attraverso across
l'attrezzatura (*f*) equipment

l'**autista** (*m or f*) driver
l'**autobus** (*m*) bus
    in autobus by bus
    automatico/a automatic
l'**autonoleggio** (*m*) care hire
l'**autore, l'autrice** author
l'**autorimessa** (*f*) garage (*for repairs*)
l'**autostrada** (*f*) motorway
l'**autunno** (*m*) autumn
  avanti! go! come in!
    in avanti forward (*movement*)
  avere to have
    avere la febbre to have a temperature
l'**aviazione** (*f*) **militare** air force
l'**avvocato/a** lawyer

B

  baciare to kiss
il **bacio** kiss
i **baffi** moustache
i **bagagli** luggage, baggage
    i **bagagli a mano** hand luggage
  bagnato/a wet
il **bagnino** lifeguard
il **bagno** bath, bathroom
la **baia** bay
  ballare to dance
il **balsamo** conditioner
i **bambini** children
il **bambino** baby, child
la **banconota** bank note
la **bandiera** flag
il **barattolo** can
la **barca** boat
    la **barca a vela** sailing boat
  basso/a low

  basta: basta così? is that enough?
il **bastone** stick
il **battello** boat
  battere a macchina to type
la **batteria** battery (*car*)
  bello/a beautiful, lovely, fine (*weather*)
  bene well
    ben cotto well done (*steak*)
la **benzina** petrol
    la **benzina senza piombo** lead-free petrol
  bere to drink
la **biancheria** laundry, underwear
  bianco/a white
    bianco e nero black and white
la **Bibbia** the Bible
la **biblioteca** library
il **bicchiere** glass (*for drinking*)
la **bicicletta** bicycle
il **bidone** bin
la **biglietteria** ticket office
il **biglietto** ticket
il **binario** platform
  biondo/a blond, fair (*hair*)
la **birra** beer
    la **birra bionda** lager
    la **birra alla spina** draught beer
il **biscotto** biscuit
  bisogna it requires
il **bisogno** need
    avere bisogno di to need
  bloccato/a blocked
  blu blue
la **bocca** mouth
il **bollitore** kettle
la **bombola di gas** gas bottle

la bomboletta di gas gas refill
la Borsa stock exchange
la borsa (hand)bag
il borsellino purse
il bosco wood
la bottiglia bottle
bravo/a good; clever
britannico/a British
la brocca jug
la bronchite bronchitis
bruciare to burn
bruciato/a burnt
brutto/a bad, ugly
il bucato washing
buona: alla buona plain (*cooking*)
buono/a good
  buon giorno good morning
  buona notte good night
  buona sera good afternoon/evening
il burro butter
bussare to knock (*on a door*)
la busta envelope
la bustina di tè tea bag

C

la cabina cabin
  la cabina telefonica telephone kiosk
cadere to fall
caduto/a fallen
il caffè coffee
  il caffè decaffeinato decaffeinated coffee
il calcio football
caldo/a hot, warm
  fa caldo oggi it's warm today
il calmante painkiller

calmo/a calm
il calore heat
le calze stockings
i calzini socks
i calzoncini corti shorts
i calzoncini da bagno swimming trunks
cambiare to change, exchange
  cambiare casa to move house
  cambiare idea to change one's mind
cambiarsi to change one's clothes
il cambio exchange rate
la camera room
  la camera da letto bedroom
  la camera doppia double room
  la camera singola single room
la cameriera waitress
il cameriere waiter
la camicia shirt
il camion lorry
camminare to walk
la campagna country(side)
la campana bell
il campanello (front door) bell
il campione sample; champion
il campo field; court, pitch (*sports*)
  il campo di corso racecourse
cancellare to cancel
il cancello gate
il cancro cancer
la candeggina bleach
la candela candle**

il **cane** dog
la **canna da pesca** fishing rod
la **canottiera** vest
la **cantina** cellar
la **canzone** song
i **capelli** hair
capire to understand
  non capisco I don't
  understand
la **capitale** capital city
il **capo** boss
il **Capodanno** New Year's Day
la **capolinea** bus terminus
il **capostazione** station master
il **capotreno** guard
la **cappella** chapel
il **cappello** hat
il **cappotto** coat
carino/a pretty
la **carne** meat
  la **carne macinata** mince
caro/a dear, expensive
il **carro** cart
  il **carro attrezzi** breakdown
  truck
la **carrozza** carriage, coach
  (*rail*)
la **carrozzina** pram
la **carta** paper, card
  la **carta d'imbarco**
  boarding card
  la **carta igienica** toilet
  paper
  la **carta da scrivere** writing
  paper
  la **carta telefonica**
  telephone card
la **cartolina** postcard
la **casa** house, home
  a **casa** at home
la **casalinga** housewife

caso: in caso di in case
  per caso by chance
la **cassetta** box
  la **cassetta delle lettere**
  letterbox
  la **cassetta di pronto**
  soccorso first-aid kit
il **cassetto** drawer
il **castello** castle
cattivo/a bad
il **cavallo** horse
il **cavatappi** corkscrew
il **cavo** rope
  il **cavo da rimorchio** tow
  rope
c'è there is
la **cena** dinner (*evening*)
centrale central
il **centro** centre
  il **centro città** city centre
la **cera** wax
cercare to look for
il **cerotto** sticking plaster
certo of course
certo/a certain
il **cervello** brain
il **cestino** basket
il **cetriolo** cucumber
che what, who, which
chi? who?
  chi è? who is it?
chiamare to call
chiamarsi to be called
  come ti chiami? what's
  your name?
  mi chiamo ... my name
  is ...
la **chiamata** call (*telephone*)
chiaro/a clear, light
la **chiave** key
chiedere to ask

la **chiesa** church
chiudere to close
   chiudere a chiave to lock
chiuso/a closed
ci us, to us, ourselves; there
ciao hello, goodbye
   (*informal*)
il **cibo** food
il **ciclismo** cycling
il **ciclomotore** moped
cieco/a blind
il **cielo** sky
la **cima** top, summit
il **cimitero** cemetery
la **cintura** belt; waist
   la cintura di sicurezza
   safety belt
la **cioccolata** chocolate
la **cipria** face powder
circa about, approximately
il **circo** circus
il **circolo** circle
circondato di surrounded by
ci sono there are
la **città** city, town
la **classe** class
il **clima** climate
la **clinica** clinic
la **coda** queue
il **codice postale** post code
la **cognata** sister-in-law
il **cognato** brother-in-law
il **cognome** surname
la **coincidenza** connection
   (*travel*)
i **collant** tights
la **collina** hill
il **colore** colour
colpire to hit
il **coltello** knife
combattere to fight

come like, as
   com'è? what's it like?
   come sono? how are they?/
   what are they like?
   come stai? how are you?
   come va? how's it going?
cominciare to begin
il/la **commerciante** dealer
il **commesso, la commessa** sales
   assistant
il **commissariato** police station
comodo/a comfortable,
   convenient
il **compartimento** compartment
il **compleanno** birthday
completo complete
   al completo full up
comprare to buy
compreso/a included
comune common
comunque in any case,
   nevertheless
con with
il **concerto** concert
confermare to confirm
confronto a compared with
congelare to freeze (*food*)
il **coniglio** rabbit
conoscere to know (*a person*)
la **consegna** delivery
la **conservazione** conservation
consigliare to recommend,
   advise
il **consolato** consulate
i **contanti** cash
contare to count
il **contatore** meter
contento/a pleased, content
il **conto** bill
il **contraccettivo** contraceptive
controllare to check

il **controllore** inspector
la **coperta** blanket
la **copia** copy
coraggioso/a brave
il **corpo** body
la **corrente** current (*electricity*)
    la **corrente d'aria** draught
    (*air*)
correntemente fluently
correre to run
correttamente properly
corretto/a correct, right
il **corridoio** corridor
il/la **corrispondente** penfriend
il **corso** course (*of lessons*);
    avenue
corto/a short
la **cosa** thing
cosa? what?
    cosa c'è? what's wrong?
così so, like (this)
    così tanto so much
la **costa** coast
costare to cost
il **costo** cost
costruire to build
il **costruttore** builder
il **costume da bagno** bathing
    costume
il **cotone** cotton
la **cravatta** tie
credere to think, believe
    credo di sì I think so
la **crema** lotion, cream
    la **crema per il viso** face
    cream
la **croce** cross
la **crociera** cruise
crudo/a raw
la **cuccetta** couchette
il **cucchiaino** teaspoon

il **cucchiaio** spoon
la **cucina** kitchen, cooker
la **cugina** cousin (*female*)
il **cugino** cousin (*male*)
il **cuoio** leather
il **cuore** heart
la **curva** bend
il **cuscino** cushion

D

da from
da nessuna parte nowhere
dappertutto everywhere
da qualche parte anywhere
da (quando) since
dare to give
    dare da mangiare to feed
la **data** date (*day*)
davanti front
    davanti a in front of
davvero really, indeed
il **dazio** customs duty
il **debito** debt
decidere to decide
del, della, dello of the . . .;
    some
dei, delle, degli of the . . .;
    some
delizioso/a delicious
deluso/a disappointed
il **dente** tooth
la **dentiera** dentures
il **dentifricio** toothpaste
il/la **dentista** dentist
dentro inside, among
il **dépliant** brochure, leaflet
il **deposito** deposit
descrivere to describe
destra right
    a destra to the right

il detersivo detergent
il dettaglio detail
deve . . . you/he/she/must
. . .
la deviazione diversion
di of, by
di là that way
di qua this way
la diapositiva slide (*camera*)
la diarrea diarrhoea
dichiarare to declare
dietro behind
di dietro back, rear
dietro (di) at the back (of),
behind
il difetto fault, defect
difettoso/a faulty
difficile difficult
dimenticare to forget
Dio God
dipende . . . it depends . . .
dire to say, to tell
diretto/a direct (*route*)
il direttore, la direttrice
director, manager;
headmaster/mistress;
producer (*radio, television*)
la direzione direction
diritto/a, dritto/a straight
sempre dritto straight on
il disco disc
il disco orario parking disc
disegnare to draw
il disegno design
disoccupato/a unemployed
la dispepsia indigestion
dispiace: mi dispiace I'm
sorry
il dito finger
la ditta firm, company
diverso/a different
divertente amusing, funny

il divertimento entertainment
divertirsi to enjoy oneself
divertiti! enjoy yourself!
divorziato/a divorced
la doccia shower
dolce sweet
dolorante sore
il dolore ache, pain
i dolori mestruali period
pains
doloroso/a painful
la domanda question
domani tomorrow
la donna woman
la donna d'affari business
woman
dopo after, afterwards
dopodomani the day after
tomorrow
doppiato/a dubbed
doppio/a double
dormire to sleep
dove? where?
dov'è . . .? where is . . .?
dovere to have to; to owe
dritto/a *see* **diritto**
le droghe drugs
dunque well, so, therefore
il duomo cathedral
durante during
durare to last
duro/a hard

205

E

e and
è is (*see 'to be', p. 174*)
eccetto except
eccitato/a excited
eccolo, eccola here it is
eccoli, eccole here they are

l'economia (f) economy
economico/a cheap
l'edicola (f) newspaper kiosk
l'edificio (m) building
educato/a polite
l'elenco (m) list, directory
  l'elenco telefonico
  telephone directory
l'elettricista (m) electrician
l'elettricità (f) electricity
l'elezione (f) election
l'emergenza (f) emergency
l'emicrania (f) migraine
l'emorragia (f) nasale
  nosebleed
l'energia (f) energy, power
  l'energia nucleare nuclear
  power
entrare to come in, enter
eppure and yet
l'erba (f) grass
  le erbe aromatiche herbs
l'errore (m) mistake
l'esame (m) exam
esattamente exactly
esatto/a exact
esaurito/a sold out
l'esempio (m) example
  per esempio for example
esente da dogana duty-free
l'esercizio (m) exercise
esportare to export
espresso/a express
essenziale essential
essere to be (see Basic
  grammar, p. 167)
essere d'accordo to agree
  (with an opinion)
l'est (m) east
l'estate (f) summer
estero/a foreign

all'estero abroad
l'estintore (m) fire
  extinguisher
l'etichetta (f) label
evitare to avoid

F

fa ago
  due anni fa two years ago
la fabbrica factory
il facchino porter (station)
la faccia face
facile easy
facoltativo/a optional
i fagioli beans
i fagiolini French beans
falso/a false
la fame hunger
  avere fame to be hungry
la famiglia family
fantastico! great!
fare to make, to do
  fare compere to go
  shopping
  fare della vela to go sailing
  fare footing to go jogging
  fare l'autostop to hitchhike
  fare male to hurt
  fare marcia indietro to
  reverse
  fare un bagno to have a
  bath, to bathe
  fare un numero to dial
la farina flour
farsi la barba to shave
il fatto fact
  fatto: fatto a mano hand
  made
la fattoria farm
il fazzoletto handkerchief

i **fazzoletti di carta** tissues
la **febbre** fever
felice happy
la **femmina** female
femminile feminine
ferire to injure
ferito/a injured
fermarsi to stop
fermi! stop!
fermo/a firm
il **ferro** iron (*metal*)
il **ferro da stiro** iron
la **ferrovia** railway
la **festa** festival
la **festa nazionale** public holiday
la **fetta** slice
a **fette** sliced
i **fiammiferi** matches
fidanzato/a engaged (*to be married*)
la **fiera** fair
la **fiera campionaria** trade fair
la **figlia** daughter
la **figliastra** step-daughter
i **figliastri** step-children
il **figliastro** step-son
il **figlio** son
la **fila** row
la **fine** end
la **finestra** window
il **finestrino** window (*car, train*)
finire to finish
fino a until
il **fiore** flower
la **firma** signature
firmare to sign
il **fiume** river
il **fondo** bottom

fondo: in fondo a at the back of, at the bottom of
la **fontana** fountain
il **footing** jogging
la **foratura** puncture
le **forbici** scissors
la **forchetta** fork
forma: in forma fit, healthy
il **formaggio** cheese
il **fornello** stove
il **fornello a petrolio** primus stove
forse perhaps
forte strong, loud
fortunato/a lucky
fra among, between
fra poco soon
francamente frankly
il **francobollo** stamp (*postage*)
il **fratellastro** step-brother
il **fratello** brother
freddo/a cold
fresco/a fresh
la **fretta** rush, haste
avere fretta to be in a hurry
il **frigorifero** refrigerator
fronte: di fronte a opposite
la **frontiera** border, frontier
la **frutta** fruit
fumare to smoke
la **funivia** cable car
funzionare to work, function
non funziona it doesn't work
il **fuoco** fire
fuori out, outside
fuori (da) out (of)
il **furgone** van
il **furto** robbery
il **fusibile** fuse

207

G

la **galleria** gallery, tunnel
la **gamba** leg
il **gas butano** butane gas
il **gasolio** diesel
gassoso/a fizzy
il **gatto** cat
il **gelato** ice-cream
gelido/a icy (*weather*)
i **gemelli** twins
generale general
generalmente generally, in general
il **genero** son-in-law
i **genitori** parents
la **gente** people
gentile kind, generous
gettare (via) to throw (away)
il **ghiaccio** ice
già already
la **giacca** jacket
giallo/a yellow
il **giardino** garden
giocare to play (*sports*)
il **giocattolo** toy
il **gioco** game
   il **gioco d'azzardo** gambling
il **giornale** newspaper
la **giornata** day (*the whole day*)
il **giorno** day
   il **giorno feriale** weekday
   il **giorno festivo** holiday, weekend
giovane young
la **gioventù** youth
il **giradischi** record player
girare to turn
il **giro** tour, excursion
la **gita** trip

giù down, downstairs
il **giubbotto salvagente/di salvataggio** lifejacket
il **giudice** judge
gli the; to him/her; to you
gocciolare to drip
la **gola** throat
la **gomma** rubber
gonfiare to pump up
gonfiato/a swollen
la **gonna** skirt
il **governo** government
il **gradino** step
grande big, tall
il **grande magazzino** department store
grasso/a fat, greasy
gratis free
grato/a grateful
grave serious
grazie thank you
   tante grazie thank you very much
grigio/a grey
la **grotta** cave
il **gruppo** group
guadagnare to earn
il **guanciale** pillow
i **guanti** gloves
guardare to look (at)
il **guasto** breakdown
guasto/a bad (*food*), out of order
la **guerra** war
   la **prima/seconda guerra mondiale** the First/Second World War
la **guida** guidebook
guidare to drive
il **guscio** shell (*egg, nut*)

I

i the
l'idratante (m) moisturiser
l'idraulico (m) plumber
ieri yesterday
   l'altro ieri the day before
   yesterday
il the
imbarazzante embarrassing
l'imbarcadero (m) pier
imbarcare to embark
imparare to learn
l'impermeabile (m) raincoat
importa: non mi importa
   I don't mind, it doesn't
   matter
l'imposta (f) duty (tax)
impressionante impressive
improvvisamente suddenly
in in
   in più extra, spare
incartare to wrap up
l'inchiostro (m) ink
l'incidente (m) accident
incinta pregnant
incontrare to meet
l'incontro (m) meeting
   (accidental)
l'incrocio (m) crossroads
indietro backwards
indisposto/a unwell
indubbiamente definitely
l'infarto (m) heart attack
infatti in fact, indeed
infelice miserable, unhappy
l'infermiera (f) nurse
l'infiammazione (f)
   inflammation
le informazioni information
l'ingegnere (m) engineer
l'ingegneria (f) engineering

l'Inghilterra (f) England
inglese English
ingombrare to obstruct
l'ingorgo (m) traffic jam
l'ingresso (m) entrance,
   admission, hall (in house)
l'inizio (m) beginning
in ogni modo anyway
inoltre besides
l'inquinamento (m) pollution
inquinato/a polluted
l'insegnante (m or f) teacher
insegnare to teach
l'insettifugo (m) insect
   repellent
l'insetto (m) insect
insieme together
l'insolazione (f) sunstroke
insolito/a unusual
interessante interesting
interessato/a interested
interno/a interior, inside
l'interrato (m) basement (of
   shop)
l'interruzione (f) di corrente
   power cut
interurbano/a long distance
   (telephone call)
l'intervista (f) interview
l'intossicazione (f) alimentare
   food poisoning
inutile useless
invece di instead of
l'inverno (m) winter
io I
irritato/a annoyed
l'isola (f) island
l'istituto (m) superiore college
l'istruttore (m) instructor
l'IVA VAT

209

L

la the; her; it
il labbro lip
il ladro thief
il lago lake
la lampada lamp
la lampadina light bulb
la lana wool
lanciare to throw
largo/a broad, wide
lasciare to leave
il lato side
la latta can
il latte milk
    il latte scremato skimmed
    milk
la lattina can
la lattuga lettuce
il lavabo wash basin
il lavandino sink
lavare to wash
    lavare i piatti to wash up
lavorare to work
i lavori stradali roadworks
il lavoro work, job
le the; them; to her/it
la legge law
leggere to read
leggero/a light (*weight*)
il legno wood
lei she
lei you
lentamente slowly
le lenti a contatto contact
    lenses
lento/a slow
il lenzuolo sheet
il leone lion
la lettera letter
il lettino cot
il letto bed

il letto matrimoniale
    double bed
la levata collection (*post*)
li them
lì there
libero/a free, vacant
la libertà freedom
il libretto d'iscrizione (*car*)
    registration document
il libro book
il limite di velocità speed limit
la linea line
la linea aerea airline
la lingua language, tongue
i liquori spirits
liscio/a smooth
lo the; him; it
lontano/a distant, far
loro they, them; to them;
    their
loro you; to you; your
la luce light
lui he
la luna moon
    la luna di miele
    honeymoon
il luna park amusement park
lungo along
lungo/a long
il luogo place

M

ma but
la macchina car, machine
    in macchina by car
    la macchina fotografica
    camera
    la macchina da scrivere
    typewriter
il macchinista train driver
il macinato mince

la madre mother
la maggior parte (di) most (of)
la maglia jumper
la maglieria knitwear
la maglietta T-shirt
magro/a thin
mai ne /er, ever
il maiale pig
malato/a ill
la malattia illness
il male pain, ache
    il mal di denti toothache
    il mal di gola sore throat
    il mal di mare sea-sickness
    il mal di stomaco stomach-ache
    il mal di testa headache
maleducato/a rude
mancare to miss, to be missing
la mancia tip
mandare to send
mangiare to eat
la maniglia handle
la mano hand
la marca make, label
marcio/a rotten
il mare sea
la marea tide
il marinaio sailor
il marito husband
la marmellata jam
marrone brown
la maschera mask
maschile masculine
il maschio male
la matita pencil
la matrigna step-mother
il matrimonio wedding
la mattina morning
maturo/a ripe

le mazze golf clubs
me me
il medico doctor
medio/a medium, intermediate
la medusa jellyfish
meglio better
meno less
mensile monthly
mentre while, during
meraviglioso/a marvellous, wonderful
il mercato market
il mese month
la messa mass (church)
le mestruazioni monthly period
la metà half
    a metà prezzo half-price
la metropolitana underground, tube
mettere to put
la mezzanotte midnight
mezzo/a (adj.) half
    una mezz'ora half an hour
il mezzo middle
il mezzogiorno midday
mi me
miei, mie my, mine
il/la migliore best
mio, mia my, mine
la misura measurement, size
mite mild (temperature)
la moda fashion
    fuori moda old-fashioned
il modo way, manner
il modulo form (to fill in)
la moglie wife
il molo pier, jetty
molti many
molto very; much, a lot (of)
mondiale world

il mondo world, earth
la moneta coin
la montagna mountain
il morbillo measles
morire to die
morto/a dead
la mosca fly
mosso/a rough (*sea*)
mostrare to show
la moto motorbike
il motore engine
il motoscafo motorboat
la multa fine
muovere to move
il muro wall
le mutandine knickers, pants

N

il naso nose
il Natale Christmas
naturalmente of course
nausea: avere la nausea to feel sick
la nave ship
né ... né ... neither ... nor ...
la nebbia fog
nebbioso/a foggy
negli, nei, nel, nella, nelle, nello in the
negligente careless
il negozio shop
nero/a black
nessuno nothing, no-one
la neve snow
nevicare to snow
nevica it's snowing
niente nothing
nient'altro? anything else?

il/la nipote grandson/granddaughter; nephew/niece
i nipoti grandchildren
la noce nut
noi we
noioso/a boring
noleggiare to hire, to rent
il nome name
la nonna grandmother
i nonni grandparents
il nonno grandfather
il nord north
la nostalgia homesickness
avere nostalgia to be homesick
nostro, nostra, nostri, nostre our, ours
le notizie news
la notte night
il numero number
la nuora daughter-in-law
nuotare to swim
nuovo/a new
la nuvola cloud

O

O or
o ... o ... either ... or ...
obbligatorio/a compulsory
l'obiettivo (*m*) lens (*camera*)
gli occhiali spectacles
gli occhiali da sci ski goggles
gli occhiali da sole sun glasses
l'occhio, gli occhi (*m*) eye, eyes
occupato/a busy, engaged
l'offerta (*f*) offer
oggi today
ogni each, every

ogni tanto occasionally
l'ombra (f) shade, shadow
l'ombrello (m) umbrella
l'ombrellone (m) sunshade
omosessuale homosexual
l'onda (f) wave
opposto/a opposite
l'ora (f) hour
   che ora è? what time is it?
   l'ora di punta rush hour
l'orario (m) timetable
ordinato/a tidy
gli orecchini earrings
l'orecchio, gli orecchi (m) ear,
   ears
l'oro (m) gold
l'orologio (m) clock
l'ospedale (m) hospital
l'ospite guest, host
l'ostello (m) hostel
   l'ostello della gioventù
   youth hostel
ottimo/a excellent
l'otturazione (f) filling (dental)
ovvio/a obvious

P

il pacco packet, parcel
la pace peace
il padre father
la padrona landlady
il padrone landlord
il paesaggio countryside,
   scenery
il paese country (nation);
   village
il pagamento fee
   pagare to pay
la pagina page
il paio pair
la palla ball

pallido/a pale
il pallone football
il pane bread
   il pane integrale
   wholemeal bread
il panino bread roll
la panna cream
i pannolini nappies
i pantaloni trousers
il papa the Pope
paralizzato/a paralysed
parecchi/parecchie several
il/la parente relation
pari even (numbers)
parlare to talk, to speak
la parola word
la parte part
   in parte partly
partire to leave, to depart
la partita game, match
il passaggio gangway, passage
il passaporto passport
passare to pass, to spend
   time
passato/a past
   nel passato in the past
la passeggiata walk
   fare una passeggiata to go
   for a walk
il passeggino push-chair
la pastiglia pastille, lozenge
il pasto meal
la patata potato
le patatine crisps
la patente driving licence
il patrigno step-father
i pattini skates
la pattumiera dustbin
il pavimento floor, pavement
pazzo/a crazy, mad
il pedaggio toll

peggio worse
la pelle skin
la pellicola film (*camera*)
la penna pen
pensare to think
  penso di sì I think so
il pensionato, la pensionata
  pensioner
la pensione bed and breakfast;
  pension
  in pensione retired
la pentola pot, saucepan
per for
  per cortesia please
  per favore please
  per piacere please
perchè because, why
perdere to lose, to leak (*oil,*
  water)
perfino even
il pericolo danger
pericoloso/a dangerous
la periferia suburb
il permesso permission, licence
  permesso excuse me (*getting*
  past someone)
permettere to allow
però but
pesante heavy
pesare to weigh
pescare to go fishing
il pesce fish
il pettine comb
il pezzo piece
  il pezzo d'antiquariato
  antique
piacere to like
  mi piace I like it
piacevole pleasant
piangere to cry

piano/a full; level (flat)
il piano storey, floor
la pianta plan; plant
il pianterreno ground floor
il piattino saucer
piatto/a flat (*level*)
il piatto dish; plate
la piazza square (*in town*)
piccante hot (*spicy*)
piccolo/a small
la pietra stone
pigro/a lazy
la pinacoteca picture gallery
le pinne flippers
la pioggia rain
il piombo lead
  senza piombo unleaded
piove it's raining
il piroscafo steamer
la piscina swimming pool
la pista (ski) slope, (ski) run
  la pista di pattinaggio ice
  rink
  la pista per i principianti
  nursery slope
il pittore painter
la pittura painting
più more
  più grande bigger
  più lontano/a further
  più presto earlier
  più tardi later
  più vicino/a nearest,
  closest
  il più presto possibile as
  soon as possible
piuttosto rather
un pò a little
poi then
la polizia police
il poliziotto policeman

il pollice thumb
la polmonite pneumonia
la polvere dust
il pomeriggio afternoon
la porta door
portabile portable
il portachiavi key ring
il portafoglio wallet
portare to carry, to bring
il porto port, harbour
posare to put down
il posto place; seat
potere to be able (*see Basic grammar, p. 167*)
potrebbe (he/she/it/you) could
povero/a poor
il pranzo lunch
preferito/a favourite
il prefisso telefonico dialling code
il premio prize
prendere to take, to catch (*bus, train etc.*)
   prendere la linea to get through (*telephone*)
   prendere il sole to sunbathe
il prenome first name
prenotare to book, to reserve
la prenotazione booking, reservation
preoccupato/a worried
la presa socket
presentare to introduce
prestare to lend
presto early, soon
il prete priest
il prezzo price
la prima colazione breakfast
prima di before
la primavera spring

primo/a first
il primo ministro prime minister
principale main
il/la principiante beginner
profondo/a deep
il profumo scent
pronto hello (*on phone*)
pronto/a ready
il pronto soccorso first aid
proprio just, exactly, really
prossimo/a next
provare to try (on)
pulire to clean
pulito/a clean
pungere to sting
puntino: a puntino medium (*steak*)
la puntura sting
purtroppo unfortunately
il puzzo smell, stink

Q

qua here
il quadro picture
qualche: da qualche parte somewhere
   in qualche modo somehow
   qualche volta sometimes
qualcosa something
qualcuno someone
quale, quali which
qual è . . .? what/ which is . . .?
quando when
la quantità quantity, amount
quanti? how many?
quanto? how much?
   quanto costa/costano? how much does it/they cost?
   quanto tempo? how long?

il quartiere district (*of town*)
quasi almost
quello, quella, quei, quelle that (one)
questo, questa, questi, queste this (one)
la questura police station
qui here
    qui vicino nearby, around here
quindi so, therefore, well
quindici giorni fortnight
quotidiano/a daily

R

la rabbia rabies
il rabbino rabbi
raccogliere to collect (*post, rubbish*)
raccomandare to register
la ragazza girl, girlfriend
il ragazzo boy, boyfriend
il raggio X X-ray
raggiungere to reach
la ragione reason
    avere ragione to be right
ragionevole reasonable, sensible
RAI Italian radio and television
il rappresentante sales representative
il re king
il regalo present, gift
la regina queen
la regione district, region
registrare to record (*music*)
il registratore tape recorder
il rene kidney
il reparto department
respirare to breathe

restare to stay
la rete net
ricco/a rich
la ricetta prescription; recipe
ricevere to receive, to get
il ricevitore receiver (*telephone*)
la ricevuta receipt
riconoscere to recognise
ricordare to remember
ricuperare to recover
ridere to laugh
riempire to fill (*in*)
i rifiuti litter, rubbish
rimanere to remain, to stay
rimborsare to reimburse
il rimborso refund
rimorchiare to tow
riparare to repair, mend
il riparo shelter
ripido/a steep
riposarsi to rest
il riscaldamento heating
    il riscaldamento centrale central heating
riserva: in riserva spare
risparmiare to save (*money*)
rispondere to answer, reply
la risposta answer, reply
il risultato result
il ritardo delay
    in ritardo late, delayed
il ritratto portrait
la riunione meeting (*business*)
riuscire to succeed
la rivista magazine
rompere to break
rosso/a red
la rotatoria roundabout
rotondo/a round
rotto/a broken
la roulotte caravan

rovinare to spoil, ruin
le rovine ruins
il rubinetto tap
il rumore noise
rumoroso/a noisy
la ruota wheel
    la ruota di scorta spare wheel
il ruscello stream
ruvido/a rough (*surface*)

S

il sacchetto di plastica plastic bag
la sala room, living room
    la sala da pranzo dining room
il saldo sale
il sale salt
salire to go up, to get on (*bus etc.*)
il salone lounge (*in hotel*)
saltare to jump; to miss
la salute health
salute! cheers!
il salvagente lifebelt
salvare to save
il sangue blood
    al sangue rare (*steak*)
sanguinare to bleed
sano/a healthy
santo/a holy
sapere to know (*see Basic grammar, p. 167*)
la saponetta soap
il sapore flavour, taste
    ha un buon sapore it tastes good
sbadigliare to yawn
sbagliarsi to make a mistake
sbagliato/a mistaken, wrong

la scala staircase, ladder
    la scala mobile escalator
le scale stairs
scarico/a flat (*car battery*)
lo scarico drain
le scarpe shoes
    le scarpe da tennis plimsolls
gli scarponi ski boots
la scatola tin, box
    la scatola dei fusibili fuse box
    in scatola tinned
scegliere to choose
la scelta choice
scendere to get/go down, to get off (*bus etc.*)
lo schermo screen
lo scherzo joke
lo sci skiing
    lo sci da fondo cross-country skiing
la scialuppa di salvataggio lifeboat
sciare to ski
lo sciopero strike
la sciovia ski-lift
scivoloso/a slippery
la scodella bowl, basin
scomodo/a uncomfortable
lo sconosciuto. la sconosciuta stranger
lo sconto reduction
lo scontrino receipt, ticket
sconvolto/a shocked, upset
scorso/a last (*year, month, week*)
scorta: di scorta spare
la scottatura sunburn
scritto/a written
scrivere to write

scrivere a macchina to type
la scuola school
scuro/a dark
scusa sorry
scusi: mi scusi sorry, excuse me
sdraiarsi to lie down
se if
sebbene although
il secchiello bucket
secco/a dry
secondo me in my opinion
il sedano celery
sedersi to sit down
la sedia chair
  la sedia a sdraio deckchair
seduto/a sitting (down)
la seggiovia chair lift
il segnale sign, signal
  il segnale di linea dialling tone
il segreto secret
seguire to follow
selvatico/a wild
il semaforo traffic light
sembrare to seem
semplice simple
sempre always
  sempre dritto straight on
se non unless
il sentiero path, track
sentire to hear
sentirsi to feel
  sentirsi male/bene to feel bad/good
senza without
la sera evening
la serratura lock
i servizi facilities
sete: avere sete to be thirsty
la settimana week
settimanale weekly

sgradevole unpleasant
sicuro/a certain, sure, safe
Signor Mr
Signora Mrs, madam
la signora woman, lady
il signore gentleman, sir
Signorina Miss
la signorina young woman
simile similar
simpatico/a nice, friendly
il sindacato trade union
singolo/a single
sinistro/a left
lo slittino toboggan
so: (non) lo so I (don't) know
sobrio/a sober
la società society, company (*business*)
il socio member
soffice soft
il soffitto ceiling
il soggiorno living room
solamente only
il sole sun
solitario/a lonely
solito: di solito usually
solo only
solo/a alone
soltanto only
sono am, are (*see 'to be', p. 174*)
sopra above, over
  di sopra upstairs
sordo/a deaf
la sorella sister
sorpassare to overtake
la sorpresa surprise
sorridere to smile
il sorriso smile
sotto below, under
il sottopassaggio underpass
i sottotitoli subtitles

lo spazio space, room
la spazzatura rubbish
la spazzola brush
lo spazzolino da denti toothbrush
lo specchio mirror
specialmente especially
spedire to post
spegnere to turn off/out (*light etc.*)
spendere to spend (*money*)
spento/a out, off (*light etc.*)
sperare to hope
spero di sì I hope so
le spese expenses; donations
spesso often
spesso/a thick
lo spettacolo performance
le spezie spices
gli spiccioli small change
spiegare to explain
la spina plug (*electrical*)
spingere to press, to push
spogliarsi to undress
sporco/a dirty
sporgersi to lean out
la sposa bride
sposarsi to get married
sposato/a married
lo sposo bridegroom
stagionato/a mature (*cheese*)
la stagione season
la stampa print; press
stanco/a tired
la stanza room
stare to be
stare in piedi to be standing up
starnutire to sneeze
lo stato state
la stazione station
la stazione delle autolinee/ di autobus bus station

la stazione di servizio petrol station
la stazione di testa terminus
la stella star
stesso/a same
lo stipendio wage
la stitichezza constipation
gli stivali boots
la stoffa fabric
stordito/a dizzy
la storia history, story
storto/a sprained, twisted
lo straccio cloth
la strada street, road
la stradina lane
straniero/a foreign
strano/a strange, odd
stretto/a tight; odd
la striscia stripe
a strisce striped
lo strofinaccio tea-towel
su on; about (*relating to*)
subito immediately
succedere to happen
il sud south
il sughero cork
suo, sua, suoi, sue his, her, hers, its
suo, sua, suoi, sue your, yours
il suocero father-in-law
suonare to play (*musical instrument*)
il suono sound
superiore advanced (*level*); upper
surgelato/a frozen (*food*)
la sveglia alarm clock
svegliare to wake
sviluppare to develop

T

il tacco heel (*shoe*)
taciturno/a quiet (*person*)
la taglia size
tagliare to cut
il taglio di capelli haircut
il tailleur suit (*for women*)
tale such
il tallone heel
la tariffa charge
la tasca pocket
la tassa tax
la tavola table
la tazza cup
il tè tea
il telone impermeabile groundsheet
il temperino penknife
il tempo time; weather
la tenda tent
tenere to hold, to keep
tenero/a tender (*meat*)
la terra earth, ground, land
il terremoto earthquake
terribile awful
terzo/a third
il tessuto cloth
   il tessuto di jeans denim
la testa head
tinta: in tinta unita plain (*material*)
il tipo type, sort
il tirante guy rope
toccare to touch
togliere to remove, take off
tornare to come back, to return
la torre tower
la torta cake, flan
tossire to cough
tradurre to translate

la traduzione translation
il traghetto ferry
tranquillo/a quiet
il trattamento treatment
triste sad
troppo too
trovare to find
tu you
il tubo tube
tuffarsi to dive
tuo, tua, tuoi, tue your, yours
la tuta da ginnastica tracksuit
tutti everyone
tutto everything
tutto/a all

U

ubriaco/a drunk
ufficiale official
uguale equal
ultimo/a last
umido/a damp
un one, a
una one, a
l'unghia (*f*) nail
uno one, a
l'uno o l'altro either
gli uomini men, gentlemen
l'uomo (*m*) man
   l'uomo d'affari businessman
l'uovo (*m*) egg
   l'uovo sodo boiled egg
uscire to go/get out
l'uscita (*f*) exit
utile useful

V

va bene fine, O.K.
le vacanze holidays

in vacanza on holiday
la vacca cow
la valanga avalanche
vale: non vale la pena it's not worth it
la valigia suitcase
il valore value
    di valore valuable
i valori valuables
il vapore steam
vecchio/a old
vedere to see
la vedova widow
il vedovo widower
il veleno poison
velenoso/a poisonous
veloce fast
velocemente quickly
la velocità speed
vendere to sell
venire to come
il vento wind
veramente really
vero/a true, real, genuine
    è vero it's true
versare to pour
verso around, towards
vestirsi to get dressed
i vestiti clothes
il vestito dress
la vetrina shop window
il vetro glass
viaggiare to travel
il viaggio journey
    buon viaggio! safe journey
il vicino, la vicina neighbour
vicino/a near
    qui vicino nearby
    vicino a next to
vietato/a forbidden, prohibited

la vigilia di Natale Christmas Eve
i vigili del fuoco fire brigade
la vigna vineyard
vincere to win
    chi ha vinto? who won?
viola purple
violentare to rape
la visita guidata guided tour
visitare to visit, to tour
la vista view, sight
il visto visa
la vita life
il vocabolarietto phrase book
la voce voice
voi you
il volantino fly sheet
volare to fly
volere to want
    voglio I want
    vorrei I would like
    che vuol dire questo? what does that mean?
    ci vuole un'ora it takes an hour
il volo flight
la volta time
    una volta once
    due volte twice
vostro, vostra, vostri, vostre your, yours
votare to vote
vuoto/a empty

Z

lo zaino rucksack
la zia aunt
lo zio uncle
lo zucchero sugar

There is a list of car parts on page 43, and parts of the body on page 157. Numbers are inside the front cover.

A

a, an **un, uno, una**
abbey **l'abbazia** (f)
about (*relating to*) **su**
  (*approximately*) **circa**
above **sopra**
abroad **all'estero**
abscess **l'ascesso** (m)
to accept **accettare**
accident **l'incidente** (m)
accommodation **l'alloggio** (m)
according to **secondo**
account (*bank*) **il conto**
accountant **il ragioniere/la ragioniera**
ache **il dolore**
acid **l'acido** (m)
across **attraverso**
  (*on the other side*) **dall'altra parte di**
acrylic **acrilico/a**
to act **recitare**
activity **l'attività** (f)
actor **l'attore** (m)
actress **l'attrice** (f)
adaptor (*electrical*) **il riduttore**
to add (*count*) **sommare**
addicted (*drink etc.*) **dedito/a a**
address **l'indirizzo** (m)
adhesive tape **il nastro adesivo**
admission **l'ingresso** (m)
  admission charge **il prezzo del biglietto del ingresso**
adopted **adottato/a**
adult **l'adulto** (m)
advance: in advance **in anticipo**
advanced (*level*) **superiore**
advertisement, advertising **la pubblicità**
aerial **l'antenna** (f)
aeroplane **l'aeroplano** (m)
afford: I can't afford it **non posso permettermelo**
afraid: I'm afraid **ho paura**
after(wards) **dopo**
afternoon **il pomeriggio**
aftershave **il dopobarba**
again **ancora**
against **contro**
age **l'età** (f)
agency **l'agenzia** (f)
ago **fa**
  a week ago **una settimana fa**
to agree **essere d'accordo**
  I agree with you **sono d'accordo con te**
AIDS **AIDS**
air **l'aria** (f)
  by air **per aerea**
  (by) air mail **via aerea**
air conditioning **l'aria** (f) **condizionata**
air force **l'aviazione** (f) **militar**
airline **la linea aerea**
airport **l'aeroporto** (m)
aisle **il passaggio**
alarm **l'allarme** (m)
  alarm clock **la sveglia**
alcohol **l'alcool** (m)
alcoholic (*content*) **alcolico/a**
  (*person*) **un alcolico/un'alcolica**

222

alive **vivo/a**
all **tutto**
allergic to **allergico/a contro**
the alley **il vicolo**
to allow **permettere**
    allowed **permesso**
allowance (*duty-free*) **la quantità permessa**
all right (*O.K.*) **va bene**
almond **la mandorla**
alone **solo/a**
    I'll do it alone **lo faccio da solo/a**
along **lungo**
already **già**
also **anche**
although **sebbene**
always **sempre**
am (*see 'to be', p. 174*) **sono**
ambassador **l'ambasciatore** (*m*)
ambition **l'ambizione** (*f*)
ambitious **ambizioso/a**
ambulance **l'ambulanza** (*f*)
among **fra**
amount (*quantity*) **la quantità**
amusement park **il luna park**
anaesthetic **l'anestetico** (*m*)
    general anaesthetic **l'anestesia** (*f*) **generale**
    local anaesthetic **l'anestesia** (*f*) **locale**
and **e**
angry **arrabbiato/a**
animal **l'animale** (*m*)
anniversary **l'anniversario** (*m*)
annoyed **irritato/a**
anorak **la giacca a vento**
another (one) **un altro/un'altra**
answer **la risposta**
to answer **rispondere**

antibiotic **l'antibiotico**
antifreeze **l'antigelo** (*m*)
antique **il pezzo d'antiquariato**
antiseptic **l'antisettico** (*m*)
anxious **ansioso/a**
any: have you any bread? **ha del pane?**
anyone: I can't see anyone **non vedo nessuno**
anything **qualcosa**, (*nothing*) **niente**
    anything else? **nient'altro?**
anyway **in ogni modo**
anywhere **da qualche parte**
apart (*from*) **a parte di**
apartment **l'appartamento** (*m*)
aperitif **l'aperitivo** (*m*)
appendicitis **l'appendicite** (*f*)
apple **la mela**
appointment **l'appuntamento** (*m*)
approximately **circa**
apricot **l'albicocca** (*f*)
arch **l'arco** (*m*)
archaeology **l'archeologia** (*f*)
architect **l'architetto/a**
are (*see 'to be', p. 174*) **sono**
argument (*debate*) **la discussione**
arm **il braccio**
armbands (*swimming*) **i bracciali**
army **l'esercito** (*m*)
around **verso**
to arrange **sistemare**
arrest: under arrest **in arresto**
arrivals **gli arrivi**
to arrive **arrivare**
art **l'arte** (*f*)
    art gallery **la galleria d'arte**
    fine arts **le belle arti**

arthritis l'artrite
artichoke il carciofo
article l'articolo (m)
artificial artificiale
artist l'artista (m or f)
as (like) come
  (while) mentre
  as far as I know per quanto me so
ash la cenere
ashtray il portacenere
to ask chiedere
asparagus gli asparagi
aspirin l'aspirina (f)
assistant (in shop) il commesso/la commessa
asthma l'asma (f)
at a
athletics l'atletica (f)
atmosphere l'atmosfera (f)
to attack attaccare
attendant (in petrol station) il benzinaio
  (in museum) il custode
attractive attraente
aubergine la melanzana
auction l'asta (f)
aunt la zia
author l'autore (m)
automatic automatico/a
autumn l'autunno (m)
avalanche la valanga
avenue il corso
avocado l'avocado (m)
to avoid evitare
away via
  it's 10 kilometres away è a dieci chilometri
awful terribile

B

baby il bambino/la bambina
  baby food gli alimenti per bambini
  baby wipes i fazzolettini pulire i bambini
baby's bottle il biberon
babysitter il/la babysitter
back (rear) di dietro
  (reverse side) il dorso
back: at the back (of) in fon a dietro (di)
backwards indietro
bacon la pancetta
bad (food) guasto/a
  (weather) brutto/a
bag la borsa
baggage i bagagli
baker il fornaio/la fornaia
baker's la panetteria
balcony il balcone
bald calvo/a
ball (tennis etc.) la palla
  (football) il pallone
  (dance) il ballo
ballet il balletto
ballpoint pen la biro
banana la banana
band (music) la banda
bandage la benda
bank la banca
banker il banchiere
bank holiday la festa nazionale
bar il bar
barber('s) il barbiere
bargain l'occasione (f)
baseball il baseball
basement (of shop) l'interr (m)
basin il bacino

basket **il cestino**
basketball **la pallacanestro**
bath **il bagno**
   to have a bath, to bathe **fare un bagno**
bathing costume **il costume da bagno**
bathroom **il bagno**
battery **la pila**
   (*car*) **la batteria**
bay **la baia**
to be (*see Basic grammar, p. 167*) **essere**
   to be fed up **essere stufo/a**
beach **la spiaggia**
beans (*kidney/haricot*) **i fagioli**
   (*French/green*) **i fagiolini**
beard **la barba**
beautiful **bello/a**
because **perchè**
bed **il letto**
bedroom **la camera da letto**
bee **l'ape** (*f*)
beef **il manzo**
beer **la birra**
beetroot **la barbabietola**
before **prima di**
to begin **cominciare**
beginner **il/la principiante**
beginning **l'inizio** (*m*)
behind **dietro di**
beige **beige**
to believe **credere**
bell **la campana**
   (*front door*) **il campanello**
to belong to **appartenere a**
below **sotto**
belt **la cintura**
bend **la curva**
bent **storto/a**
berry **la bacca**

berth **la cuccetta**
beside **accanto a**
besides **inoltre**
best **migliore**
better **meglio**
between **fra**
beyond **al di là di**
bib **il bavaglino**
Bible **la Bibbia**
bicycle **la bicicletta**
big **grande**
bigger **più grande**
bill **il conto**
bin **il bidone**
   bin liners **i sacchi per la spazzatura**
binoculars **il binocolo**
biochemistry **la biochimica**
biology **la biologia**
bird **l'uccello**
birthday **il compleanno**
biscuit **il biscotto**
bishop **il vescovo**
a bit **un pò**
to bite **mordere**
bitter **amaro/a**
black **nero/a**
   black and white (*film*) **bianco e nero**
   black coffee **il caffè nero**
blackberry **la mora**
blackcurrant **il ribes nero**
blanket **la coperta**
bleach **la candeggina**
to bleed **sanguinare**
blind **cieco/a**
blister **la vescica**
blocked **bloccato/a**
blond(e) **biondo/a**
blood **il sangue**
blouse **la camicetta**

to blow **soffiare**
to blow-dry (*hair*) **asciugare con il föhn**
blue **blu**
blusher **il fard**
to board **imbarcarsi**
boarding card **la carta d'imbarco**
boat **il battello**
  boat trip **la gita in battello**
body **il corpo**
to boil **bollire**
boiled egg **l'uovo** (*m*) **sodo**
boiler **il bruciatore del riscaldamento**
bomb **la bomba**
bone **l'osso** (*m*)
book **il libro**
to book **prenotare**
booking **la prenotazione**
booking office **la biglietteria**
booklet (*bus tickets*) **il blocchetto**
bookshop **la libreria**
boots (*shoes*) **gli stivali**
border (*edge*) **l'orlo** (*m*) (*frontier*) **la frontiera**
bored **annoiato/a**
boring **noioso/a**
boss **il capo**
both **tutti e due**
bottle **la bottiglia**
bottle opener **l'apribottiglie** (*m*)
bottom **il fondo**
bow (*ship*) **la prua** (*knot*) **il fiocco**
bowl **la scodella**
box **la scatola** (*theatre*) **il palco**
box office **il botteghino**

boy **il ragazzo**
boyfriend **il fidanzato, il ragazzo**
bra **il reggiseno**
bracelet **il braccialetto**
braces **le bretelle**
brain **il cervello**
branch (*bank etc.*) **l'agenzia** (*f*)
brand **la marca**
brandy **il brandy**
brass **l'ottone** (*m*)
brave **coraggioso/a**
bread **il pane**
  roll **il panino**
  shop **il panificio**
  wholemeal **il pane integrale**
to break (*inc. limb*) **rompere**
breakdown **il guasto**
breakdown truck **il carro attrezzi**
breakfast **la prima colazione**
breast **il seno**
to breathe **respirare**
bricklayer **il muratore**
bride **la sposa**
bridegroom **lo sposo**
bridge **il ponte**
briefcase **la cartella**
bright (*colour*) **vivace** (*light*) **luminoso/a**
to bring **portare**
British **britannico/a**
broad **largo/a**
brochure **il dépliant**
broken **rotto/a**
bronchitis **la bronchite**
bronze **il bronzo**
brooch **la spilla**
brother **il fratello**
brother-in-law **il cognato**
brown **marrone** (*hair*) **castano/a**

brown sugar **lo zucchero greggio**
bruise **il livido**
brush **la spazzola**
bucket **il secchiello**
budgerigar **il pappagallino**
buffet **il buffet**
to build **costruire**
builder **il costruttore**
building **l'edificio** (*m*)
building site **il cantiere**
bulb (*light*) **la lampadina**
bull **il toro**
bumper **il paraurti**
burn **la scottatura**
to burn **bruciare**
  burnt **bruciato/a**
bus **l'autobus** (*m*)
  by bus **in autobus**
  bus-driver **l'autista d'autobus**
  bus station **la stazione delle autolinee**
  bus stop **la fermata d'autobus**
bush **il cespuglio**
business **gli affari**
  business trip **il viaggio d'affari**
  on business **per affari**
businessman/woman **l'uomo/ la donna d'affari**
business studies **l'economia e commercio**
busy **occupato/a**
but **ma, però**
butane gas **il gas butano**
butcher's **la macelleria**
butter **il burro**
butterfly **la farfalla**
button **il bottone**

to buy **comprare**
by (*author*) **di**

C

cabbage **il cavolo**
cabin **la cabina**
cable car **la funivia**
café **il caffè**
cake **la torta**
cake shop **la pasticceria**
calculator **il calcolatore**
call (*phone*) **la chiamata**
to call **chiamare**
  to be called **chiamarsi**
calm **calmo/a**
camera **la macchina fotografica**
camomile tea **la camomilla**
to camp **campeggiare**
campbed **il lettino da campeggio**
camping **il campeggio**
campsite **il campeggio**
can (*to be able*) **potere**
  (*to know how to*) **sapere**
  (he, she, it) could **potrebbe**
can **il barattolo**
  (*tin*) **la lattina**
can opener **l'apriscatole** (*m*)
to cancel **cancellare, annullare**
cancer **il cancro**
candle **la candela**
canoe **la canoa**
capital (*city*) **la capitale**
captain **il capitano**
car **la macchina**
  by car **in macchina**
  car hire **l'autonoleggio** (*m*)
car park **il parcheggio**
carafe **la caraffa**

caravan **la roulotte**
  caravan site **il campeggio**
cardigan **il cardigan**
care: I don't care **non mi importa**
careful **attento/a**
careless **negligente**
carpenter **il carpentiere**
carpet **il tappeto**
carriage (*rail*) **la carrozza**
carrier bag **il sacchetto, la busta**
carrots **le carote**
to carry **portare**
to carry on **continuare**
  car wash **il lavaggio macchine**
case: in case **in caso di**
cash **i contanti, il liquido**
  in cash **in contanti**
to cash **incassare**
  cash desk **la cassa**
cassette **la cassetta**
castle **il castello**
cat **il gatto**
catalogue **il catalogo**
to catch (*train/bus*) **prendere**
cathedral **il duomo, la cattedrale**
Catholic **cattolico/a**
cauliflower **il cavolfiore**
to cause **causare**
caution **la prudenza**
cave **la grotta**
ceiling **il soffitto**
celery **il sedano**
cellar **la cantina**
cemetery **il cimitero**
centimetre **il centimetro**
central **centrale**
central heating **il riscaldamento centrale**

centre **il centro**
century **il secolo**
cereal **i fiocchi di cereali**
certain **certo/a**
certainly **certamente, certo**
certificate **il certificato**
CFCs **CFCs**
chain **la catena**
chair **la sedia**
  chair lift **la seggiovia**
chalet **lo chalet**
champagne **lo champagne**
change (*small coins*) **gli spiccioli**
to change **cambiare**
  (*clothes*) **cambiarsi**
  changing room **lo spogliatoio**
chapel **la cappella**
charcoal **il carbone di legna**
charge **la tariffa**
charter flight **il volo charter**
cheap **economico/a**
to check **controllare**
checked (*pattern*) **a quadri**
check-in (*desk*) **il check-in**
  to check in **fare il check-in**
cheek **la guancia**
cheeky **sfacciato/a**
cheers! **salute!**
cheese **il formaggio**
chef **lo chef**
chemist **il/la farmacista**
chemistry **la chimica**
cheque **l'assegno** (*m*)
cherry **la ciliegia**
chess **gli scacchi**
chestnut **la castagna**
chewing gum **la gomma di masticare**
chicken **il pollo**
chickenpox **la varicella**

child **il bambino/la bambina**
children **i bambini**
chimney **il camino**
china **la porcellana**
chips **le patatine fritte**
chocolate **la cioccolata**
chocolates **i cioccolatini**
to choose **scegliere**
chop (*lamb/pork*) **la costoletta**
Christian **cristiano/a**
    Christian name **il prenome**
Christmas **il Natale**
    Christmas Eve **la vigilia di Natale**
church **la chiesa**
cigar **il sigaro**
cigarette **la sigaretta**
    cigarette papers **le cartine per sigarette**
cinema **il cinema**
cinnamon **la cannella**
circle **il circolo**
    (*theatre*) **la galleria**
circus **il circo**
city **la città**
civil servant **l'impiegato/a statale**
class **la classe**
classical music **la musica classica**
claustrophobia **la claustrofobia**
to clean **pulire**
clean **pulito/a**
cleansing cream **la crema detergente**
clear **chiaro/a**
clerk **l'impiegato/a**
clever **intelligente**
cliff **la scogliera**
climate **il clima**

to climb **salire**
climber **l'alpinista** (*m or f*)
climbing **l'alpinismo**
clinic **la clinica**
cloakroom **il guardaroba**
clock **l'orologio** (*m*)
close (by) **qui vicino**
close to **vicino a**
to close **chiudere**
closed **chiuso/a**
cloth **lo straccio**
clothes **i vestiti**
clothes pegs **le mollette**
cloud **la nuvola**
cloudy **nuvoloso/a**
club **il club**
    (*golf*) **la mazza**
coach (*bus*) **il pullman**
    (*railway*) **la carrozza**
coal **il carbone**
coarse **grezzo/a**
coast **la costa**
coat **il cappotto**
coat-hanger **la gruccia**
cocktail **il cocktail**
code (*telephone*) **il prefisso**
coffee **il caffè**
coin **la moneta**
cold **freddo/a**
    to have a cold **avere un raffreddore**
collar **il collo**
colleague **il/la collega**
to collect (*post*) **raccogliere**
    collection **la collezione**
    (*post*) **la levata**
college **l'istituto superiore**
colour **il colore**
    colour blind **daltonico/a**
    colour-fast **colori solidi**
comb **il pettine**

to come **venire**
  I come **vengo**
  he, she, it comes **viene**
to come back **tornare**
to come in **entrare**
come in! **avanti!**
to come off (*e.g. button*) **staccarsi**
comedy **la commedia**
comfortable **comodo/a**
comic (*magazine*) **il giornaletto**
commercial **commerciale**
common **comune**
communion **la comunione**
communism **il comunismo**
compact disc **il compact**
company (*firm*) **la società**
compared with **confronto a**
compartment **il compartimento**
compass **la bussola**
to complain **fare un reclamo**
complaint **il reclamo**
complete **completo/a**
complicated **complicato/a**
composer **il compositore/la compositrice**
compulsory **obbligatorio/a**
computer **il computer**
  operator **l'operatore di computer**
  programmer **il programmatore di computer**
  studies **l'informatica** (*f*)
concert **il concerto**
concert hall **la sala da concerti**
concussion **la commozione cerebrale**
condition **la condizione**
conditioner **il balsamo**

condom **il condom; il preservativo**
conference **il congresso**
confirm **confermare**
conjunctivitis **la congiuntivite**
connection (*travel*) **la coincidenza**
conscious **cosciente**
conservation **la conservazione**
conservative **conservativo/a**
constipation **la stitichezza**
consulate **il consolato**
consultant **il consulente**
contact lenses **le lenti a contatto**
contact lens cleaner **il liquido per lenti a contatto**
continent **il continente**
contraceptive **il contraccettivo**
contract **il contratto**
control (*passport*) **il controllo**
convenient **conveniente, comodo/a**
convent **il convento**
cook **il cuoco/la cuoca**
to cook **cucinare**
  cooked **cotto/a**
cooker **la cucina**
cool **fresco/a**
cool box **la borsa frigorifero**
copper **il rame**
copy **la copia**
cork **il sughero**
corkscrew **il cavatappi**
corner **l'angolo** (*m*)
correct **corretto/a**
corridor **il corridoio**
cosmetics **i cosmetici**
cost **il costo**
to cost **costare**
cot **il lettino**
cottage **la casetta**

cotton **il cotone**
cotton wool **il cotone idrofilo**
couchette **la cuccetta**
cough **la tosse**
to cough **tossire**
could (*see 'can'*) **potrebbe**
to count **contare**
counter (*shop*) **lo sportello**
country (*nation*) **il paese**
country(side) **la campagna**
   in the country **nella**
    campagna
couple (*pair*) **la coppia**
courgettes **gli zucchini**
course (*lessons*) **il corso**
court (*law*) **il tribunale**
   (*tennis*) **il campo**
cousin **il cugino/la cugina**
cover **il coperchio**
   cover charge **il coperto**
cow **la vacca**
crab **il granchio**
cramp **il crampo**
crayons **i pastelli a cera**
crazy **pazzo/a**
cream **la panna**
   (*lotion*) **la crema**
   (*colour*) **crema**
   cream cheese **il mascarpone**
credit card **la carta di credito**
cricket **il cricket**
crisps **le patatine**
cross **la croce**
   Red Cross **la Croce rossa**
to cross (*border*) **attraversare**
cross-country (*skiing*) **lo sci da**
   fondo
crossing (*sea*) **la traversata**
crossroads **l'incrocio** (*m*)
crowd **la folla**
crowded **affollato/a**
crown **la corona**

cruise **la crociera**
crutch **la stampella**
to cry **piangere**
crystal **il cristallo**
cucumber **il cetriolo**
cuff **il polsino**
cup **la tazza**
cupboard **l'armadio** (*m*)
cure (*remedy*) **la cura**
to cure **guarire**
curler (*hair*) **il bigodino**
curly **ricciuto/a**
current (*electricity*) **la corrente**
curtain **la tenda**
curve **la curva**
cushion **il cuscino**
custard **la crema pasticciera**
customs **la dogana**
cut **il taglio**
to cut **tagliare**
   to cut oneself **tagliarsi**
cutlery **le posate**
cycling **il ciclismo**
cyclist **il/la ciclista**
cylinder (*car*) **il cilindro**
   (*gas*) **la bombola**
cystitis **la cistite**

D

daily **quotidiano/a**
damage **il danno**
to damage **danneggiare**
damp **umido/a**
dance **il ballo**
to dance **ballare**
danger **il pericolo**
dangerous **pericoloso/a**
dark **scuro/a**
darling **tesoro**
darts **le freccette**
data (*information*) **i dati**

231

date (*day*) la data
(*fruit*) il dattero
daughter la figlia
daughter-in-law la nuora
day il giorno
  day after tomorrow
  dopodomani
  day before yesterday l'altro
  ieri
  day after/before il giorno
  dopo/prima
dead morto/a
deaf sordo/a
dealer il/la commerciante
dear caro/a
death la morte
debt il debito
decaffeinated coffee il caffè
  decaffeinato
to decide decidere
deck il ponte

deckchair la sedia a sdraio
to declare dichiarare
deep profondo/a
deer il cervo
defect il difetto
defective difettoso/a
definitely indubbiamente
defrost sgelare
degree (*temperature*) il grado
(*university*) la laurea
delay il ritardo
delicate delicato/a
delicious delizioso/a
to deliver consegnare
delivery la consegna
demonstration la
  dimostrazione
denim il tessuto di jeans
dental dentale
dentist il/la dentista

denture la dentiera
deodorant il deodorante
to depart partire
department il reparto
department store il grande
  magazzino
departure la partenza
departure lounge la sala
  partenze
deposit il deposito
to describe descrivere
description la descrizione
design il disegno
to design disegnare
designer il disegnatore/la
  disegnatrice
dessert il dolce
destination la destinazione
detail il dettaglio
detergent il detersivo
to develop sviluppare
diabetes il diabete
diabetic diabetico/a
to dial fare un numero
dialling code il prefisso
  telefonico
dialling tone il segnale di linea
diamond il diamante
diarrhoea la diarrea
diary l'agenda (*f*)
dice i dadi
dictator il dittatore
dictionary il dizionario
to die morire
  . . . died morto
diesel il gasolio
diet la dieta
different diverso/a
difficult difficile
dining room la sala da pranzo
dinner la cena

dinner jacket **lo smoking**
diplomat **il diplomatico**
direct (*route*) **diretto/a**
direction **la direzione**
director **il/la direttore**
directory (*telephone*) **l'elenco
  (*m*) telefonico**
dirty **sporco/a**
disabled **handicappato/a**
disappointed **deluso/a**
disc **il disco**
disc jockey **il disc jockey**
disco(thèque) **la discoteca**
discount **lo sconto**
dish **il piatto**
dishwasher **la lavastoviglie**
disinfectant **il disinfettante**
dislocated **slogato/a**
disposable **a perdere**
  disposable nappies **i
  pannolini per bambini usa e
  getta**
distance **la distanza**
distilled water **l'acqua
  distillata**
district (*of country*) **la regione,
  la zona**
  (*of town*) **il quartiere**
to dive **tuffarsi**
diversion **la deviazione**
diving **il tuffo**
diving-board **il trampolino**
divorced **divorziato/a**
dizzy **stordito/a**
to do **fare**
  done **fatto**
dock **il bacino**
doctor **il medico**
documents **i documenti**
dog **il cane**
doll **la bambola**

dollars **i dollari**
dome **la cupola**
dominoes **il domino**
donkey **l'asino** (*m*)
door **la porta**
double **doppio/a**
double bed **il letto
  matrimoniale**
dough **l'impasto**
down, downstairs **giù**
drain **lo scarico**
drama **la dramma**
draught (*air*) **la corrente d'aria**
draught beer **la birra alla spina**
to draw **disegnare**
drawer **il cassetto**
drawing **il disegno**
drawing-pin **la puntina da
  disegno**
dreadful **terribile**
dream **il sogno**
dress **il vestito**
to dress, get dressed **vestirsi**
dressing (*medical*) **la benda**
  (*salad*) **il condimento**
drink **la bibita**
to drink **bere**
to drip **gocciolare**
to drive **guidare**
  driver **l'autista** (*m or f*)
  (*of train*) **il macchinista**
driving licence **la patente**
to drown **annegare**
drug **la droga**
  drug addict **il tossicomane**
drum **il tamburo**
drunk **ubriaco/a**
dry **secco/a**
dry-cleaner's **la tintoria**
dubbed **doppiato/a**
duck **l'anatra** (*f*), **l'anitra** (*f*)

dull (*weather*) **nuvoloso/a**
dumb **muto/a**
dummy (*baby's*) **la tettarella**
during **durante**
dust **la polvere**
dustbin **la pattumiera**
dusty **polveroso/a**
duty (*tax*) **l'imposta, il dazio**
duty-free **esente da dogana**
duvet **il piumino**

E

each **ogni**
ear(s) **l'orecchio, gli orecchi** (*m*)
earache **il mal d'orecchi**
eardrops **le gocce per gli orecchi**
early **presto**
earlier **più presto**
to earn **guadagnare**
earrings **gli orecchini**
earth (*soil*) **la terra**
(*world*) **il mondo**
earthquake **il terremoto**
east **l'est** (*m*)
eastern **orientale**
Easter **la Pasqua**
easy **facile**
to eat **mangiare**
economical **economico/a**
economy **l'economia** (*f*)
edible **commestibile**
egg **l'uovo** (*m*)
either: either one **l'uno o l'altro**
either...or... **o...o...**
elastic band **l'elastico** (*m*)
election **l'elezione** (*f*)
electric **elettrico/a**
electrician **l'elettricista** (*m*)

electricity **l'elettricità** (*f*)
electronic **elettronico/a**
else: anything else? **nient'altro?**
to embark **imbarcare**
embarrassing **imbarazzante**
embassy **l'ambasciata** (*f*)
emergency **l'emergenza** (*f*)
emergency exit **l'uscita di sicurezza**
emergency telephone **il telefono di emergenza/soccorso**
empty **vuoto/a**
to empty **vuotare**
enamel **lo smalto**
end **la fine**
to end **finire**
energetic **energico/a**
energy **l'energia** (*f*)
engaged (*to be married*) **fidanzato/a**
(*occupied*) **occupato/a**
engine **il motore**
engineer **l'ingegnere** (*m*)
engineering **l'ingegneria** (*f*)
England **l'Inghilterra** (*f*)
English **inglese**
to enjoy (oneself) **divertirsi**
enough **abbastanza, basta**
is that enough? **basta così?**
to enter **entrare**
entertainment **il divertimento**
enthusiastic **entusiastico/a**
entrance **l'entrata** (*f*)
envelope **la busta**
environment **l'ambiente** (*f*)
equal **uguale**
equipment **l'attrezzatura** (*f*)
escalator **la scala mobile**
especially **specialmente**

essential **essenziale**
estate **la tenuta**
estate agent **l'agente** (*m*)
  immobiliare
evaporated milk **il latte**
  concentrato
even (*including*) **perfino**
  (*not odd*) **pari**
evening **la sera**
every **ogni**
everyone **tutti**
everything **tutto**
everywhere **dappertutto**
exact **esatto/a**
exactly **esattamente**
examination **l'esame** (*m*)
example **l'esempio** (*m*)
  for example **per esempio**
excellent **ottimo/a**
except **eccetto**
excess luggage **il bagaglio in**
  eccedenza
to exchange **cambiare**
exchange rate **il cambio**
excited **eccitato/a**
exciting **emozionante**
excursion **l'escursione** (*f*)
excuse me (*sorry*) **mi scusi**
  (*when passing*) **permesso**
executive **esecutivo/a**
exercise **l'esercizio** (*m*)
exhibition **la mostra**
exit **l'uscita** (*f*)
to expect **aspettare**
expensive **caro/a**
experience **l'esperienza** (*f*)
expert **l'esperto/a**
to explain **spiegare**
explosion **l'esplosione** (*f*)
export **l'articolo** (*m*) **di**
  esportazione

to export **esportare**
express **espresso/a**
extension (*cable*) **la prolunga**
external **esterno/a**
extra (*spare*) **in più**
eye(s) **l'occhio, gli occhi** (*m*)
eyebrow **il sopracciglio**
eyebrow pencil **la matita per le**
  sopracciglia
eyelash **il ciglio**
eyeliner **la matita per occhi**
eyeshadow **l'ombretto** (*m*)

F

fabric **la stoffa**
face **la faccia**
  face cream **la crema per il**
    viso
  face powder **la cipria**
facilities **i servizi**
fact **il fatto**
  in fact **infatti**
factory **la fabbrica**
failure **il fallimento**
to faint **svenire**
fair (*haired*) **biondo/a**
  (*weather*) **bello/a**
fair **la fiera**
  trade fair **la fiera**
    campionaria
fairly **abbastanza**
faith **la fede**
fake **l'imitazione** (*f*)
to fall (*down/over*) **cadere**
false **falso/a**
  false teeth **la dentiera**
familiar **familiare**
family **la famiglia**
famous **famoso/a**

fan (*air*) **il ventilatore**
(*supporter*) **il tifoso**
fantastic **fantastico/a**
far (*away*) **lontano/a**
as far as I know **per quanto me so**
is it far? **è lontano?**
fare **la tariffa**
farm **la fattoria**
farmer **l'agricoltore** (*m*)
fashion **la moda**
fashionable/in fashion **alla moda**
fast **veloce**
fat (*adj/noun*) **grasso/a, il grasso**
fatal **fatale**
father **il padre**
father-in-law **il suocero**
fault **il difetto**
it's not my fault **non è colpa mia**
faulty **difettoso/a**
favourite **preferito/a**
fax **il fax**
feather **la piuma**
to be fed up **essere stufo/a**
fee **il pagamento**
to feed (*inc. baby*) **dare da mangiare**
to feel **sentirsi**
(*ill/well*) **sentirsi male/bene**
I don't feel well **mi sento male**
felt-tip pen **il pennarello**
female **la femmina**
feminine **femminile**
feminist **il/la femminista**
fence **il recinto**
ferry **il traghetto**
festival **la festa**

to fetch (*bring*) **portare**
fever **la febbre**
(a) few **alcuni/e**
fiancé(e) **il fidanzato/la fidanzata**
fibre **la fibra**
field **il campo**
fig **il fico**
to fight **combattere**
file (*documents*) **l'incartamento** (*m*)
(*nail, DIY*) **la lima**
to fill (out) **riempire**
filling (*dental*) **l'otturazione** (*f*)
film (*cinema*) **il film**
(*for camera*) **la pellicola**
filter **il filtro**
finance **la finanza**
to find **trovare**
fine (*O.K.*) **va bene**
(*penalty*) **la multa**
(*weather*) **bello/a**
finger **il dito**
to finish **finire**
fire **il fuoco**
fire brigade **i vigili del fuoco**
fire extinguisher **l'estintore** (*m*)
firewood **la legna**
fireworks **i fuochi d'artificio**
firm **fermo/a**
firm (*company*) **la ditta**
first **primo/a**
first aid **il pronto soccorso**
first-aid kit **la cassetta di pronto soccorso**
fish **il pesce**
to fish/go fishing **pescare**
fishing **la pesca**
fishing rod **la canna da pesca**
fishmonger's **il pescivendolo**

fit (*healthy*) **in forma**
o fit **andare bene**
   this doesn't fit me **questo non mi va bene**
fitting room **lo spogliatoio**
o fix **riparare**
fizzy **gassato/a**
flag **la bandiera**
flash **il flash**
flashbulb **la lampadina per il flash**
flat (*apartment*) **l'appartamento** (*m*)
flat (*level*) **piatto/a** (*battery*) **scarico/a**
flavour **il sapore**
flaw **il difetto**
flea **la pulce**
flight **il volo**
flight bag **la borsa da viaggio**
flippers **le pinne**
flood **l'inondazione** (*f*)
floor **il pavimento** (*storey*) on the first floor **al primo piano** ground floor **il pianterreno**
flour **la farina**
flower **il fiore**
flu **l'influenza** (*f*)
fluent(ly) **correntemente**
fluid **il fluido**
fly **la mosca**
fly sheet **il volantino**
fly spray **l'insetticida**
o fly **volare**
fog **la nebbia**
foggy **nebbioso/a**
foil **la carta stagnola**
folding (*e.g. chair*) **pieghevole**
folk music **la musica popolare**
o follow **seguire**

following (*next*) **successivo/a**
food **il cibo**
food poisoning **l'intossicazione** (*f*) **alimentare**
foot **il piede** on foot **a piedi**
football **il calcio**
footpath **il sentiero**
for **per**
forbidden **vietato**
foreign **straniero/a**
foreigner **lo straniero/la straniera**
forest **la foresta**
to forget **dimenticare**
to forgive **perdonare**
fork **la forchetta**
form **il modulo**
fortnight **quindici giorni**
forward (*movement*) **in avanti**
forwarding address **il prossimo indirizzo**
foundation (*make-up*) **il fondo tinta**
fountain **la fontana**
foyer **il ridotto**
fracture **la frattura**
frankly **francamente**
freckles **le lentiggine**
free **gratis** (*available, unoccupied*) **libero/a**
freedom **la libertà**
to freeze (*food*) **congelare**
freezer **il congelatore**
frequent **frequente**
fresh **fresco/a**
fridge **il frigorifero**
fried **fritto/a**
friend **l'amico/a**
frightened **spaventato/a**

fringe la frangia
frog la rana
from da
front davanti
    in front of davanti a
front door la porta d'ingresso
frontier la frontiera
frost la brina
frozen (*food*) surgelato/a
fruit la frutta
fruit shop il fruttivendolo
to fry friggere
frying pan la padella
fuel il carburante
full pieno/a
    full board la pensione
    completa
    full up al completo
to have fun divertirsi
funeral il funerale
funfair il luna park
funny (*amusing*) divertente
    (*peculiar*) strano/a
fur la pelliccia
furniture i mobili
further on più lontano
fuse il fusibile
fusebox la scatola dei fusibili

G

gallery la galleria
gambling il gioco d'azzardo
game (*match*) il gioco
    (*hunting*) la cacciagione
gangway il passaggio
garage la stazione di servizio
    (*repairs*) l'autorimessa (*f*)
garden il giardino
gardener il giardiniere
garlic l'aglio (*m*)
gas il gas

gas bottle/cylinder la
    bombola di gas
gas refill la bomboletta di
    gas
gastritis la gastrite
gate il cancello
    (*airport*) l'uscita (*f*)
gel (*hair*) il gel
general generale
generally, in general
    generalmente
generous generoso/a
gentle dolce
gentleman/men (*gents*) signor
    uomini
genuine vero/a
    (*antique*, *picture*) autentico,
geography la geografia
to get (*receive*) ricevere
    to get off (*bus*) scendere
    to get on (*bus*) salire
    to get through (*phone*)
    prendere la linea
gift il regalo
gin il gin
    gin and tonic il gin tonic
girl la ragazza
girlfriend la fidanzata, la
    ragazza
to give dare
glass (*for drinking*) il bicchier
    (*substance*) il vetro
glasses gli occhiali
gloves i guanti
glue la colla
to go andare
    to go away andare via,
    andarsene
    go away! via! se ne vada!
    to go down scendere
    to go in entrare
    to go out uscire

to go up **salire**
let's go! **andiamo!**
goal **il goal**
goat **la capra**
(ski) goggles **gli occhiali (da sci)**
gold **l'oro** (*m*)
golf **il golf**
  golf clubs **le mazze**
  golf course **il campo di golf**
good **buono/a**
  good day/morning **buon giorno**
  good evening **buona sera**
  good night **buona notte**
goodbye **arrivederci**
  (*casual*) **ciao!**
goods **gli articoli**
government **il governo**
gram **il grammo**
grammar **la grammatica**
grandchildren **i nipoti**
granddaughter **la nipote**
grandfather **il nonno**
grandmother **la nonna**
grandparents **i nonni**
grandson **il nipote**
grandstand **la tribuna**
grape **l'uva** (*f*)
grapefruit **il pompelmo**
grass **l'erba** (*f*)
grateful **grato/a**
greasy **grasso/a**
great! **fantastico!**
green **verde**
  green card **la carta verde**
greengrocer's **il fruttivendolo**
to greet **salutare**
grey **grigio/a**
grilled **alla griglia**
grocer's **il negozio di alimentari**

ground **la terra**
ground floor **il pianterreno**
groundsheet **il telone impermeabile**
group **il gruppo**
to grow (*cultivate*) **crescere**
guarantee **la garanzia**
guard (*on train*) **il capotreno**
guest **l'ospite** (*m or f*)
  (*in hotel*) **il/la cliente**
guest house **la pensione**
guide **la guida**
  guided tour **la visita guidata**
guidebook **la guida**
guilty **colpevole**
guitar **la chitarra**
gun **la pistola**
guy rope **il tirante**
gymnastics **la ginnastica**

H

239

habit **l'abitudine** (*f*)
hail **la grandine**
hair **i capelli**
hairbrush **la spazzola per capelli**
haircut **il taglio di capelli**
hairdresser **il parrucchiere/la parrucchiera**
hairdrier **il föhn**
hairgrip **il fermacapelli**
hairspray **la lacca per capelli**
half **la metà**
  (*adj.*) **mezzo/a**
  half board **la mezza pensione**
  half price/fare **a metà prezzo**
  half-hour/half an hour **una mezz'ora**

half past . . . *(see Time, p. 181)* . . . e mezzo
hall *(in house)* l'ingresso
  (concert) la sala da concerti
ham il prosciutto
  cooked ham il prosciutto cotto
  cured ham il prosciutto crudo
hamburger il hamburger
hammer il martello
hand la mano
  hand cream la crema per le mani
  hand luggage i bagagli a mano
  hand made fatto a mano
handbag la borsa
handicapped handicappato/a
handkerchief il fazzoletto

240

handle la maniglia
hangover i postumi di una sbornia
to hang up riattaccare
to happen succedere
happy felice
harbour il porto
hard duro/a
  (difficult) difficile
  hard shoulder la corsia d'emergenza
hat il cappello
to hate odiare
to have avere
  hay il fieno
  hay fever la febbre da fieno
hazelnut la nocciola
he lui
head la testa
  (boss) il capo
headache il mal di testa

headphones le cuffie
to heal guarire
health la salute
  health foods alimenti biologici e integrali
healthy sano/a
to hear sentire
  hearing *(facility)* l'udito *(m)*
    hearing aid l'apparecchio *(m)* acustico
heart il cuore
  heart attack l'infarto *(m)*
heat il calore
heater il termosifone
heating il riscaldamento
heaven il paradiso
heavy pesante
hedge la siepe
heel il tallone
  (shoe) il tacco
height l'altezza *(f)*
helicopter l'elicotterro *(m)*
hell l'inferno *(m)*
hello ciao!
helmet *(motorbike)* il casco
help l'aiuto *(m)*
  help! aiuto!
to help aiutare
  (to) her *(pronoun)* la, le, gli
    (adj.) suo, sua, suoi, sue
herb l'erba *(f)* aromatica
  herbal tea il tè erbale
here qui
  here is . . . eccolo, eccola
hers il suo, la sua, i suoi, le sue
hiccups: to have hiccups ave il singhiozzo
high alto/a
  high chair il seggiolone
to hijack dirottare
hill la collina

(to) him **lo, gli**
to hire **noleggiare**
his *(adj. and pronoun)* **il suo, la sua, i suoi, le sue**
history **la storia**
to hit **colpire**
to hitchhike **fare l'autostop**
hobby **l'hobby** *(m)*
to hold **tenere**
hole **il buco**
holidays **le vacanze**
    on holiday **in vacanza**
    self-catering holiday **la vacanza in residenza**
holy **santo/a**
home **la casa**
    at home **a casa**
    home address **l'indirizzo** *(m)* **abituale**
    to go home **andare a casa**
homeopathic **omeopatico/a**
to be homesick **avere nostalgia di casa**
homosexual **omosessuale**
honest **onesto/a**
honeymoon **la luna di miele**
to hope **sperare**
    I hope so **spero di sì**
horrible **orribile**
horse **il cavallo**
hose **il manicotto**
hospital **l'ospedale** *(m)*
host **l'ospite** *(m or f)*
hot **caldo/a**
    (spicy) **piccante**
hotel **l'albergo** *(m)*
hour **l'ora** *(f)*
    half-hour **una mezz'ora**
house **la casa**
housewife **la casalinga**

housework **le faccende domestiche**
hovercraft **l'aliscafo** *(m)*
how **come**
    how long? **quanto tempo?**
    how many? **quanti?**
    how much? **quanto?**
    how much does it cost/is it? **quanto costa?**
    how much do they cost? **quanto costano?**
human **umano/a**
    human being **l'umano** *(m)*
hungry: I am hungry **ho fame**
to hunt **cacciare**
hunting **la caccia**
hurry: to be in a hurry **avere fretta**
to hurt **fare male**
    it hurts **fa male**
husband **il marito**
hut **la capanna**
hydrofoil **l'aliscafo** *(m)*

I

I **io**
ice **il ghiaccio**
ice-cream **il gelato**
ice rink **la pista di pattinaggio**
icy **ghiacciato/a**
    weather **gelido/a**
idea **l'idea** *(f)*
if **se**
ill **malato/a**
illness **la malattia**
imagination **la fantasia**
to imagine **immaginare**
immediately **subito**
immersion heater **il boiler**
impatient **impaziente**
important **importante**

impossible **impossibile**
impressive **impressionante**
in **in**
included **compreso/a**
income **il reddito**
indeed **infatti, davvero**
independent **indipendente**
indigestion **la dispepsia**
indoors **dentro**
industrial **industriale**
industry **l'industria** (f)
infected **infetto/a**
infection **l'infezione** (f)
infectious **contagioso/a**
inflamed **infiammato/a**
inflammation **l'infiammazione** (f)
influenza **l'influenza** (f)
informal **informale**
information **le informazioni**
    information desk/office **l'ufficio** (m) **informazioni**
injection **l'iniezione** (f)
to injure **ferire**
    injured **ferito/a**
injury **la ferita**
ink **l'inchiostro** (m)
inner **interno/a**
innocent **innocente**
insect **l'insetto** (m)
    insect bite **la puntura d'insetto**
    insect repellent **l'insettifugo** (m)
inside **dentro**
insist **insistere**
inspector **il controllore**
instant coffee **il caffè solubile**
instead of **invece di**
instructor **l'istruttore** (m)
insulin **l'insulina** (f)
insult **l'insulto** (m)

insurance **l'assicurazione** (f)
    insurance certificate **il certificato di assicurazione**
to insure **assicurare**
    insured **assicurato/a**
intelligent **intelligente**
interested **interessato/a**
interesting **interessante**
interior **interno/a**
intermediate **medio/a**
international **internazionale**
to interpret **interpretare**
interpreter **l'interprete** (m or f)
interval (*theatre etc*) **l'intervallo** (m)
interview **l'intervista** (f)
into **in**
to introduce **presentare**
invitation **l'invito** (m)
to invite **invitare**
iodine **l'iodio** (m)
Ireland **l'Irlanda** (f)
Irish **irlandese**
iron (*metal*) **il ferro**
    (*for clothes*) **il ferro da stiro**
to iron **stirare**
ironmonger's **il negozio di ferramenta**
is (*see 'to be', p. 174*) **è**
    is there . . .? **c'è . . .?**
island **l'isola** (f)
it **lo, la**
Italy **l'Italia** (f)
itch **il prurito**

J

jacket **la giacca**
jam **la marmellata**
jar **il vasetto**
jazz **il jazz**
jeans **i jeans**

jelly (*pudding*) la gelatina
jellyfish la medusa
Jesus Christ Gesù Cristo
jetty il molo
jeweller's la gioielleria
Jewish ebreo/a
job il lavoro
to jog fare footing
jogging il footing
joke lo scherzo
journalist il/la giornalista
journey il viaggio
judge il giudice
jug la brocca
juice il succo
to jump saltare
jump leads i cavi per fa partire
  la macchina
jumper la maglia
junction l'incrocio (*m*)
just (*only*) solamente

K

kaolin mixture il kaoline
to keep tenere
kettle il bollitore
key la chiave
  key ring il portachiavi
kidney il rene
to kill uccidere
kilo(gram) un chilo
kilometre un chilometro
kind (*sort*) il tipo
  (*generous*) gentile
king il re
kiss il bacio
to kiss baciare
kitchen la cucina
knickers le mutandine
knife il coltello
to knit fare a maglia

knitting il lavoro a maglia
  knitting needle il ferro da
  calza
to knock (*on door*) bussare
knot il nodo
to know (*someone*) conoscere
  (*something*) sapere
  as far as I know per quanto
  me so

L

label l'etichetta (*f*)
lace il pizzo
ladder la scala
lady la donna
  ladies donne
lager la birra bionda
lake il lago
lamb l'agnello (*m*)
lamp la lampada
lamp post il lampione

land la terra
to land atterrare
landing (*house*) il pianerottolo
  (*plane*) lo sbarco
landlady la padrona
landlord il padrone
lane (*country road*) la stradina
language la lingua
large grande
last ultimo/a
  (*week, month*) scorso/a
to last durare
late tardi
  (*train*) in ritardo
later più tardi
laugh la risata
to laugh ridere
launderette la lavanderia
laundry la biancheria
law la legge

lawyer l'avvocato, l'avvocata
laxative il lassativo
lazy pigro/a
lead il piombo
    lead-free senza piombo
leaf la foglia
leaflet il dépliant
to lean out sporgersi
to learn imparare
learner il/la principiante
least: at least almeno
leather il cuoio
to leave (message etc) lasciare
    (to go away) partire
lecturer il professore/la
    professoressa
left sinistro/a
left-handed mancino/a
left luggage (office) il deposito
    bagagli
leg la gamba
legal legale
lemon il limone
lemonade la limonata
to lend prestare
length la lunghezza
lens (camera) l'obiettivo (m)
less meno
lesson la lezione
to let (allow) permettere
    (rent) affittare
letter la lettera
letterbox la cassetta delle
    lettere
lettuce la lattuga
leukaemia la leucemia
level (height, standard) il livello
level (flat) piano/a
level crossing il passaggio a
    livello
library la biblioteca

licence (driving) la patente
    (fishing etc) il permesso
lid il coperchio
to lie down sdraiarsi
life la vita
lifebelt il salvagente
lifeboat la scialuppa di
    salvataggio
lifeguard il bagnino
lifejacket il giubbotto
    salvagente/di salvataggio
lift l'ascensore (m)
light la luce
    light bulb la lampadina
light (coloured) chiaro/a
    (weight) leggero/a
to light (fire) accendere
lighter (cigarette) l'accendino
    (m)
lighter fuel il gas per
    l'accendino
lightning il fulmine
like (similar to) come
    like this/that così
    what is . . . like? com'è . . .?
    what are . . . like? come sono
    . . .?
to like piacere
    I like it mi piace
likely probabile
limited limitato/a
line (underground) la linea
lion il leone
lip il labbro
lipstick il rossetto
liqueur liquore
liquid il liquido
list l'elenco (m)
to listen (to) ascoltare
litre il litro
litter i rifiuti

little **piccolo/a**
a little **un pò**
to live **abitare**
liver **il fegato**
living-room **il soggiorno**
loaf **il pane**
local **locale**
lock **la serratura**
to lock **chiudere a chiave**
locker **l'armadietto** (*m*)
London **Londra**
lonely **solitario/a, solo/a**
long (*inc. hair*) **lungo/a**
long-distance (*call*)
 interurbano
to look (at) **guardare**
to look after **badare**
to look for **cercare**
to look like **assomigliare**
loose (*clothes*) **ampio/a**
lorry **il camion**
lorry-driver **il camionista**
to lose **perdere**
lost property (office) **l'ufficio**
 (*m*) **oggetti smarriti**
a lot (of) **molto**
lotion **la lozione**
lottery **la lotteria**
loud **forte**
lounge (*airport*) **la sala d'attesa**
 (*hotel*) **il salone**
love **l'amore** (*m*)
to love **amare**
lovely **bellissimo/a**
low **basso/a**
lower **più basso/a**
lozenge **la pastiglia**
LP **LP (ellepi)**
lucky: to be lucky **essere**
 fortunato/a
luggage **i bagagli**

luggage allowance **il**
 bagaglio permesso
lump **la zolla**
 (*swelling*) **il nodulo**
lunch **il pranzo**

M

machine **la macchina**
machinist **il/la macchinista**
mad **pazzo/a**
madam **signora**
magazine **la rivista**
mail **la posta**
main **principale**
make (*car*) **la marca**
to make **fare**
make-up **il trucco**
male **il maschio**
man **l'uomo** (*m*)
manager **il direttore**
managing director
 l'amministratore (*m*)
 delegato
many **molti**
 not many **non molti**
map **la carta**
marble **il marmo**
margarine **la margarina**
market **il mercato**
married **sposato/a**
 to get married **sposarsi**
mascara **il mascara**
masculine **maschile**
mask (*diving*) **la maschera**
mass (*church*) **la messa**
matches **i fiammiferi**
 (*game*) **la partita**
material (*cloth*) **il tessuto**
mathematics **la matematica**
matter: it doesn't matter **non**
 importa

what's the matter? **cosa c'è?**
mattress **il materasso**
  air mattress **il materassino**
mature (*cheese*) **stagionato/a**
mayonnaise **la maionese**
me **mi, me** (*after prepositions*)
  with me **con me**
meadow **il prato**
meal **il pasto**
mean: what does this mean?
  cosa vuol dire questo?
meanwhile **nel frattempo**
measles **il morbillo**
  German measles **la rubella**
to measure **misurare**
measurement **la misura**
meat **la carne**
  cold meats **i salami**
mechanic **il meccanico**
medical **medico/a**
medicine **la medicina**
medieval **medievale**
Mediterranean **il
  Mediterraneo**
medium **medio/a**
  (*steak*) **a puntino**
  (*wine*) **abboccato**
to meet **incontrare**
meeting (*accidental*) **l'incontro**
  (*m*)
  (*business*) **la riunione**
melon **il melone**
member **il socio**
men **gli uomini**
to mend **riparare**
menu **il menù**
message **il messaggio**
metal **il metallo**
meter **il contatore**
metre **il metro**

microwave oven **il forno a
  microonde**
midday **il mezzogiorno**
middle **il mezzo**
middle-aged **di mezza età**
midnight **la mezzanotte**
migraine **l'emicrania** (*f*)
mild (*temperature*) **mite**
  (*taste*) **delicato/a**
mile **il miglio**
milk **il latte**
milkshake **il frullato**
mill **il mulino**
mince **la carne macinata**
mind: do you mind if . . .? **Le
  da fastidio se . . .?**
  I don't mind **non mi import**
mine (*of me*) **il mio, la mia, i
  miei, le mie**
minibus **il pulmino**
minister **il ministro**
minute (*time*) **il minuto**
mirror **lo specchio**
Miss **Signorina**
to miss (*bus etc*) **perdere**
  (*nostalgia*) **mancare**
mist **la foschia**
mistake **l'errore** (*m*)
  to make a mistake **sbagliars**
mixed **misto/a**
mixture **la mescolanza**
model **il modello**
modern **moderno/a**
moisturiser **l'idratante** (*m*)
monastery **il monastero**
money **i soldi**
month **il mese**
monthly **mensile**
monument **il monumento**
moon **la luna**
moped **il ciclomotore**

more **più**
  no more **non più**
morning **la mattina**
mortgage **l'ipoteca** (*f*)
mosquito **la zanzara**
mosquito net **la zanzariera**
most (of) **la maggior parte (di)**
mother **la madre**
mother-in-law **la suocera**
motor **il motore**
motorbike **la moto**
motorboat **il motoscafo**
motor racing **le corse automobilistiche**
motorway **l'autostrada** (*f*)
mountain **la montagna**
mountaineering **l'alpinismo** (*f*)
moustache **i baffi**
mouth **la bocca**
to move **muovere**
  to move house **cambiare casa**
Mr **Signor**
Mrs **Signora**
much **molto**
  not much **non molto**
mug **il tazzone**
mugs **i boccali**
to murder **assassinare**
museum **il museo**
mushrooms **i funghi**
music **la musica**
musical **la commedia musicale**
musician **il musicista**
must: you must . . . **deve**
mustard **la senape**
my **mio, mia, miei, mie**
mystery **il mistero**

N

nail (*DIY*) **il chiodo**
  (*finger/toe*) **l'unghia** (*f*)
nail clippers/scissors **le forbici per unghie**
nail file **la lima per unghie**
nail polish **lo smalto per le unghie**
nail polish remover **l'acetone** (*m*)
naked **nudo/a**
name **il nome**
  my name is . . . **mi chiamo . . .**
  what is your name? **come ti chiami?**
napkin **il tovagliolo**
nappies **i pannolini per bambini**
  disposable nappies **i pannolini usa e getta**
narrow **stretto/a**
national **nazionale**
nationality **la nazionalità**
natural **naturale**
  naturally **naturalmente**
naughty **birichino/a**
navy **la marina**
navy blue **il blu marino**
near (to) **vicino/a (a)**
  nearby **qui vicino**
nearest **più vicino/a**
nearly **quasi**
necessary **necessario**
necklace **la collana**
to need **avere bisogno di**
  I need a doctor **ho bisogno di un medico**
needle **l'ago** (*m*)
negative (*photo*) **il negativo**
neighbour **il vicino/la vicina**

neither . . . nor né . . . né . . .
nephew il nipote
nervous nervoso/a
net la rete
never mai
new nuovo/a
New Year il Capodanno
news le notizie
newspaper il giornale
newspaper kiosk l'edicola (f)
next prossimo/a
nice (person) simpatico/a
niece la nipote
night la notte
nightclub il night
nightdress la camicia da notte
no no
nobody nessuno/a
noise il rumore
noisy rumoroso/a
non-alcoholic analcolico/a
none nessuno
non-smoking non fumatori
normal normale
normally normalmente
north il nord
nose il naso
nosebleed l'emorragia (f)
nasale
nostril la narice
not non
note (bank) la banconota
notepad il bloc-notes
nothing niente
nothing else nient'altro
now adesso
nowhere da nessuna parte
nuclear nucleare
nuclear power l'energia (f)
nucleare
number il numero

nurse l'infermiera (f)
nursery slope la pista per
principianti
nut la noce
(DIY) il dado
nylon il nylon

O

oar il remo
object l'oggetto (m)
obvious ovvio/a
occasionally ogni tanto
occupied (seat) occupato/a
odd strano/a
(not even) dispari
of di
of course naturalmente
off (power) spento/a
offended offeso/a
offer l'offerta (f)
special offer l'offerta
speciale
office l'ufficio (m)
officer (police) il poliziotto
official ufficiale
often spesso
how often do you go? ogni
quanto ci va?
oil l'olio (m)
OK va bene
old vecchio/a
how old are you? quanti
anni hai?
how old is he/she/are you?
quanti anni ha?
I am . . . years old ho . . .
anni
old-fashioned fuori moda
olive l'oliva (f)
olive oil l'olio (m) d'oliva

on **su**
  (*light*) **acceso/a**
once **una volta**
onion **la cipolla**
only **soltanto**
open **aperto/a**
to open **aprire**
opera **l'opera** (*f*)
operation **l'operazione** (*f*)
opinion: in my opinion
  secondo me
opposite **opposto/a**
  opposite the house **di fronte
  alla casa**
optician **l'ottico** (*m*)
optional **facoltativo/a**
or **o**
orange (*fruit*) **l'arancia** (*f*)
  (*colour*) **arancione**
to order **ordinare**
ordinary **comune**
original **originale**
other **l'altro/a**
  others **altri**
our **nostro, nostra, nostri,
  nostre**
ours **il nostro/la nostra**
out (of) **fuori (da)**
outdoor **fuori**
over **sopra**
overcast **coperto/a**
overcoat **il cappotto**
to overtake **sorpassare**
to owe **dovere**
  I owe you . . . **ti devo . . .**
owner **il proprietario/la
  proprietaria**

P

package tour **il viaggio
  organizzato**
packet **il pacco**
paddle (*canoeing*) **la pagaia**
padlock **il lucchetto**
page **la pagina**
pain **il dolore**
painful **doloroso/a**
painkiller **il calmante**
paint **la vernice**
to paint **dipingere**
  (*walls, door*) **verniciare**
painter **il pittore**
painting **il quadro**
pair **il paio**
palace **il palazzo**
pale **pallido/a**
pants **le mutande**
paper **la carta**
paper clip **il clip**
paraffin **il cherosene**
paralysed **paralizzato/a**
parcel **il pacco**
pardon? **come?**
parents **i genitori**
park **il parco**
to park **parcheggiare**
parking **il parcheggio**
  parking disc **il disco orario**
  parking meter **il
  parchimetro**
parliament **il parlamento**
part **la parte**
parting (*hair*) **la riga**
partly **in parte**
partner **il/la partner**
party **la festa**
to pass (*on road*) **sorpassare**
  (*salt etc*) **passare**
passenger **il passeggero**

passion **la passione**
passport **il passaporto**
  passport control il **controllo passaporti**
past **passato/a**
  in the past **nel passato** (*Time, see p. 181*)
pasta **la pasta**
pastille **la pastiglia**
pastry **la pasta**
path **il sentiero**
patient (*hospital*) **il/la paziente**
pattern **il disegno**
pavement **il pavimento**
to pay **pagare**
peas **i piselli**
peace **la pace**
peach **la pesca**
peanut **l'arachide** (*f*)
pear **la pera**
pedal **il pedale**
pedal-boat **il pedalò**
pedestrian **il pedone**
pedestrian crossing il **passaggio pedonale**
to peel **sbucciare**
peg **la molletta**
pen **la penna**
pencil **la matita**
pencil sharpener il **temperamatite**
penfriend **il/la corrispondente**
penicillin **la penicillina**
penknife **il temperino**
pension **la pensione**
pensioner **il pensionato/la pensionata**
people **la gente**
pepper **il pepe**
  (*sweet green/red*) **il peperone**
peppermint **la menta**

per **per**
  per hour **all'ora**
  per week **alla settimana**
perfect **perfetto/a**
performance **lo spettacolo**
perfume **il profumo**
perhaps **forse**
period (*menstrual*) le **mestruazioni**
  period pains i **dolori mestruali**
perm **la permanente**
permit **il permesso**
to permit **permettere**
person **la persona**
personal **personale**
personal stereo **il walkman**
petrol **la benzina**
petrol can **la latta di benzina**
petrol station **la stazione di servizio**
petticoat **la sottogonna**
philosophy **la filosofia**
photocopy **la fotocopia**
to photocopy **fotocopiare**
photo(graph) **la foto(grafia)**
photographer il **fotografo/la fotografa**
photography **la fotografia**
phrase book **il vocabolarietto**
physics **la fisica**
piano **il pianoforte**
to pick (*choose*) **scegliere**
  (*flowers etc*) **cogliere**
to pick up (*fetch*) **venire a prendere**
  can you pick me up? **mi puoi venire a prendere?**
picnic **il picnic**
picture **il quadro**
  (*painting*) **la pittura**

piece il pezzo
pier l'imbarcadero (m)
pierced (ear) bucato/a
pig il maiale
(the) pill la pillola
pillow il guanciale
pillowcase la federa
pilot il pilota
pilot light la fiammella di
  sicurezza
pin lo spillo
pineapple l'ananas (m)
pink rosa
pipe (smoking) la pipa
  (drain) il tubo
place il luogo
  (seat) il posto
plain (food) alla buona
  (material) in tinta unita
plan (of town) la pianta
plane l'aereo (m)
plant la pianta
plaster (sticking) il cerotto
plastic di plastica
plastic bag il sacchetto di
  plastica
plate il piatto
platform il binario
play (theatre) la commedia
to play (instrument) suonare
  (record/tape) mettere un
    disco
  (sport) giocare
pleasant piacevole
please per favore, per piacere,
  per cortesia
pleased contento/a
plenty (of) abbastanza
pliers le pinze
plimsolls le scarpe da tennis

plug (bath) il tappo
  (electrical) la spina
plumber l'idraulico (m)
pneumonia la polmonite
pocket la tasca
point la punta
poison il veleno
poisonous velenoso/a
pole il palo
police la polizia
police car la macchina della
  polizia
police station il
  commissariato, la questura
polish (for shoes) il lucido
polite educato/a
political politico/a
politician il politico
politics la politica
polluted inquinato/a
pollution l'inquinamento (m)
pool (swimming) la piscina
poor povero/a
pop (music) la musica pop
Pope il papa
popular popolare
pork il maiale
port il porto
portable portabile
porter (hotel) il portiere
  (station) il facchino
porthole l'oblò
portion la porzione
portrait il ritratto
positive (sure) sicuro/a
  (photo) positivo/a
possible possibile
  as . . . as possible il più . . .
    possibile
possibly forse
post (mail) la posta

to post **spedire**
postbox **la cassetta delle lettere**
postcard **la cartolina**
postcode **il codice postale**
poster **il poster**
postman **il postino**
post office **l'ufficio** (*m*) **postale**
to postpone **rinviare**
pot (*for cooking*) **la pentola**
potato **la patata**
pottery **la ceramica**
potty (*child's*) **il vasino**
pound (*sterling*) **la sterlina**
to pour **versare**
powder **la polvere**
  (*talcum*) **il talco**
powdered milk **il latte in polvere**
powdery (*snow*) **polveroso/a, farinoso/a**

power (*electricity*) **l'energia** (*f*)
power cut **l'interruzione** (*f*) **di corrente**
pram **la carrozzina**
to prefer **preferire**
pregnant **incinta**
to prepare **preparare**
prescription **la ricetta**
present (*gift*) **il regalo**
press (*newspapers*) **la stampa**
  press office **l'ufficio** (*m*) **stampa**
pretty **carino/a**
price **il prezzo**
priest **il prete**
prime minister **il primo ministro**
primus stove **il fornello a petrolio**
prince **il principe**

princess **la principessa**
print (*photo*) **la stampa**
to print **stampare**
prison **la prigione**
private **privato/a**
prize **il premio**
probably **probabilmente**
problem **il problema**
producer (*radio/TV/film*) **il direttore/la direttrice**
profession **la professione**
professor **il professore/la professoressa**
profit **il profitto**
programme **il programma**
prohibited **vietato/a**
to promise **promettere**
to pronounce **pronunciare**
  how do you pronounce it? **come si pronuncia?**
properly **correttamente**
property (*land*) **la proprietà**
protestant **protestante**
public (*noun*) **il pubblico**
  (*adj*) **pubblico/a**
public holiday **la festa nazionale**
public relations **le pubbliche relazioni**
to pull **tirare**
to pump up **gonfiare**
puncture **la foratura**
pure **puro/a**
purple **viola**
purse **il borsellino**
to push **spingere**
push-chair **il passeggino**
to put (*insert*) **mettere**
to put down **posare**
pyjamas **i pigiama**

Q

quality **la qualità**
quarter **il quarto**
quay **il molo**
queen **la regina**
question **la domanda**
queue **la coda**
quick **veloce**
quickly **velocemente**
quiet **tranquillo/a**
    (*person*) **taciturno/a**
quite **abbastanza**

R

rabbi **il rabbino**
rabbit **il coniglio**
rabies **la rabbia**
racecourse **il campo di corso**
racing (*horse*) **la corsa dei**
    cavalli
    (*motor*) **le corse**
    automobilistiche
racket (*tennis*) **la racchetta**
radiator **il radiatore**
radio **la radio**
radioactive **radioattivo/a**
radio station **la stazione radio**
raft **la zattera**
railway **la ferrovia**
railway station **la stazione**
rain **la pioggia**
to rain: it's raining **piove**
raincoat **l'impermeabile** (*m*)
to rape **violentare**
rare **raro/a**
    (*steak*) **al sangue**
rash **lo sfogo**
raspberries **i lamponi**
rate (*speed*) **la velocità**
    (*tariff*) **la tariffa**

rather (*quite*) **piuttosto**
raw **crudo/a**
razor **il rasoio**
razor blades **le lamette**
to reach **raggiungere**
to read **leggere**
reading **la lettura**
ready **pronto/a**
real (*authentic*) **vero/a**
really **veramente, davvero**
rear **di dietro**
reason **la ragione**
receipt **la ricevuta**
receiver (*telephone*) **il ricevitore**
reception **la reception, il**
    ricevimento, la ricezione
receptionist **il/la receptionist**
recipe **la ricetta**
to recognise **riconoscere**
to recommend **consigliare**
record **il disco**
to record (*music*) **registrare**
record-player **il giradischi**
to recover **ricuperare**
red **rosso/a**
    Red Cross **la croce rossa**
reduction **la riduzione**
refill (*gas*) **la bomboletta**
refrigerator **il frigorifero**
refugee **il rifugiato/la rifugiata**
refund **il rimborso**
to refund **rimborsare**
region **la regione**
to register **raccomandare**
registration document (*car*) **il**
    libretto d'iscrizione
registration number **il numero**
    di targa
relation **il/la parente**
religion **la religione**
to remain **rimanere**

to remember **ricordare**
to remove **togliere**
rent **l'affitto** (*m*)
to rent **affittare**
(*car*) **noleggiare**
to repair **riparare**
to repeat **ripetere**
reply **la risposta**
to reply **rispondere**
report **il rapporto**
to report **presentarsi**
to rescue **salvare**
reservation **la prenotazione**
to reserve **prenotare**
reserved **prenotato/a**
responsible **responsabile**
to rest **riposarsi**
restaurant **il ristorante**
restaurant-car **il vagone
ristorante**
result **il risultato**
retired **in pensione**
return **il ritorno**
(*ticket*) **di andata e ritorno**
to return **tornare**
to reverse **fare marcia indietro**
reverse-charge call **una
chiamata in 'erre'**
rheumatism **il reumatismo**
ribbon **il nastro**
rice **il riso**
rich **ricco/a**
to ride a bicycle **andare in
bicicletta**
to ride a horse **andare a cavallo**
right (*correct*) **giusto/a**
(*place*) **destra**
on the right **a destra**
to be right **avere ragione**
ring (*jewellery*) **l'anello** (*m*)
ripe **maturo/a**

river **il fiume**
road (*main*) **la strada**
roadworks **i lavori stradali**
roast **arrosto/a**
to rob **rubare**
robbery **il furto**
roll (*bread*) **il panino**
rollers (*hair*) **i bigodini**
roof **il tetto**
room **la camera**
(*space*) **lo spazio**
rope **il cavo**
rose **la rosa**
rosé **rosato/a**
rotten **marcio/a**
rough (*surface*) **ruvido/a**
(*sea*) **mosso/a**
round **rotondo/a**
roundabout **la rotatoria**
row (*theatre etc*) **la fila**
to row **remare**
rowing boat **la barca a remi**
royal **reale**
rubber **la gomma**
rubbish **la spazzatura**
rucksack **lo zaino**
rude **maleducato/a**
ruins **le rovine**
ruler (*for measuring*) **il righello**
rum **il rum**
to run **correre**
rush hour **l'ora** (*f*) **di punta**
rusty **rugginoso/a**

S

sad **triste**
safe (*strongbox*) **la cassaforte**
safe **sicuro/a**
safety pin **la spilla di sicurezza**
sail **la vela**
to sail **fare della vela**

sailboard il **sandolino**
sailing la **vela**
sailing boat la **barca a vela**
sailor il **marinaio**
saint il **santo**/la **santa**
salad l'**insalata** (*f*)
salami il **salame**
sale il **saldo**
sales representative il **rappresentante**
salmon il **salmone**
salt il **sale**
salty **salato/a**
same **stesso/a**
sample il **campione**
sand la **sabbia**
sandals i **sandali**
sandwich il **panino**, il **tramezzino**
   toasted sandwich il **toast**
sandy **sabbioso/a**
sanitary towels gli **assorbenti**
sauce la **salsa**
saucepan la **pentola**
saucer il **piattino**
sauna la **sauna**
sausage la **salsiccia**
o save **risparmiare**
   (*rescue*) **salvare**
o say **dire**
scald la **scottatura**
scales la **bilancia**
scarf la **sciarpa**
scene la **scena**
scenery il **paesaggio**
scent l'**odore** (*m*)
school la **scuola**
science la **scienza**
scientist il **scienziato/la scienziata**
scissors le **forbici**
scooter la **motoretta**

score i **punti**
what's the score? qual è il **risultato?**
Scotland la **Scozia**
Scottish **scozzese**
scratch il **graffio**
to scratch **graffiare**
screen lo **schermo**
screw la **vite**
screwdriver il **cacciavite**
sculpture la **scultura**
sea il **mare**
seafood i **frutti di mare**
seasick il **mal di mare**
season la **stagione**
season ticket l'**abbonamento** (*m*)
seat la **sedia**
   (*train, theatre*) il **posto**
seatbelt la **cintura di sicurezza**
second **secondo/a**
second (*time period*) il **secondo**
secret il **segreto**
secretary la **segretaria**
section la **sezione**
to see **vedere**
to seem **sembrare**
   it seems to me mi **sembra**
self-catering (*holiday*) la **vacanza in residenza**
self-service **self-service**
to sell **vendere**
to send **mandare**
senior citizen l'**anziano/a**
sensible **ragionevole**
   (*person*) di **buon senso**
sentence la **frase**
separate(d) **separato/a**
septic tank la **fossa settica**
serious **grave**

to serve **servire**
  service (*charge*) **il servizio**
    (*church*) **la messa**
  set (*collection*) **la serie**
  setting lotion **la lozione
    fissativa**
  several **parecchi/parecchie**
to sew **cucire**
  sewing **la cucitura**
  sex **il sesso**
  shade (*not sun, shadow*)
    l'ombra (*f*)
  shampoo **lo shampoo**
  shampoo and set **shampoo e
    messa in piega**
  sharp **affilato/a**
    (*pain*) **acuto/a**
to shave **farsi la barba**
  shaving cream/foam **la crema
    da barba**
  she **lei**
  sheep **la pecora**
  sheet **il lenzuolo**
  shelf **lo scaffale**
  shell (*egg, nut*) **il guscio**
  shellfish **i frutti di mare**
  shelter **il riparo**
  sherry **lo sherry**
  shiny **lucido/a**
  ship **la nave**
  shirt **la camicia**
  shock (*electric*) **la scossa**
    (*emotional*) **lo shock**
  shocked **sconvolto/a**
  shoe **la scarpa**
  shoelace **la stringa**
  shoe polish **il lucido per le
    scarpe**
  shoe repairer's **il calzolaio**
  shoe shop **la calzoleria**
  shop **il negozio**

  shop assistant **il commesso/
    commessa**
  shopping: to go shopping **fa
    compere**
  shopping centre **il centro
    commerciale**
  short **corto/a**
  shorts **i calzoncini corti**
  shout **il grido**
  show **lo spettacolo**
to show **mostrare**
  shower **la doccia**
to shrink **restringersi**
  shrunk **rattrappito/a**
  shut **chiuso/a**
  shutter **l'otturatore** (*m*)
  sick (*ill*) **malato/a**
    to be sick **vomitare**
    to feel sick **avere la nausea**
  side **il lato**
  sieve **il colino**
    (*for flour*) **il setaccio**
  sight (*vision*) **la vista**
    (*tourist*) **lo spettacolo**
  sightseeing **il turismo**
  sign **il segnale**
to sign **firmare**
  signal **il segnale**
  signature **la firma**
  silent **silenzioso/a**
  silk **la seta**
  silver **l'argento** (*m*)
  similar **simile**
  simple **semplice**
  since **da (quando)**
to sing **cantare**
  single (*room*) **singolo/a**
    (*ticket*) **di andata**
    (*unmarried*) **non sposato/a**
  single (*record*) **il singolo**
  sink **il lavandino**

sir **Signore**
sister **la sorella**
sister-in-law **la cognata**
to sit (*down*) **sedersi**
sitting (*down*) **seduto/a**
size **la misura**
    (*clothes*) **la taglia**
    (*shoes*) **il numero**
skates (*ice*) **i pattini**
    (*roller*) **i pattini a rotelle**
to skate **pattinare**
ski **lo sci**
to ski **sciare**
ski boots **gli scarponi**
skiing **lo sci**
    cross-country skiing **lo sci da fondo**
ski-lift **la sciovia**
skimmed milk **il latte scremato**
skin **la pelle**
skindiving **le attività subacquee**
skirt **la gonna**
ski-run/slope **la pista**
ski stick **il bastone da sci**
sky **il cielo**
to sleep **dormire**
sleeper/sleeping-car **il vagone letto**
sleeping bag **il sacco a pelo**
sleeve **la manica**
slice **la fetta**
sliced **a fette**
slide (*film*) **la diapositiva**
slim **magro/a**
slip (*petticoat*) **la sottoveste**
slippery **scivoloso/a**
slow **lento/a**
slowly **lentamente**
small **piccolo/a**

smell **il profumo**
    (*unpleasant*) **il puzzo**
to smell **sentire**
    it smells of . . . **sa di . . .**
    (*bad/good*) **cattivo/buono**
smile **il sorriso**
to smile **sorridere**
smoke **il fumo**
to smoke **fumare**
smoked **affumicato/a**
smooth **liscio/a**
to sneeze **starnutire**
snorkel **il boccaglio**
snow **la neve**
snow chains **le catene di neve**
to snow **nevicare**
    it's snowing **nevica**
so **così**
    (*therefore*) **dunque**
    so much **così tanto**
soap **la saponetta**
sober **sobrio/a**
socialism **il socialismo**
socialist **socialisto/a**
social worker **l'assistente** (*m or f*) **sociale**
sociology **la sociologia**
socket **la presa**
socks **i calzini**
soda (*water*) **la soda**
soft **soffice**
soft drink **l'analcolico** (*m*)
soldier **il soldato**
sold out **esaurito/a**
solicitor **l'avvocato** (*m*)
solid **solido/a**
some **di**
    some wine **del vino**
    (*plural*) **alcuni, alcune**
somehow **in qualche modo**
someone **qualcuno**

something **qualcosa**
sometimes **qualche volta**
somewhere **da qualche parte**
son **il figlio**
song **la canzone**
son-in-law **il genero**
soon **fra poco, presto**
    as soon as possible **primo possibile**
sore (*inc. throat*) **dolarante**
sorry: I'm sorry **mi scusi**
    (*regret*) **mi dispiace**
sort **il tipo**
sound **il suono**
soup **la minestra**
sour **aspro/a**
south **il sud**
souvenir **il souvenir**
space **lo spazio**
spade **la paletta**
spanner **la chiave**
spare **di scorta, di riserva**
spare time **il tempo libero**
spare tyre **la ruota di scorta**
sparkling (*wine*) **spumante**
to speak **parlare**
special **speciale**
    offer **l'offerta** (*f*) **speciale**
specialist **il/la specialista**
speciality **la specialità**
spectacles **gli occhiali**
speed **la velocità**
speed limit **il limite di velocità**
to spend (*money*) **spendere**
    (*time*) **passare**
spices **le spezie**
spicy **piccante**
spinach **gli spinaci**
spirits **i liquori**
splinter **la scheggia**
to spoil **rovinare**

sponge (*bath*) **la spugna**
spoon **il cucchiaio**
sport **lo sport**
spot **il punto**
    (*place*) **il posto**
sprain **la storta**
sprained **storto/a**
spray **lo spray**
spring (*season*) **la primavera**
square (*in town*) **la piazza**
    (*shape*) **il quadrato**
stadium **lo stadio**
stain **la macchia**
stainless steel **l'acciaio** (*m*) **inossidabile**
stairs **le scale**
stalls (*theatre*) **la platea**
stamp (*postage*) **il francobollo**
stand (*stadium*) **la tribuna**
to stand **stare in piedi**
    to stand up **alzarsi**
staple **la graffetta**
stapler **la cucitrice**
star **la stella**
    (*film etc.*) **il divo/la diva**
start **l'inizio** (*m*)
to start **cominciare**
starter (*food*) **l'antipasto** (*m*)
state **lo stato**
station **la stazione**
station master **il capostazione**
stationer's **la cartoleria**
statue **la statua**
to stay **restare**
    (*in a hotel*) **stare**
steak **la bistecca**
to steal **rubare**
steam **il vapore**
steamer **il piroscafo**
steel **l'acciaio** (*m*)
steep **ripido**

step il gradino
step-brother il fratellastro
step-children i figliastri
step-daughter la figliastra
step-father il patrigno
step-mother la matrigna
step-sister la sorellastra
step-son il figliastro
stereo lo stereo
sterling: pound sterling la sterlina
steward (*air*) lo steward
stewardess (*air*) la hostess
stick il bastone
sticking plaster il cerotto
sticky appiccicoso/a
sticky tape il nastro adesivo
stiff rigido/a
still fermo/a
  (*non-fizzy*) non gassato/a
sting la puntura
to sting pungere
stock cube il dado
stock exchange la Borsa
stockings le calze
stolen rubato/a
stomach lo stomaco
stomach-ache il mal di stomaco
stone la pietra
stop (*bus*) la fermata
to stop fermarsi
  stop! ferma!
stopcock il rubinetto principale
story la storia
stove il fornello
straight diritto/a
straight on sempre dritto
strange strano/a
stranger lo sconosciuto/la sconosciuta

strap la cinghia
straw (*drinking*) la cannuccia
strawberries le fragole
stream il ruscello
street la strada
street light il lampione
stretcher la barella
strike lo sciopero
string lo spago
stripe la striscia
striped a strisce
strong forte
stuck bloccato/a
student lo studente/la studentessa
studio (*radio/TV*) lo studio
to study studiare
stupid stupido/a
style lo stile
styling mousse il fissatore
subtitled con sottotitoli
subtitles i sottotitoli
suburb la periferia
to succeed riuscire
success il successo
such tale
suddenly improvvisamente
sugar lo zucchero
sugar lump la zolletta
suit (*for men*) l'abito (*m*)
  (*for women*) il tailleur
suitcase la valigia
summer l'estate (*f*)
sun il sole
to sunbathe prendere il sole
sunburn la scottatura
sunglasses gli occhiali da sole
sunny assolato/a
sunshade l'ombrellone (*m*)
sunstroke l'insolazione (*f*)
suntan oil l'olio (*m*) solare

supermarket il **supermercato**
supper la **cena**
supplement il **supplemento**
suppose: I suppose so **credo di
sì**
suppository la **supposta**
sure **sicuro/a**
surface la **superficie**
surname il **cognome**
surprise la **sorpresa**
surprised **sorpreso/a**
surrounded by **circondato di**
to sweat **sudare**
sweater il **maglione**
sweatshirt la **felpa**
to sweep **spazzare**
sweet **dolce**
sweetener il **dolcificante**
sweets le **caramelle**
swelling il **gonfiore**

to swim **nuotare**
swimming il **nuoto**
swimming pool la **piscina**
swimming trunks i **calzoncini
da bagno**
swimsuit il **costume da bagno**
switch l'**interruttore** (*m*)
to switch off (*light etc.*) **spegnere**
    switched off **spento/a**
to switch on (*light etc.*) **accendere**
    switched on **acceso/a**
swollen **gonfio/a**
symptom il **sintomo**
synagogue la **sinagoga**
synthetic **sintetico/a**
system il **sistema**

T

table la **tavola**
tablet la **pastiglia**
table tennis il **ping-pong**

tailor il **sarto**
to take (*bus etc.*) **prendere**
    (*carry*) **portare**
    (*exam/test*) **sostenere**
    (*photo*) **fare**
    it takes an hour **ci vuole
    un'ora**
taken (*seat*) **occupato/a**
to take off (*clothes*) **togliere**
    (*plane*) **decollare**
talcum powder il **talco**
to talk **parlare**
tall **alto/a**
tame **addomesticato/a**
tampons i **tamponi**
tap il **rubinetto**
tape (*adhesive*) il **nastro**
    (*cassette*) la **cassetta**
tape measure il **metro a nastro**
tape recorder il **registratore**
taste il **sapore**
to taste: it tastes good **ha un buon
    sapore**
tax la **tassa**
taxi il **tassì, il taxi**
taxi rank la **stazione di taxi**
tea il **tè**
teabag la **bustina di tè**
to teach **insegnare**
teacher l'**insegnante** (*m or f*)
team la **squadra**
teapot la **teiera**
to tear **strappare**
teaspoon il **cucchiaino**
teat (*for baby's bottle*) la
    tettarella
tea-towel lo **strofinaccio**
technical **tecnico/a**
technology la **tecnologia**
teenager l'**adolescente** (*m or f*)
telegram il **telegramma**

telephone **il telefono**
telephone box **la cabina telefonica**
telephone card **la carta telefonica**
telephone directory **l'elenco telefonico**
to telephone **telefonare**
television **la televisione**
telex **il telex**
to tell **dire**
temperature **la temperatura**
  to have a temperature **avere la febbre**
temporary **temporaneo/a**
tender (*meat*) **tenero/a**
tennis **il tennis**
tennis court **il campo da tennis**
tennis shoes/trainers **le scarpe da tennis**
tent **la tenda**
tent peg **il picchetto**
tent pole **il palo**
terminal (*airport*) **l'aerostazione** (*f*)
terminus (*bus*) **la capolinea** (*station*) **la stazione di testa**
terrace **la terrazza**
terrible **terribile**
terrorist **il/la terrorista**
thank you (very much) **(tante) grazie**
that (one) **quello, quella**
the **il, la, lo, i, le, gli**
theatre **il teatro**
their **loro**
theirs **il/la loro**
them (*direct object*) **li** (*indirect object*) **loro**
then **poi**
there **lì**

there is/are **c'è/ci sono**
therefore **quindi**
thermometer **il termometro**
these **questi, queste**
they **loro**
thick **spesso/a**
thief **il ladro**
thin **magro/a**
thing **la cosa**
to think **pensare** (*believe*) **credere**
  I (don't) think so **penso di sì/(no)**
third **terzo/a**
thirsty: I'm thirsty **ho sete**
this (one) **questo, questa**
those **quei, quelle**
thread **il filo**
throat **la gola**
throat lozenges/pastilles **le pastiglie**
through **attraverso**
to throw **lanciare**
to throw away **gettare via**
thumb **il pollice**
thunder **il tuono**
ticket **il biglietto**
ticket office **la biglietteria**
tide **la marea**
tidy **ordinato/a**
tie **la cravatta**
to tie **legare**
tight **stretto/a**
tights **i collant**
till (*until*) **fino a**
time (*once etc.*) **la volta**
time (*see p. 181*) **il tempo**
timetable **l'orario** (*m*)
tin **la scatola**
tin foil **la carta stagnola**
tinned **in scatola**

tin opener l'apriscatole (m)
tip (in restaurant etc.) la mancia
tired stanco/a
tissues i fazzoletti di carta
to a
toast il pane tostato
toasted sandwich il toast
tobacco il tabacco
tobacconist's il tabaccaio
toboggan lo slittino
today oggi
together insieme
toiletries gli articoli da toletta
toilet(s) la toilette
toilet paper la carta igienica
toilet water l'acqua (f) colonia
toll il pedaggio
tomato il pomodoro
tomorrow domani
tongue la lingua
tonic water l'acqua (f) tonica
tonight stasera
too troppo
  (as well) anche
tool l'attrezzo (m)
tooth il dente
toothache il mal di dente
toothbrush lo spazzolino da
  denti
toothpaste il dentifricio
toothpick lo stuzzicadenti
top (summit) la cima
  on top of sopra
torch la pila
torn strappato/a
total il totale
to touch toccare
tough (meat) duro/a
tour il giro
to tour visitare
tourism il turismo

tourist il/la turista
tourist office l'ufficio (m) del
  turismo
to tow rimorchiare, trainare
towards verso
towel l'asciugamano (m)
tower la torre
town la città
town centre il centro città
town hall il municipio
tow rope il cavo da rimorchio
toy il giocattolo
track il sentiero
  (rail) il binario
tracksuit la tuta da ginnastica
trade union il sindacato
traditional tradizionale
traffic il traffico
traffic jam l'ingorgo (m)
traffic lights il semaforo
trailer il rimorchio
train il treno
  by train con il treno
training shoes (trainers) le
  scarpe di ginnastica
tram il tram
tranquilliser il calmante
to translate tradurre
translation la traduzione
to travel viaggiare
travel agency l'agenzia (f) di
  viaggio
traveller's cheques i traveller
  (cheques)
travel sickness (car) il mal
  d'auto
tray il vassoio
treatment il trattamento
tree l'albero (m)
trip la gita
trousers i pantaloni

trout **la trota**
truck **l'autocarro** (*m*)
true **vero/a**
    that's true **è vero**
to try (attempt) **provare**
to try on **provare**
T-shirt **la maglietta**
tube **il tubo**
    (*underground*) **la metropolitana**
tuna **il tonno**
tunnel **la galleria**
to turn **girare**
to turn off (*light*) **spegnere**
twice **due volte**
twin beds **i letti gemelli**
twins **i gemelli**
twisted **storto/a**
type **il tipo**
to type **scrivere/battere a macchina**
typewriter **la macchina da scrivere**
typical **tipico/a**

U

ugly **brutto/a**
ulcer **l'ulcera** (*f*)
umbrella **l'ombrello** (*m*)
uncle **lo zio**
uncomfortable **scomodo/a**
underground (*tube*) **la metropolitana**
under(neath) **sotto**
underpants **le mutande**
underpass **il sottopassaggio**
to understand **capire**
    I don't understand **non capisco**
    understood **capito**
underwater **sott'acqua**

underwear **la biancheria**
to undress **spogliarsi**
unemployed **disoccupato/a**
unfortunately **purtroppo**
unhappy **infelice**
uniform **l'uniforme** (*f*)
university **l'università** (*f*)
unleaded petrol **la benzina senza piombo**
unless **se non**
    unless they arrive **se non arrivano**
unpleasant **sgradevole**
to unscrew **svitare**
until **fino a**
unusual **insolito/a**
unwell **indisposto/a**
up **su**
upper **superiore**
upstairs **di sopra**
urgent **urgente**
urine **l'orina** (*f*)
us **ci**
use **l'uso** (*m*)
to use **usare**
useful **utile**
useless **inutile**
usually **di solito**

V

vacant **libero/a**
vacuum cleaner **l'aspirapolvere** (*m*)
vacuum flask **il thermos**
valid **valido/a**
valley **la valle**
valuable **di valore**
valuables **i valori**
van **il furgone**
vase **il vaso**
VAT **l'IVA** (*f*)

veal il vitello
vegetables le verdure, la verdura
vegetarian il vegetariano/la vegetariana
vehicle il veicolo
vermouth il vermut
very molto
vest la canottiera
vet il veterinario
via via
video cassette la videocassetta
video recorder il video
view la vista
villa la villa
village il paese
vinegar l'aceto (m)
vineyard la vigna
virgin la vergine
  Virgin Mary la Beatissima Vergine
visa il visto
visit la visita
to visit visitare
visitor l'ospite (m or f)
vitamin la vitamina
vodka la vodka
voice la voce
volleyball la pallavolo
voltage il voltaggio
to vote votare

W

wage lo stipendio
waist la cintura
waistcoat il gilè
to wait (for) aspettare
waiter il cameriere
waitress la cameriera
waiting room la sala d'attesa, la sala d'aspetto

Wales il Galles
to walk camminare
to go for a walk fare una passeggiata
walking stick il bastone da passeggio
wall il muro
wallet il portafoglio
walnut la noce
to want volere
  I want voglio
  I would like vorrei
war la guerra
warm caldo
  it's warm today fa caldo oggi
to wash lavare
  to wash up lavare i piatti
washable lavabile
wash-basin il lavabo
washing il bucato
washing machine la lavatrice
washing powder il detersivo
washing-up liquid il detersivo per i piatti
wasp la vespa
wastepaper basket il cestino
watch l'orologio (m)
to watch (e.g. TV) guardare
watchstrap il cinturino dell'orologio
water l'acqua (f)
water heater lo scaldabagno
water melon il cocomero
waterfall la cascata
waterproof impermeabile
water-skiing lo sci d'acqua
wave (sea) l'onda (f)
wax la cera
way (manner) il modo
  (route) la strada
  that way di là

this way **di qua**
way in **l'entrata** (f)
way out **l'uscita** (f)
we **noi**
weather **il tempo**
  what's the weather like?
    com'è il tempo?
weather forecast **il bollettino meteorologico**
wedding **il matrimonio**
week **la settimana**
weekday **il giorno feriale**
weekend **il week-end**
weekly **settimanale**
to weigh **pesare**
weight **il peso**
well **bene**
  as well **anche**
well done (*steak*) **ben cotto**
Welsh **gallese**
west **l'ovest** (m)
western **occidentale**
  (*film*) **il western**
wet **bagnato/a**
wetsuit **la muta**
what **che**
  what? **che?**
  what is . . . **cos'è . . .?**
wheel **la ruota**
wheelchair **la sedia a rotelle**
when **quando**
  when? **quando?**
where **dove**
  where? **dove?**
  where is/are . . . **dov'è/dove sono . . .?**
which **che**
  which? **quale?**
while **mentre**
whisky **il whisky**

whisky and soda **il whisky e soda**
white **bianco/a**
  (*with milk*) **con latte**
  white coffee **il caffellatte**
who? **chi?**
  who **che**
  who is it? **chi è?**
whole **tutto/a**
wholemeal bread **il pane integrale**
why? **perchè?**
  why not? **perchè no?**
wide **largo/a**
widow **la vedova**
widower **il vedovo**
wife **la moglie**
wild **selvatico/a**
to win **vincere**
  who won? **chi ha vinto?**
wind **il vento**
windmill **il mulino a vento**
window **la finestra**
  (*car/train*) **il finestrino**
  (*shop*) **la vetrina**
to windsurf **fare il windsurf**
windy: it's windy **c'è vento**
wine **il vino**
  dry wine **vino secco**
  medium-dry wine **vino abboccato**
  sweet wine **vino dolce**
wine merchant/shop **il vinaio**
wing **l'ala** (f)
winter **l'inverno** (m)
with **con**
without **senza**
woman **la donna**
wonderful **meraviglioso/a**
wood **il legno**
  (*forest*) **il bosco**

wool **la lana**
word **la parola**
work **il lavoro**
to work (*job*) **lavorare**
  (*function*) **funzionare**
world (*noun*) **il mondo**
  (*adj*) **mondiale**
  First/Second World War **la
  prima/seconda guerra
  mondiale**
worried **preoccupato/a**
worse **peggio**
worth: it's worth . . . **vale . . .**
  it's not worth it **non vale la
  pena**
(I) would like: (*see 'to want',
  p. 175*) **vorrei**
wound **la ferita**
to wrap (up) **incartare**
to write **scrivere**
writer **l'autore/l'autrice**
writing paper **la carta da
  scrivere**
wrong (*incorrect*) **sbagliato/a**

X

X-ray **il raggio X**

Y

yacht **lo yacht**
to yawn **sbadigliare**
year **l'anno** (*m*)
  leap year **l'anno bisestile**
yellow **giallo/a**
yes **sì**
yesterday **ieri**
yet **ancora**
yoghurt **lo yogurt**
you **tu, voi, lei** (*see Basic
  grammar, p. 167*)

young **giovane**
your **suo, sua, suoi, sue; tuo,
  tua, tuoi, tue; vostro, vostra,
  vostri, vostre**
yours **il suo, la sua; il tuo, la
  tua; il vostro, la vostra**
youth **la gioventù**
youth hostel **l'ostello** (*m*) **della
  gioventù**

Z

zip **la cerniera**
zoo **lo zoo**
zoology **la zoologia**

EMERGENCIES

(*See also* Problems and complaints, *page 159*; Health, *page 149*)

You may want to say

Help!	**Aiuto!**
	iy-ooto
It's urgent!	**È urgente!**
	e oorjente
It's an emergency!	**È un'emergenza!**
	e oon emerjentsa
You must help me!	**Deve aiutarmi!**
	deve iyootarmee
Quickly!	**Subito!**
	soobeeto
Be careful!	**Sta attento!**
	sta attento
Police!	**Polizia!**
	poleetsee-a
Fire!	**Al fuoco!**
	al fwoko
Ambulance!	**Ambulanza!**
	amboolantsa
Go away!	**Via!**
	vee-a
Stop!	**Fermi!**
	fermee
Stop thief!	**Al ladro!**
	al ladro
Look!	**Guarda!**
	gwarda

EMERGENCY TELEPHONE NUMBERS

The number for all the emergency services in Italy is 113.

You may want to say

Phoning the emergency services

(I need an) ambulance
(Ci vuole un') ambulanza
chee vwole oon amboolantsa

(I need the) police
(Ci vuole la) polizia
chee vwole la poleetsee-a

(I need the) fire brigade
(Ci vogliono i) pompieri
chee volyono ee pompyeree

I've been robbed
Mi hanno rubato
mee anno roobato

There's been an accident
È stato un incidente
e stato oon eencheedente

There's a fire
C'è fuoco
che fwoko

There's someone injured/ill
Qualcuno è ferito/malato
kwalkoono e fereeto/malato

I've been attacked
Sono stato attaccato/a
sono stato attakkato/a

I've been raped
Sono stata violentata
sono stata vyolentata

My husband/son/boyfriend is very ill
Mio marito/figlio/fidanzato è molto ammalato
mee-o mareeto/feelyo/feedantsato e molto ammalato

My wife/daughter/girlfriend is very ill
Mia moglie/figlia/fidanzata è molto ammalata
mee-a molye/feelya/feedantsata e molto ammalata

Please come immediately
Per favore, venite subito
per favore, veneete soobeeto

Come to . . .
Venite a . . .
veneete a . . .

My name is . . .
Mi chiamo . . .
mee kyamo . . .

The telephone number is . . .
Il numero di telefono è . . .
eel noomero dee telefono e . . .

Where is the police station?
Dov'è la questura?
dove la kwestoora

Where is the hospital?
Dov'è l'ospedale?
dove lospedale

Can anyone speak English?
C'è qualcuno che parla inglese?
che kwalkoono ke parla eengleze

Is there a doctor who speaks English?
C'è un medico che parla inglese?
che oon medeeko ke parla eengleze

Can you call the British Embassy?
Può chiamare l'ambasciata britannica?
pwo kyamare lambashata breetanneeka

Can you call the British Consulate?
Può chiamare il consolato britannico?
pwo kyamare eel konsolato breetanneeko

I need a lawyer
Ho bisogno di un avvocato
o beezonyo dee oon avvokato

I want to speak to a woman
Voglio parlare con una donna
volyo parlare kon oona donna

You may hear

Pronto, polizia
pronto poleetsee-a
Hello, police

Centotredici
chentotredeechee
113

Come si chiama?
kome see kyama
What is your name?

Qual è il suo indirizzo?
kwal e eel soo-o eendeereetso
What's your address?

Che cosa è successo?
ke koza e soochesso
What happened?

Dov'è successo?
dove soochesso
Where did it happen?

Quando è successo?
kwando e soochesso
When did it happen?

Può descrivere . . .?
pwo deskreevere
Can you describe . . .?

Venga con me/noi alla questura
venga kon me/noy alla kwestoora
Come with me/us to the police station

La dichiaro in arresto
la deekyaro een arresto
You're under arrest

Deve andare all'ospedale
deve andare allospedale
You have to/he/she has to go to hospital

Dov'è che fa male?
dove ke fa male
Where does it hurt?

Quanto tempo è stato/stata così?
kwanto tempo e stato/stata kozee
How long have you/has he/she been like this?

Quatro billetti per Venezia
per favore.

Per due adulti e
due bambini.

Andata e ritorno

Per il treno de 4.15
per ~~Roma~~ Venezia

C

Ritorno

fra Firenze de 18.10

C'è un supplemento?

Quale binario per

Venecia?

Permesso?

NOTES

Buon giorno

Può aiutarmi.

Parlo poco italiano.

È mio figlio.

Gli fa male qui.

l'orecchio.

C'è un infezione il.

Ha

NOTES

NOTES

NOTES

NOTES

NOTES

NOTES

NOTES

NOTES

NOTES

NOTES

NOTES

NOTES

NOTES

ALL-PURPOSE PHRASES

Hello
Ciao!
chow

Good morning/Good day
Buon giorno
bwonjorno

Good afternoon/evening
Buona sera
bwonasera

Good night
Buona notte
bwonanotte

Goodbye
Arrivederci
arreevederchee

Yes
Si
see

No
No
no

Thank you (very much)
Grazie (mille)
gratsye meelle

Pleasure
Prego
prego

I don't know
Non lo so
non lo so

I don't understand
Non capisco
non kapeesko

I speak very little Italian
Parlo pochissimo italiano
parlo pokeesseemo eetalyano

Pardon?
Come?
kome

Can you repeat that?
Può ripetere?
pwo reepetere

Slowly
Lentamente
lentamente

Can you show me in the
book?
Può mostrarmi nel libro?
pwo mostrarmee nel leebro

Can you write it down?
Può scriverlo?
pwo skreeverlo

Do you speak English?
Parla inglese?
parla eengleze